DO NOT REMOVE
CARDS FROM POCKET

A NEW
FEDERAL TAX
SYSTEM

A NEW FEDERAL TAX SYSTEM

Richard W. Lindholm

PRAEGER SPECIAL STUDIES • PRAEGER SCIENTIFIC

New York • Philadelphia • Eastbourne, UK
Toronto • Hong Kong • Tokyo • Sydney

Library of Congress Cataloging in Publication Data

Lindholm, Richard Wadsworth, 1914-
   A new federal tax system.

   Bibliography: p.
   Includes index.
   1. Taxation--United States.   I. Title.
HJ2381.L515 1984   336.2'05'0973   83-24791
ISBN 0-03-070734-X (alk. paper)

Published in 1984 by Praeger Publishers
CBS Educational and Professional Publishing
a Division of CBS Inc.
521 Fifth Avenue, New York, NY 10175 USA
© 1984 by Praeger Publishers

56789 052 98765432

Printed in the United States of America
on acid-free paper

CONTENTS

LIST OF TABLES AND FIGURES

ix

PREFACE

The <u>Wall Street Journal</u> reported on January 12, 1983, that President Reagan would include in his 1983 state-of-the-union message an outline of a major restructuring and simplification of the federal tax system. This, as we all know, did not take place.

One cannot help but be intrigued by what the administration had in mind. One official was reported to have said that the president favored a proposal alongside the current tax reductions. It would be a totally new tax system that is simple, fair, and equitable; it would produce as much revenue as the existing system.

To a degree the analyses in this book describe an entirely new and fair tax system to replace the current hodgepodge. The replacement taxes recommended are tried and workable, and they are currently used by many advanced industrial nations. The proposed tax system might well be what the administration had in mind. It is also a proposal that would change very substantially the fiscal interaction between business and the federal government.

ACKNOWLEDGMENTS

I wish to thank Professor Reed Hansen of Washington State University and Professor Glen Atkinson of the University of Nevada-Reno for their careful reading and evaluation of the tax philosophy underlying this proposed major change in the U. S. approach to taxation. I also benefited in many ways from the in-house comments and analyses of Professor Tom Calmus and Lecturer Charlie Cole. The encouragement and analyses offered by Sol Price of the Weingart Foundation are greatly appreciated. It goes without saying that the manuscript typists of the College of Business Administration were most helpful and careful throughout the developing process. Finally, assembly of the materials and other preparations for publication were aided greatly by my graduate assistant, Linda Pocan. Any shortcomings in the analysis and approach are mine, and much of the strengths arose from the cooperative efforts of those mentioned above.

We are all hopeful that the time is arriving when basic U. S. tax reform can be accomplished and that the discussions in this book will hasten the process and increase the likelihood of sound and fundamental corrections.

INTRODUCTION

The first question that must be considered, and answered, in developing a major reform of the U.S. federal tax system is, What are the basic qualities that a national tax system of an advanced non-dictatorship and noncommunist nation needs to have?

Digging into the distribution of benefits from the loopholes in estate and gift taxes of the current federal individual and corporate income tax system is not enough. Neither is it enough to introduce one or two special, high windfall-profit or luxury-expenditure taxes while keeping the framework, if not the current rates, of the existing federal tax system.

If the trauma certain to arise from a "real" major reform of the U.S. federal tax system is to be initiated, there had better be some very convincing assured gains, including in particular, a sharp reduction of total administrative effort. One cannot even lightly recommend a minor change, as for example, the treatment of depreciation, without carefully evaluating the administrative impacts of all kinds. Simplicity, especially for the citizen taxpayer, is a sine qua non of tax reform legislation.

In the example of the treatment of depreciation, the impacts would vary between industries and between domestic and foreign plant-location decisions. These are examples of basically private sector considerations related to a change in the treatment of depreciation as a method to reduce business income tax payments. Public sector impacts would include (1) sources to be used to replace lost revenue where expenditure cuts or increases would be made and (2) the effect of these on both the speed of economic development and the level of unemployment. The last two considerations are obviously of interest to both the private and public sectors, as is actually true to a greater or lesser extent of all the impacts of this and all other tax shifts.

The policy formation study presented in this book avoids the weakness of all complicating income and estate tax reforms by eliminating individual and corporate income taxes, the estate tax, and the gift tax at the federal level. Its objective is not a tax reform that would modify the revenue-raising capabilities of these major federal taxes and in some uncertain and complex way move toward (or maybe through lobbying, move away from) the general qualities the federal tax system should possess. Of course, the approach adopted here does not eliminate all possible impact complexities. However, the "all-the-way" approach does avoid doing over and over again the analyses of what would result from changing the treatment of depreciation or a whole list of other adjustments in establishing a reformed income and estate tax liability.

So here we are. It is a new world. The federal government has eliminated three of its major tax groups and has adopted a major value-added tax (VAT) and a major net wealth tax (NWT). No longer will decisions be determined by federal income or estate tax considerations. After all, perhaps the United States is the right nation to be first to go all the way and eliminate the corporate income tax. For it was the United States that originally provided the example and leadership resulting in adoption of the corporate income tax by other nations.

The taxes to be introduced to provide the revenues lost by the repealed taxes are broad-based taxes with bases that include all of economic accumulation and production. The largest of the two replacement revenue sources is the value-added tax. The VAT and NWT bases include the value of all production sold in the marketplace, private natural resources, and man-produced capital goods.

The essential philosophy of this book can be summarized in six basic points.

First, increasing the welfare of the general citizenry is best accomplished by expenditures financed with government revenues, not by using taxes in a manner that actively attempts to make its levies on the basis of some concept of ability-to-pay.

Second, tracing and identifying the location of a tax's economic burden can only be carried out in a very partial way, and little is accomplished and maybe much harm is done by highlighting a tax's impact in a manner that assumes impact and incidence to be identical.

Third, the experience of the past 20 years has demonstrated the concept of a cyclically balanced budget to be unworkable. In addition, a tax producing stable revenues is to be preferred over one having wide fluctuations in collections.

Fourth, simplicity in the administration of a major tax is a characteristic much to be desired.

Fifth, tax harmonization and international impacts of the federal tax system must always be carefully considered in setting federal tax policy.

Sixth, the accepted level of government expenditures is so large that great care must be taken in taxing and borrowing so that private investment and savings are adequate to support a growing and risk-taking society.

1

FISCAL
DEVELOPMENTS

ATTITUDES AND ECONOMIC QUANTITIES

The recognized failure of simple, economic model building and
mathematical manipulation has led to a new economics. The new economic emphasis is best characterized as more humanistic. Emphasis
shifts from analysis of growth or decline of trend rates and monetarist
explanations to the complicated emotional attitudes of groups as diver-
gent as college students and retirees. The analysis must be in terms
of absorption of messages sent by the communications industry and
how this affects decisions and work attitudes.

Information that led to the shift in understanding of economic
operations and forecasting events is familiar to everyone. Productivity did not increase as wages rose. A growing money supply did not
lead to lower real-interest rates. Finally, a word was coined to include the results of the new economics. It was stagflation.

Stagflation

Supply-side economics and its emphasis on production of goods
and services became an explanation of stagflation. As a forecasting
replacement its performance has been less than earthshaking. There
continue to be strong doubts as to the helpfulness of emphasizing that
supply is not demand driven.

Today, the forecasts presented by economists, business leaders,
and government leaders are hesitant and the assumptions, always the
most important part of a forecast, continue to resemble the old economics.

Humanistic Forecast of Trends

If a humanistic forecast were attempted, the first data gathered would concern changes in management's dealings with its employees. These shifts would form the basis of forecasts for expanded productivity and a sound competitive position. This, of course, would lead directly to an understanding of some of what is being done properly and where the problems exist.

The burden of bureaucratic regulatory activity is another area a humanistic forecast would emphasize. Reducing this basically unproductive use of resources would stimulate the economy. The major area of government regulation is the tax system. Movement toward greater tax complexity, as is the case for 1983, must be considered to be a limiting element in economic growth. The humanistic estimation would also replace much of the Keynesian emphasis on monetary developments.

Other important elements of a humanistic forecast would include the manner in which personnel departments and labor unions are being managed, the influence on policy of individual members, and the movement of industrial decision making toward the individual.

In the meantime management and ownership have evolved into a group less closely associated with operations and more outside the daily functioning of the plant. The potential of this humanistic development to reduce negotiating difficulties is high. Failure to identify this evolving problem and to work to defuse the showdown must be seen as another humanistic aspect of economic trends.

The final humanistic characteristic of an industrial nation's economic forecast is found in the ability to plan for economic well-being based on individual, rather than government, decisions. If financing of retirement, medical care, and education, as examples, cannot be done with individual economic resources but must be provided under government programs, the private sector has been weakened. Tax collections and deficits will be high, and the political pressures for unsound government fiscal policy will be irresistible. Again, these are very important humanistic elements in making an economic forecast.

Minimal data are being gathered currently to quantify and understand the basic elements of an economic forecast based on new economic determinants. As demonstrated by the failure of forecasts based on old procedures, the time has come to rectify this situation. Ways must be developed to understand and interpret labor elections, new management appointments, growth or decline of regulations, and changes in the economic independence of the citizenry. These are the basic elements of a useful economic forecast, not money supply or deficits. For example, on October 6, 1983, the <u>Wall Street Journal</u> reported in an editorial titled "Population on Parade" that "no sane Swede has worked overtime in years." This attitude certainly has arisen largely from the 65 percent marginal tax rate the workers of Sweden must pay on their wages, even at the lower income levels.

NEW RELATIONSHIPS

The thrashing about of economists and others to explain and develop recommendations for improving the economy is proof of the unsatisfactory nature of existing explanations of stagflation. The increased demand for energy and the oligopolistic marketing position of a substantial portion of usable energy undoubtedly are important explanations for the shortage of investment activity and the resulting weakly sustained level of economic growth. However, this is not the emphasis of our immediate discussion, which concerns the other great shift in the economy since 1950, that is, the increase in federal government revenue collections.

In a manner of speaking, however, the energy crisis and the growth of federal tax collections are similar. The similarity exists in that they both drain off potential savings, thereby increasing interest costs and reducing the size of the flow of capital for use by enterprises, large and small, both private and public.

The federal government has properly continued to use the payroll tax to finance social security. It should remain as the dominant source of social security financing. However, this will not be possible if the individual income tax continues to provide about 46 percent of federal government tax collections. Realistically, the payroll tax cannot be relied upon to finance social security when the individual income tax continues to be a major federal tax. There is, of course, no real justification for using the individual income tax with all of its enforcement costs if it is going to be used as just another federal tax.

Big government, perhaps with some decline in defense spending, is here to stay. This has been learned by all industrial democracies, even by Japan in these later days. Acceptance of this reality is a first step in bringing about a reform of the tax system. The change needs to be such that funding on an immense scale can be carried out while stimulating savings and encouraging innovative investment decisions. The quantities of funds required by the federal government are so large that great care must be exercised in raising them. Retardation of initiatives must be avoided while encouraging careful consumption decisions and dynamic savings programs.

Revenue Estimates

Table 1.1 shows the bare numbers of the new federal tax system that is supported, developed, and analyzed in this discussion. The left-hand side of Table 1.1 gives current collections from application of the existing federal tax system. The right-hand side reflects the two tax introductions and the four tax eliminations. The table assumes the new federal tax system would be as productive of revenues as the existing system. This revenue level would be reached by use of appropriate rates and base exemptions. The value-added tax (VAT) and net wealth tax (NWT) rates are sufficiently high to result in revenue levels equal to current collections with a tax base that is broad but that also leaves space for some traditional exemptions.

To provide the $265 billion in federal tax collections estimated for 1983 by applying a VAT with no exemptions, the rate required is

TABLE 1.1

Federal Tax Collection Estimates, Fiscal Year 1983
(in billions of dollars)

Existing System		New System	
Individual income tax		Value-added tax	
Top rate of 50 percent	285	15 percent flat rate	265
Customs duties	9	Excise taxes	40
Corporate income tax		Net wealth tax	
Top rate of 46 percent	35	2 percent flat rate	60
Excise taxes	40	Customs duties	10
Estate and gift tax			
Top rate of 50 percent	6	Miscellaneous	15
Miscellaneous	15		
Estimated total	390	Total	390

Much of Stagflation Is Tax Caused and Can Be Tax Erased

High rates, narrow base, and volatile collections from corporate income tax	Low rates, broad base, and stable collections

Source: U.S. Department of the Treasury data and new tax estimates.

about 11 percent. A rate of 15 percent would permit exemption of about one-quarter of the total VAT base produced. If basic governmental productive activities were exempt, the 15 percent rate would permit exemption of about 15 percent of private economic production and still would meet the allocated revenue requirement of $265 billion.

As the nations of Western Europe have introduced their VATs, they have made estimates of both the administrative problems and costs and the revenues to be expected. The administrative difficulties turned out in the great majority of instances to be less than expected and tax collections more than estimates had established (Mehus 1969).

One must conclude that VAT and NWT possess the economic strength to provide the revenues allocated to them in Table 1.1. The rough estimates made here are adequate for our purposes at this time. Two important aspects of the revenue estimates are that the rates are low and that the tax system remains an ability-to-pay system. Both wealth and purchases are proving to be bases more associated with ability-to-pay than are personal income and profits (Studenski 1940; Carlson 1980).

The quantities of collections given for VAT and NWT arise from an assumed tax rate level combined with the portion of the tax base used by both taxes in applying the legislated tax rates. The tax base available to both VAT and NWT is very substantial. This means the quantity of revenues arising from each tax can be altered substantially through relatively minor exemption changes and rate shifts. This characteristic has been exploited by nations using VAT in particular. The NWT shifts have been less frequent, but the potential exists for substantial adjustment activity here also.

The NWT-allocated tax provision of $60 billion requires that a 2 percent tax be applied to a base of $3,000 billion. The estimated net wealth privately controlled in the United States is about $10,000 billion. Therefore, the estimated NWT collections to provide $60 billion at a 2 percent rate must be applied to only one-third of the estimated base available.

Table 1.2, based upon data reported in the 1983 Economic Report of the President, provides a summary of federal tax and debt data. The weakness of the current tax system is demonstrated by the substantial decline of the corporate income tax collections and the slight decline in individual income tax collections. Estate and gift taxes remain stable at a low level of collections. Legislation already adopted will result in decreased revenues through the years.

The federal taxes slated for elimination in the tax program developed in these analyses are politically and economically weak. Failure of the existing federal tax system to meet the need for substantial and stable revenues is demonstrated by the growth of the federal debt. The taxes being used to finance desired services simply cannot meet the challenge.

TABLE 1.2

Federal Tax and Debt Data
(in billions of dollars)

	Fiscal Year		
	1979	1981	1983*
Total federal deficit	-27.7	-57.9	207.7
Gross federal debt	833.7	1,003.9	1,383.7
Budget receipts			
Individual income tax	217.8	285.9	285.2
Corporate income tax	65.7	61.1	35.3
Social security tax and con-			
tributions	139.0	182.7	210.3
Excise tax	18.7	40.8	37.2
Estate and gift taxes	5.4	6.8	6.1
Customs duties	7.4	8.1	8.8
Miscellaneous receipts			
Federal reserve earnings	8.3	12.8	13.4
All other	0.9	0.9	1.1
Total receipts	463.3	599.3	597.5

*Estimates

Source: Council of Economic Advisers, Economic Report of the President, 1983 (Washington, D.C.: U.S. Government Printing Office, 1983).

During the period 1979–83 the federal debt has increased by over one-half trillion dollars. The increase during the first six months of 1984 is expected to be more than an additional $200 billion. The net interest paid by the federal government has expanded along with the deficits; thus, it is now over $100 billion annually. This is equal to about one-half of total federal expenditures for national defense.

Consumption Label

The wrong impression of VAT's relation to prices is given when the term consumption is used to describe the VAT used in Europe. The label consumption was attached by France to its expanded production tax, which became the taxe sur la valeur ajoutée (TVA, or VAT), in order to gain General Agreement on Tariffs and Trade (GATT) approval to refund TVA payments on exported goods and to levy a border tax equal to domestic TVA on imports. In other words, to gain acceptance in treating TVA under the destination principle, it had to be a tax on consumption. (See the discussion of VAT and international trade in Chapter 3.)

Actually, of course, VAT is no more a consumption tax than any other broad-based tax. The end result of all economic activity is consumption. Capital goods contribute their value to consumption as they wear out and become out of date. The Western European VAT is a consumption tax only because it avoids double taxation of capital and raw materials. The VAT tax on capital goods and raw materials is no greater than the tax on goods and services destined for consumption, nor is it any less.

To gain this relationship, the VAT paid and due on capital goods and raw materials is deductible from the VAT due from the firm that purchased capital and raw materials. The price of capital goods purchased includes the VAT levied on parts and similar items used in constructing the capital good. This VAT under the Western European approach is deductible from the VAT the firm purchasing the capital good owes on the sales it has made. These sales may be made to consumers and final users or they may be made to other firms as equipment; it does not affect the tax treatment accorded capital goods and raw materials.

The other replacement tax is a net wealth tax (NWT), which is levied on wealth in all forms. However, federal constitutional provisions may somewhat restrict the inclusion of land in the base. Also, NWT often has progressive rates and exempts wealth of a given quantity controlled by a single economic group.

The Additive Value-Added Tax

There are several varieties of VAT. The subtractive VAT is used by Western Europe (see Chapter 7). The additive VAT is used by Michigan and is called the Single Business Tax (SBT). (See Figure 1 for a computation outline of the Michigan VAT.) The base of the tax to which the legislated rate is applied is developed by adding up the firm's profits, net interest, wages, and net rents. These, of course, add up to the amounts earned by the factors of production (that is, land, capital, labor, and entrepreneurship) used by the taxable firm. The base to which the VAT rate would be applied is somewhat less than what it would be when the subtractive method is used. This occurs because taxes other than VAT become a portion of the selling price and are therefore included in the base of a subtractive

FIGURE 1

Computation of Michigan Value-Added Tax

Add:	Total compensation = salaries and wages (W-2), FICA payments, unemployment insurance tax, worker's compensation premium, health insurance premium, pension, profit-sharing cost
Subtotal	
Add:	Taxable income from federal return
Add:	Net interest (paid less received)
Add:	All depreciation taken on federal return for assets purchased before January 1, 1976
	All depreciation taken on federal return for assets purchased after January 1, 1976
Subtotal:	Gross tax base
Subtract:	28 percent of depreciation on federal return for assets purchased before January 7, 1976
	Full value of real and personal-property capital acquisitions
Subtotal:	Adjusted gross tax base
	Apportion by three-factor formula to determine Michigan tax base
Subtotal:	Michigan tax base
Subtract:	Small-business, low-profit exclusion, if eligible
Subtotal:	Adjusted tax base
Subtract:	Gross-receipts limitation, if eligible
Subtract:	Labor-intensity deduction, if eligible
Total tax base	
Multiply by tax rate	
Tax liability	

VAT, but they are generally not included in the earnings of production factors and therefore are not included in the base used in the additive VAT. Otherwise, the base under the two VAT approaches is the same.

The additive VAT applies the rate more directly to productive activities of the economy. It makes VAT more obviously a tax on total value added through business activities. Emphasis on the sales transaction activity, so obvious when VAT is calculated on the subtractive basis, is substantially reduced when the additive procedure is used.

A LOOK AT THE RICH

It is generally believed that a degree of economic equality is worth striving for. On one side, the rich side, inequality harms by pampering. On the other side, inequality vulgarizes and is depressing. A society must minimize both of these products of inequality in order to live and grow.

Although the degree of equality of wealth is generally considered to be a very important element in the functioning of a society, little effort has been exercised to measure the existing equality. Because the wealthy concentrate their holdings in common stocks and real estate, the fortunes enjoyed by these investments strongly affect the portion of total wealth controlled by the richest 0.5 percent of the population.

The approximately one million persons making up 0.5 percent of the U.S. population in 1969 accounted for 29.9 percent of the net worth, or about $3,003 billion. British data tend to show that there are vast differences in wealth within this group. The very rich are much richer than the average rich person included in the 0.5 percent of the richest.

A detailed study of rich people who died in the period 1956-73 in Britain identifies that inheritance is the major determiner of wealth inequality. Only about one-third of those dying wealthy were born poor.

These findings demonstrate rather conclusively that the high estate tax rates introduced in the 1940s in Britain did little or nothing to reduce inequality of wealth. The importance, at least in Britain (similar U.S. studies have not been made), of the contribution of inheritance in maintaining wealth inequality was the same in the 1950s as in the 1920s. Apparently, in Britain the tendency is high for sons about to inherit considerable wealth to marry women also about to inherit wealth. In fact, the tendency of marriage to constantly work toward greater wealth concentration is at least as great as the impact of estate taxes to reduce wealth concentration.

Finally, the data gathered in Britain demonstrate that the estate tax has stimulated tax avoidance procedures. This effort has reduced the quantity of wealth passing through probate. More of the wealth is given away or assigned to others before death. This is particularly true of those dying when over 60 years of age.

TAX AND DEBT TRENDS

Figure 2 shows the trend of federal internal revenue sources during the past 30 years. No adjustment for inflation rates has been attempted. The trend definitely has an upward sweep. The total of employment taxes (social security and unemployment insurance of the federal government) with 1950 at zero have increased over 350 percent. The next greatest percentage increase took place in individual income taxes. These two areas of federal tax collections are the largest revenue providers and are rising most rapidly. These are the taxes levied most directly on individuals. Also, the salary base that is taxed is concentrated in urban areas.

Until 1972 the estate and gift taxes proceeded upward at approximately the same rate as the other personal taxes. Since 1972, and particularly since 1978, estate and gift taxes have provided revenues at a lower, stable base at a level about 250 percent of increase.

The corporate income tax does not demonstrate a strong cyclical characteristic except in 1959 and 1968. Collection trends for the periods 1976-79 and 1962-67 were the strongest, with the 1962-67 period being the only time when corporate income tax collections kept up with individual income and employment (payroll) taxes for a period of substantial length.

Taxation Growth

The strong upward movement of individual income taxes was owing largely to bracket creep arising from graduated rates and inflation. The strength of employment taxes is tied closely to increases in the covered wage of employees and to higher rates. The employment tax changes were politically acceptable because they were considered necessary to meet the financing needs of social programs attached to this financing source.

The strong, generally upward sweep of taxes shown in Figure 2 gives a rather accurate impression of the constant, substantial increase in taxes year after year. Of course, during this period the federal debt was also rising almost yearly, starting with $256.7 billion in 1950 and reaching $914 billion in 1980. The federal government's financing needs are huge. The way in which these immense amounts are collected has a very substantial effect on level of business activity, direction of consumer expenditures and business investment, and location and rate of growth of pockets of unemployment.

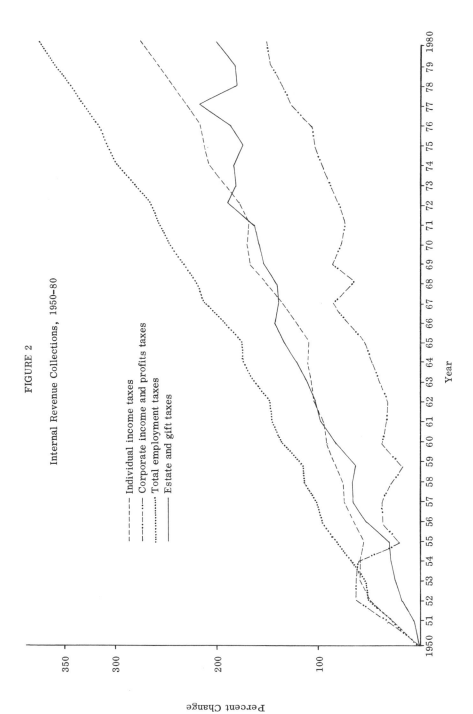

FIGURE 2

Internal Revenue Collections, 1950–80

------- Individual income taxes
—··— Corporate income and profits taxes
·········· Total employment taxes
——— Estate and gift taxes

Percent Change

Year

11

Causes of Stagflation

One method of explaining stagflation, which is usually assumed rather than spelled out, emphasizes the reduced incentives to save and invest of the participant decisions in the current economic environment. If one assumes that incentives are weak because the federal government is too large in many areas, including regulation, then wise budget reduction is required to cut back on stagflation.

If the large federal deficits are at fault, then flat-rate tax increases combined with budget cuts can eliminate stagflation. However, if it is assumed that (1) the budget cannot be cut substantially because of military needs and social commitments and (2) income taxes and profit taxes need to be cut, not increased, if savings and investment stimulants are required, then a basic fiscal shift is a must (Laffer 1982; Bell 1976).

The New Approach

Discussions in this section are largely concerned with development of a meaningful alternative to the existing federal revenue system.

Federal income taxes, estate taxes, and profit taxes would be eliminated under the fiscal shift I propose. Very substantial revenues would be lost at the federal level from this action, but the states would at the same time gain a substantial tax base. In addition, billions of dollars and thousands upon thousands of skilled accounting, legal, and tax-expert manpower hours would be released for use in hundreds of specialties. The dollars of profits would remain largely under the control of those engaged in enterprises providing productive working opportunities. This would actively encourage both savings and investment.

This possibility is not pie in the sky. The following discussions will demonstrate that big government of the type modern democratic societies appear to need requires a new approach to taxation. If basic tax reforms are not completed, the result will be continued stagflation and a society unable to employ its resources in a democratic-capitalistic manner while enjoying the planning efficiency of stable prices.

INFLATION AND TAXATION

Argentina and Brazil among the major nations have experienced the most rapid rates of inflation. They also have been most active in experimenting with new taxation approaches. Basically, their tax systems are completely indexed. This is true of both business and personal taxation.

Very few nations have done anything substantial toward adjustment for inflation. The United States is one of many countries that have done very little to face up to the broad revenue-raising adjustments that inflation both requires and brings about. In the Economic Recovery Tax Act of 1981 the United States has finally taken some hesitant steps toward indexing the income tax.

Indexing

Canada has the most complete inflation-recognition program of any country experiencing relatively normal rates of inflation. Canada automatically indexes personal income tax rates, exemptions, and allowances. Along with France, Japan, and West Germany, Canada has special provisions allowing reduction of income from inventory write-ups.

One important result of a nation's failure to adjust income and profits taxes to account for inflation is the increase of real tax collections without undergoing the political difficulty of raising tax rates. Most governments ignore this built-in characteristic of graduated personal income taxes and taxes on corporate profits. The real increase of tax revenues is largely seen as a fortunate aspect of the system. Undoubtedly, worldwide inflation combined with governments' typical treatment of higher real tax collections have combined to increase the size of the public sector.

Political Impact

Most nations are interested in stimulating investment and economic development. In reaching this aim the treatment of inflation in taxation legislation can be a two-edged sword if nothing is done. The debt burden of the firm is reduced as the monetary unit declines in value. This encourages additional investment. Also, the profits arising from operations increase, resulting in higher income taxes. This discourages investment.

When an inflation fueled with budget deficits is under way, action aimed at control without large unemployment levels leads to use of direct controls. The adopted approach often includes rationing of foreign exchange and establishing maximum prices on certain products. These direct-control actions have been spawned by tax policy. For if the budget had been kept in balance, the inflation would have been less violent and fewer direct controls would have been introduced.

One can even go a step further and identify taxation as an important social phenomenon. Taxes that are complex and have high rates are by their very nature only partially administered and/or levied in a nonuniform fashion. This results in reduced citizen confidence in the honesty and efficiency of government personnel, which in turn fuels an underground economy, a reduced tax base, and higher deficits. In developed nations the underground economy is concerned largely with schemes to reduce taxable income and profits. In developing nations the underground economy consists largely of actions to smuggle out and in goods that have been placed under direct price controls and/or that have favorable access to foreign exchange.

Underground Economy

The underground economy, whether tax or foreign-exchange centered, arises from ineffective governmental efforts to reach economic stability. Generally, the government's failure becomes obvious. In addition, there is a carry-over impact: the people's confidence in government's ability to carry out any program is weakened. This in turn weakens governmental efforts to initiate corrective policy. Inflation works its destructive will.

The first rule in eliminating the tax-underground economy is to have the tax be simple and to give the ordinary citizen a chance to see if favoritism exists or if tax dodging is being practiced. It is amazing that all or a substantial portion of the substance of this rule is violated in all the major industrial nations as well as in developing countries. When the existing fiscal policy violates this first rule, the tax system becomes a kind of con game.

The second rule requires that local property taxes be limited to land as a base. Everyone can see land, and when values are made public they can be usefully judged by citizens.

The third rule requires that income and property of individuals and businesses be treated alike.

One can go on—but enough has been said to make even a casual observer realize that the tax policies now generally followed need a major overhaul. Maybe an entirely different approach is required.

2

PROGRAM
ACTIVATION

THE FISCAL CRISIS AND ITS PHILOSOPHICAL BASE

Introduction

The fiscal crisis of the Western world today is very different from those experienced in the past. This, of course, is always true of a crisis. In fact, being different as well as being massive is what moves a problem into the crisis classification.

The current fiscal crisis is different because huge war expenditures or wasteful, unproductive public works did not cause it. There is, however, an expenditure aspect. It has arisen from expanding welfare and annuity programs—the so-called transfer payments.

Another important difference is in the conception of the federal government's abilities to move the economy in what is perceived to be the desirable direction. As often mentioned here and elsewhere, new expenditures financed with new federal borrowing no longer stimulate; rather, the action frightens. A new medicine to cure a down economy is needed—or maybe the federal government can no longer cure. To look to federal government action is not appropriate at crisis time. Rather, action to stabilize the economy through fiscal policy is required.

If this is the appropriate relationship between the economy and the federal government, new tools are needed. Tax revenues must be rather uniform during good and bad times, and government expenditures should not fluctuate widely.

This seems to be a common-sense approach until it is considered more closely. For instance, if government revenues have declined, should expenditures be held up to their old level? Or if government revenues are going above old levels, should expenditures be increased, or should government debt be retired, or should taxes be cut? One could go on and on listing choices.

What is obviously needed is some procedure to make the government's fiscal impact stabilizing. This stabilization impact, however, cannot go much further than that arising from levels and types of actions that have not changed greatly. Experience during the early 1980s showed that stabilization through counterinstability turns out in practice to exert pressure resulting in serious fiscal policy problems.

The federal corporate income tax collections must by their very nature decline sharply when the economy contracts and expand substantially when the economy expands. This tax has been designated as countercyclical—and because of this substantial fluctuation in revenues, it is a tax contributing to economic stability. The graduated personal income tax acts to a considerable degree in the same manner.

New Approach to Economic Problems

It is now being realized that the desirable collection–fluctuation qualities of income taxes as seen through the eyes of Keynesian economics are not desirable when seen through the eyes of current conditions. In terms of federal government fiscal policy the taxation of profits and the progressive personal income tax are bad because of their instability. These very same qualities gave these taxes added luster during the 40-year period before the Keynesian world was destroyed through development of immunity to the Keynesian medicine.

One can correctly ask at this stage, Can the federal government through fiscal policy make a major contribution to national and local economic stability and growth? If the answer is yes, then one must consider the current position to be unique or one must see on the horizon a revolution in economic thinking approaching the size of the Keynesian revolution.

The revolution required would be both political and economic, as was true of the Keynesian revolt. One possible revolt would be initiated through action to take away from the national government the power to change the quantity of assets having value, that is, its legal power to declare a piece of paper legal tender. If the national government had to rely on funds collected as taxes or borrowed on the money market without the power to create "money," how would the existing and future power of government to stimulate action be affected?

The national government in its debt–carrying ability would be reduced basically to the level now enjoyed by the states. The budget's negative imbalances would be limited to the sum of total debt–carrying charge costs plus repayment schedules. This would mean that the federal government's ability to act through an increase of indebtedness would be limited by both the aggregate debt-carrying ability and the stability of revenue receipts. If this is the new revolution in the wings, because of the inability of national governments to restrict their deficits, then the feasibility of realistically looking to the federal government to provide the means to abort fiscal crises will be substantially decreased.

Under these conditions it would also be true that national governments will be pressed to develop new revenue sources possessing a great deal of stability. No longer would the old corporate and graduated personal income taxes fill the requirements for federal economic stability activity. The new political, legislative, and economic research findings would point to a need for greater stability of fiscal programs and a limited federal role.

Under these conditions, looking to the federal government to correct a dangerous and highly undesirable economic situation would not be a useful approach. The possibility of unwise fiscal policies would be sharply increased. The efficient would be encouraged through unwise federal fiscal policy to bail out the inefficient.

THE TIME IS RIPE

The first comment usually made by a person examining the tax proposal offered above is something along this line: "A good approach, but it could never gain political support." The basis for this forecast must rest on observation of all the efforts that have been put forward to reform the tax system in relatively small ways and on the results of such efforts. For example, even after years of inflation the income tax has not been indexed. A decision to change the treatment of income-in-kind of homeowners never gains enough support to be adopted, and so it goes. As efforts are made to simplify the income tax, the result is a more complex tax (Brinner 1981).

The basic difference in the tax reform proposed here and the reform that has been going on over the years is that the change proposed here is not a patch job but a change in the system. Actually, when one considers the useful developments in tax policy, it is evident that shifts came as basic reforms and not as changes here and there. When looking at the record, one is inclined to conclude that efforts to make small changes are doomed to fail. The goal of simplification is not met, the shift in revenue-flow goal desired is not reached, and so forth.

Tax Reform

On the other hand, the reform of the 1890s up to 1913 was aimed at eliminating the tariff as the principal revenue-raiser of the federal government and replacing it with an income tax. It was a change of direction. It was a major change; so major, in fact, that it required a new amendment to the United States Constitution, the Sixteenth Amendment.

Take another example. In the 1930s property valuations fell dramatically. The property tax, which supplied nearly all local taxes and a large portion of state revenues, was not up to its revenue-raising responsibilities. The problem was not solved by reforms here and there, although this approach was tried over and over again. It was the general introduction of the retail sales tax at the state level, and to some extent at the local government level, that rectified the situation. Again, it was a major reform and not patches here and there that did the job.

During World War II, with its huge growth of federal expenditures, a basic revenue shift was required. Again, patches would not do the job. The income tax was changed from a tax paid by the few to a mass tax. The deed was done by introducing tax withholding from income earned as wages were received.

Tax reform to solve a major problem must be major. Boys should not be assigned to do a man's work. Also, if we expect a "man-sized" job to be accomplished, major tax shifts must be introduced.

Today, the general public is beginning to realize that a major tax reform is needed. We cannot continue to go on running huge deficits during an economic downturn and changing the law so that new complexities and tax expenditures (loopholes) arise.

But what to do and how to do it? Is the answer to be found in current reforms under way? Hardly. Can another major tax reform find political acceptance? Must we go from one fight to get this minor shift (like the withholding of 10 percent on dividend and interest income) to another fight for another improvement and so forth down the political/fiscal road of unfulfilled needs?

The new situation regarding quantity and use of revenues is as demanding of new approaches as was the development of a modern industrial society in the 1890s, fighting a world war in 1917, and adjusting to the great deflation of the 1930s. Today, we need a fiscal approach that raises huge and stable revenues, and which does so without reducing private initiative and savings. If the requirements of these goals are not met, the consequences can be very serious, as we are learning day by day as the fiscal problem remains unsolved. We are also learning day by day that a patch here and a rate shift there do not solve the difficulty but, instead, add to it.

For the moment let us accept that to continue down the existing fiscal road leads to a severe social crisis. If this is happening, a new road must be given the highest priority. Where shall we look for this new road? More than likely it must be constructed out of roads being followed and theoretically possible roads. These practices must be combined with adjustments to meet our domestic requirements.

When one looks around the world, successful use of a number of different roads is found. Also, there are a number of theories of the result to be expected by following this or that fiscal road. I suppose the first effort must abandon realized income, defined in a thousand different ways, as the tax base. Possible replacements are really only two in number—wealth and/or expenditures.

Countries going down these alternative fiscal roads, while abandoning income and estates entirely, do not really exist. However, there are many examples of considerable development of the alternative bases—expenditures and wealth—while not abandoning income. Because of its huge economic base, the United States need not suffer the regulatory costs of following all three roads. The United States is wealthy enough and possesses a sufficiently developed state and local tax system to eliminate income and estates as a federal tax base. The U.S. tax system at the national level can be more streamlined with a lower cost (costs of all kinds) fiscal system than that of other national governments. This potential should be realized.

In order to realize this fiscal policy potential, however, the U.S. tax reform must be more dramatic and complete than that being undertaken in other countries. The income and estate tax base must be entirely removed, of course. The tax reform program developed here does this. It faces up to the historic experience that change of direction in a major tax becomes the politically acceptable approach when the fiscal crisis is acknowledged. This is the case now. A major shift is needed in the fiscal road being followed, and it is politically acceptable to do so. This has been demonstrated by U.S. fiscal history.

Transaction-Based Taxes

The Advisory Commission on Intergovernmental Relations (ACIR) reports a growing support for taxes based on sales. If additional taxes are needed, some 52 percent of a national sample favor introduction of a federal sales tax and only 24 percent favor higher individual income tax collections. This trend toward transaction taxes and away from the individual income tax has been growing (see Chapter 7, Table 7.3). It is demonstrated by an increasing number of ACIR survey respondents reporting the federal individual income tax to be the worst tax now widely used (Wall Street Journal 1983a).

The Broad Picture

The existing federal tax system is based on the surplus or net income realized as individuals and businesses sell the goods and services over which they have control. In the case of the individual income tax the deductions made to arrive at the tax base have lost any relationship they ever had to a cost figure that could be used to calculate net income. The corporate income tax has stayed much closer to the fundamental relationship of the tax, that is, it is a tax on profits; but here also the tax has wandered far afield from its original theoretical character. Finally, the gift and estate tax has proved (1) to be a tax concept only justified because of failure of income taxes to reach all net incomes and (2) to possess many weaknesses of its own, both administrative and conceptual.

Elimination of these taxes at the federal level is called for because of the evolution that has taken place both in the taxes themselves and in the economic environment in which they function. Their abandonment would leave the federal government short somewhere between $350 billion and $400 billion, which would have to be made up with new taxes. To avoid the existing fiscal system's influence in terms of stimulating inefficiency and retarding private savings, the new taxes would have to be very broad based in order to maintain low rates while providing substantial and stable revenues. The two tax bases fitting these requirements rather well, while being balanced between wealth and consumption, are net wealth and the sale of value added as goods or services.

These two taxes, at rates and bases corresponding rather well to the manner in which they are used in other countries, would provide the revenues lost through repeal of federal income taxes and the federal gift and estate tax. Therefore, the potential exists to shift the federal tax system to a net wealth tax possessing a high ability-to-pay characteristic, and a value-added tax assessed as a productivity is marketed.

Concurrent with the occurrence of the major federal tax reform (a reform that would shift the federal tax system away from retarding and inefficient effects), the state and local governments' tax systems would be encouraged to improve the ability-to-pay characteristics of their revenue systems. State government's reliance on income and land taxes would most likely increase. State income taxes would expand, having been given up by the federal government. State land taxes would be initiated because land is likely to be excluded from the federal net wealth tax for constitutional reasons. A state land tax would appear to provide a more just manner in which the nation's new tax system could function.

THE BIG SHIFT REQUIRED

Very serious consideration along the lines outlined here would be an important step toward raising vast amounts of revenue from transaction and net wealth taxes, while repealing progressive taxes on income and estates. Such a tremendous shift in the U.S. tax structure requires, first, that substantial weaknesses be identified as built-in characteristics of the current system. In addition, a substitute approach must have the qualities required of a basic replacement tax system. Finally, replacement procedures must be practical.

The political acceptability of the current system obviously existed at one time in the past. Also, as has been mentioned, major tax system shifts take place only when serious crisis conditions exist. Therefore, the first requirement for a major tax shift is the realization that a serious fiscal crisis exists, that the crisis can be remedied only through a substantial fiscal shift, and that the economic requirements to remedy the problem exist in tested tax legislation in force in major industrial and developing nations (that is, the substitute must be a proved program).

The value-added tax (VAT) and the net wealth tax (NWT) replacements have been in place and used by mature industrial nations and by developing nations. The ability of VAT and NWT to fully demonstrate their potentials in the nations where they are used has been limited by continued use of income and profit taxes with progressive and substantial rates. This tendency to add a new tax while keeping the old taxes continues to work against efforts to gain the adoption of VAT in the United States and of NWT in the United Kingdom.

Because of the bureaucratic tendency to layer taxes and the recognition of this proclivity in the United States, the tax program recommended provides for complete elimination of the old. Also, VAT and NWT are completely new taxes in the United States at the national level. No provision is needed for adding a bit of new to the old.

Obviously, procedures must be created for a step-by-step repeal of old income and estate taxes and for introduction of the new VAT and NWT taxes. To a degree problems of tax introduction and repeal have been faced before at one time or another by all nations. For example, the nations of Western Europe faced this problem as they introduced their VATs. In the United States the introduction of retail sales taxes to replace state property taxes is another example.

In order to provide some insight into the types of adjustments the United States would have to make in adopting a new fiscal structure, a few obvious possibilities should be briefly considered.

New Taxes

The first major step would be to introduce a VAT along the lines of VATs now used in Western Europe. The adjustment step would substantially increase the level of exempt personal and corporate income. The VAT rate applicable during the adjustment period would be at the level needed to replace revenues lost as additional incomes were exempted from the income tax. The second and third annual steps would move in the same direction. At the end of the three-year period all income taxes would be repealed. The VAT rate would have moved up to about 15 percent to replace all individual and some corporate income taxes.

The NWT would be introduced at the full 2 percent rate. This rate would be applied to wealth data gathered during the three-year adjustment period. Thus, NWT would be first collected three years after initiation of the tax reform. The minimum base to be subject to NWT would in the first instance be set at $700,000.

Tax Repeal

The estate tax would also be repealed at the end of the three-year adjustment period. Estates subject to the estate tax but in the process of being assessed and taxed would be subject to the regular estate tax. All estate tax liabilities would be established during the three-year adjustment period. Estates becoming taxable after this period would be adjudicated under legislation adopted to limit windfall gains.

An interesting aspect of the repeal of income and estate taxes is the effect it would have on values of income and capital assets. Provision under the income tax law of a tax credit against taxable income would be worthless because the income tax would no longer exist. Special exemptions of all kinds would lose their value.

One particularly important impact is the effect the abolition of income and estate taxes would have on charitable giving. Of course, the gift would no longer be the source of lower tax liabilities. The income tax would be gone. A system of federal grants to equal tax deduction now in effect could be introduced to correct difficulties arising from repeal of income taxes.

Another broadly gauged impact would arise in the municipal bond field. Here, tax-exempt interest has resulted in lower interest levels on these securities. Elimination of the income tax would cause the prices of regular securities to rise and the market value of municipals to decline. The general effect on the bond market of repeal of the income tax would be stimulating. This would not be true, however,

of the municipal securities market. Those who had purchased municipals to avoid the income tax would find themselves only one group of
the universe now enjoying tax-free interest income.

The adjustments likely to take place are too numerous to consider at this time. The problems that would actually arise are likely
to be both short run and less serious than expected prior to introduction of the new tax system. The reform, of course, would have a generally desirable effect. These generally good developments cannot be
matched directly with the troubles to be expected, but they certainly
outweigh even the immediate troubles and in the long run far outweigh
the adjustment problems.

All levels of governments around the world have gone through
major tax adjustments. The adoption of VAT in Germany and the
United Kingdom, for example, was expected to cause many more difficulties than arose. The market forces adjusted in relatively short
order.

MONETARY AND FISCAL BURDENS

The current fiscal crisis can be usefully divided into the following five parts for purposes of analysis and solution: (1) the size of
government debt and the current monetary growth rate, (2) the economic effect of high income taxes on the availability of savings for
domestic investment, (3) the huge cost of carrying the debt at current
interest rates, (4) the instability of tax revenues and the failure of
countercyclical fiscal policy, and (5) the inability to meet defense
and transfer-payment budgetary demands, that is, unproductive expenditures.

The accumulation of government indebtedness stated in monetary units that are not adjusted for per-unit loss of value means a
decline in the well-being of the holders of this debt. The federal government's real debt burden declines if inflation continues. At the
same time all individuals and pension funds that have invested in government debt suffer a decline in real net worth unless their savings
continue to expand more rapidly than the rate of inflation. Inflation
plus a large outstanding government debt spell government absorption
of savings and a decline in the growth of net worth and, therefore,
the potential for private investment and economic productivity.

In monetary terms the debt may be expanding at the same time
as it is declining as a claim to economic resources. Because of this
relationship, one way to carry and reduce the economic burden of a
large government debt is to adopt and carry through policies that expand the inflation rate.

The federal government debt, by increasing at a 6-to-7-percent annual rate when an equal rate of inflation exists (as was the approximate situation between 1981 and 1982), is not a fiscal policy that increases the burden of federal debt. The rate of debt increase is approximately the rate of inflation. Reduction of the inflation rate below the rate of growth of the federal debt would be needed to increase the burden of federal debt. Following this approach, we arrive at the policy conclusion that the best way to keep the burden of federal debt low is to have an inflation rate above the federal debt increase rate. Acceptance of this analysis requires a policy recommendation to increase the federal debt in monetary terms at a lower rate than that of inflation, that is, to reduce the growth rate of federal debt while increasing the general inflation rate. This is perhaps best accomplished through commodity and wage price-support programs. Second, there is the impact on investment of high income taxes. High income taxes reduce savings, as these taxes hit middle-income people and corporations. They are the providers of much of our savings. High income taxes also increase the return rate necessary to justify a new investment.

Debt Management

If debt growth is to be retarded under the present fiscal system, either income and/or payroll taxes must be increased or expenditures must be decreased. Reduction of government spending in areas of pensions and the like does not decrease the rate of productivity expansion. Reduction of government spending for highways and research acts to reduce productive stimulants provided by government spending.

If high income taxes are used to finance production-increasing investments, the possibility exists for high income taxes to be as productive a use of resources as is stimulated by low income and profit taxes and high transaction taxes. However, for this to be the case an additional hurdle must be overcome. The government must supervise and select highly productive uses for funds collected as taxes. This second area of efficiency, in which governments have not proved to be particularly effective, must be improved.

On the other hand, when transaction taxes (which absorb much less savings) are used, the second hurdle is lowered. High tax collections are only useful as retardants to the growth of deficits and the quantity of government borrowing.

The huge cost of carrying a gross public federal debt of over $1.2 trillion is a third element of the serious fiscal crisis. The carrying cost, of course, declines as interest rates fall. However, the required higher taxes decrease productivity expansion along with reduced profits and a reduced savings pool. Another aspect of the impact of high interest costs is the instability of rate levels. These combine to make the fiscal impact of the carrying costs of a huge debt an important aspect of the fiscal crisis.

The government security market, with its $1.2 trillion of outstanding obligations, is comparable to the $1.6 trillion of real estate debt and is about four times the outstanding consumer credit. Policies followed in managing this huge sum affect the interest rate differences between long- and short-term debt and the availability of different categories of credit to the private securities market.

Recent (1982) heavy use of short-term securities by the federal government pushed up short-term interest rates to new highs. This, in turn, acted to drain funds out of savings institutions and reduced the availability of consumer and housing credit at reasonable rates. At the same time, the federal government's lower-than-normal use of long-term interest rates acted to push long-term interest rates below the level justified by the rate of inflation. As a result, businesses and private investors lengthened the maturity of their borrowing above what prudence would indicate with the existing inflation rate. Consequently, a serious liquidity crisis developed that sharply reduced the ability of housing contractors and businesses generally to meet their liquidity needs.

Concluding Remarks

As a result of these developments, bankruptcies multiplied, causing serious unemployment levels and a very low level of investment. The crisis that developed was not entirely the result of federal debt management policies, but the role they played was very important in combination with cyclically sensitive taxes.

The final element in the crisis arising from the huge federal debt is the influence of its carrying costs on the federal government's ability to meet expanding defense and transfer-payment budgetary demands. Here again, we face the problem of trying to meet legitimate spending demands with an inadequate financing base. Heavy use of the income and profits tax base, combined with their economic impact, causes the general economic base to deteriorate. The result is the creation of crisis conditions.

The expenditures are needed. The debt is already huge. It acts to retard the economy, which has already been battered from the impact of higher income and profit taxes. Use of taxes that reduce investment possibilities, absorption of savings by the federal deficits, and accumulation of debt all combine to create the fiscal crisis.

PAYING FOR WHAT HAS TO BE DONE

It costs the federal government a lot of money to develop new jobs for the unemployed. In addition, it is more than likely that normal governmental costs will continue to grow by about $332 (1982 dollars) annually for each person (assuming a population increase of about two million per year). To provide the expanding coverage will cost about $700 million (1982 dollars) more each year. Putting the unemployed back to work, rather than using job programs and welfare, would push the costs of government even higher.

Raising this amount of revenue is an essential responsibility of the federal government. Almost all groups in our society believe this to be the case, yet recent administrations have not really been up to it. The federal debt more than doubled in real dollars since 1971, just 12 years! Prior to 1983 the number of unemployed had increased and the quality of government services had declined. The federal debt, as noted before, has increased from less than $0.5 billion to over $1 trillion (Taylor et al. 1977).

During that same 12-year period, when the federal government's gross debt was expanding at an unheard-of rate, the value of the dollar was falling to less than one-half its 1971 value. Undoubtedly, there was a relationship between these two trends. But just exactly why they existed along with rising unemployment remains uncertain to this day.

There are many forces whirling around the markets and workshops of the United States and the world. One of them is the effects of U.S. inability to balance the budget. One can say with some certainty, however, that the federal revenue-expenditure problem is not the only reason. Nevertheless, the failure to adjust the nation's tax system to the new economic conditions faced by other nations must have been an important shortcoming.

The Income Tax System

The individual income tax and the corporate income tax provide nearly 60 percent of total federal taxes collected. When social security contributions are eliminated, as more than likely they should be in this type of comparison, the portion increases to about 80 percent.

Why the individual and corporate income taxes are used to approximate the full federal tax base, which is used to meet the federal government's fiscal obligations, has proved to be hard to explain; yet regarded from a different perspective, perhaps it is very simple.

It happened because the United States was a very rich nation, it had good local and state government revenue-raisers, and the U.S.

dollar was the only truly international currency. This was a very comfortable situation for the nation's government; but as it turned out, it was also fraught with temptations and dangers. The dangers ranged from unnecessary revenue instability to high tax rates that were difficult to administer; discouragement of savings; huge federal deficits; and a related, expanding money supply.

The taxable base provided by individual and corporate income taxes was continually narrowed. This was owing to the political pressure of high tax rates and serious economic downturns. Actions to grant tax shelters were, of course, self-defeating. Legislation to raise the needed revenues became increasingly difficult; so difficult, in fact, that the government and the taxpayers generally accepted rationalizations of why large deficits were run and why traditional spending responsibilities (such as the military) declined. Also, more than in any other nation, the U.S. voter believed in two ideas: (1) that the income tax was really an ability-to-pay tax, and perhaps the only one, and that all national taxes should be collected according to ability-to-pay, and (2) that a major shift should not be made in the way the national government collected its taxes.

To demonstrate how tax collection at the national level declined and how reliance had to be placed on borrowing, a review of some data is in order.

Individual and corporate income taxes were 11 percent of gross national product (GNP) in 1971. In 1982 the percentage was about the same, 11 percent. But in 1971 the federal deficit was $23 billion and in 1982 it was $111 billion.

Income taxes remained at the same percentage of GNP despite the expansion impact of inflation on the collections of a graduated income tax and the overstatement of taxable corporate profits owing to high inventory and capital replacement costs. Congressional actions narrowing the tax base had such a great influence that even though inflationary conditions existed, corporate taxes were among the highest in the world, and personal income taxes were not indexed, the United States in 1982 had to go into debt by around $111 billion. The forecast deficit for 1984 is in the range of $200 billion.

Maybe, just maybe, the federal government's income taxes are overburdened. Maybe income taxes are really a bad way to raise needed revenues at the federal level. At least the possibility of this relationship must be included in tax reform studies. This possibility has not been generally accepted nor has it been perceived by influential tax policy makers as a basic element for establishing tax reform directions.

What is required, but what has not been done, is fiscal reform action based on the actual requirements of a good federal tax approach in today's social, political, and economic environment. The federal income tax arose from the financial necessities of a war and from a belief that graduated income taxes could reduce wealth concentration. These goals are no longer appropriate. The United States is not at war, and wealth concentration has not been reduced after 20 years of trying.

Concluding Remarks

Let it be agreed that reform of the income tax within a federal system that does not include a major VAT and a major NWT is bad policy. The policy is bad because (1) the current system cannot provide the needed funds and (2) by trying to provide these funds it reduces the productivity of the whole economy. In addition, expanded tax collections based on income will cause serious administrative problems ranging from a growing underground economy to unstable revenues. Therefore, a switch in the direction of the federal tax system is required.

The basic fiscal needs of the federal government are productivity and stability. These are not to be found in the current system. Existing revenue sources are constantly being revised. The tax collection productivity varies sharply with economic shifts. These conditions and others require basic remedial tax legislation.

TAXES AND STAGFLATION

During World War II the groundwork was laid for the U.S. income tax to become a major peacetime revenue-raiser. Prior to this the income tax had been primarily a war tax plus a peace tax just productive enough to maintain revenues after import tariffs had been reduced. The income tax was not a major provider of government revenues. The big shift to withholding income taxes on wages, coupled with higher interest rates and inflation, made the income tax a mass tax that really cut back on savings and stimulated consumer indebtedness. The basic results of these tax shifts turned out to be a shortage of productive investment and a weak dollar. This shift in impact of the income tax was accelerated by new international fiscal and monetary relationships. Interactions of the primary tax developments with adjustments to alleviate the situation combined to develop an economic environment that came to be called stagflation (Stein and Foss 1981).

The combination of high inflation and high unemployment was considered in the late 1960s to be a phenomenon limited to developing countries such as Pakistan or Bolivia. It could not happen in great industrial nations such as Britain and the United States. How wrong the seers were.

Finally, in the late 1970s the business of finding out the causes of stagflation in the United States got under way. However, few worthwhile policy shifts developed. For example, income and profit taxes were not identified as the principal culprits. Emphasis was placed instead on secondary aspects of the society, that is, government waste and monetary policy.

A basic tenet of popular Keynesianism of the 1960s was that an increase in money supply reduces quoted interest rates. This turned out to be incorrect, except in the short run. Another truth stated that highly industrial nations tend to oversave. This also turned out to be wrong, as did the third basic position that consumer goods and services always move toward a surplus.

Therefore, it was concluded that economic policy for economic productivity needed to be aimed at (1) increasing consumer demand, (2) maintaining prices of agricultural products and other raw materials, and (3) using taxes that were cyclically sensitive. Again, time has proved the basic assumptions to be incorrect.

So much being wrong with the basic economic assumptions, a lot of new thinking was needed. However, little was forthcoming from economic research centers or from popular economic publicists (Thurow 1982). Also, policy makers, who were watching the destruction of economic growth they had fought for, failed to sound the alarm in any concerted fashion.

Why the professional observers were so wrong has become a major issue in the analysis of stagflation existing in major industrial nations as well as in developing countries. Certainly both inflation and unemployment are complex and undesirable elements of the functioning of our own society and that of many other developed nations.

More than likely the explanation is relatively simple and deeply rooted in the functioning of our society. The answer must deal with a relationship of growing importance and it must affect many private sector decisions that are social and philosophical as well as economic.

When one searches for the type of activity fitting this relatively simple but necessarily powerful element operating in the Western industrial nations, the culprit is not difficult to identify. Of course, this does not mean that differences of opinion as to the villain's identity will not exist. Very often something obvious, such as the trend of energy use and the control over its supply, can be missed in efforts to understand what is going on and what is likely to result in the future. Certainly, this was the case in 1972.

Cause of Stagflation

In 1984 there is a very obvious but overlooked element that is responsible for stagflation. The powerful explanatory phenomenon is the reliance on the graduated personal income tax, the corporate profits tax, and the estate tax. Each of these taxes is aimed at reducing the savings available for private investment, creating huge deficits during a recession, encouraging spending for consumption, decreasing private sector risk taking with accumulated resources, and cutting back on the productivity of professional and other workers. In addition, all three taxes stimulate tax-avoidance decisions that lead to less-than-most-efficient use of resources.

These shortcomings can be absorbed when the public sector demands 10 percent or so of GNP. Such absorption cannot be expected when taxes are around one-third of GNP. Tax aggregates are just too large for us to neglect their effects on society's decisions from the length of the workday to allocation of earnings and the direction of business decisions. Also, these taxes have proved to be very complex to administer and costly to taxpayers.

Concluding Remarks

While suffering from the major weaknesses pointed out, the individual income tax, the corporate profits tax, and the estate tax are nevertheless used so intensively in the United States that they combine to provide about $400 billion annually for the U.S. Treasury. This amounts to about 60 percent of all federal government budgetary receipts, including social security collections. These are important monies that push our society in ways that make stagflation its fundamental characteristic. They are also large revenue resources that cannot be abandoned without initiating revenue replacements that are approximately as productive. New revenue sources must bring along fewer impact weaknesses than the current approach and must possess some important pluses to stimulate creative development decisions and reduced centralization of government.

The value-added and net wealth taxes with their broad bases and low taxpayer compliance costs are the logical replacements. The reform direction is obvious.

3

GENERAL
PROBLEM
AREAS

ECONOMIC CONCEPTS

The new economics that has developed out of the failure of simple model building and mathematical manipulation is perhaps best characterized as humanistic (see Chapter 1). The attitude of workers and managers and the spirit they demonstrate in carrying out their domestic and secular functions have become important determinants of social progress and of the direction and success of economic policy (Jump 1980).

Worker Directions

Workers and their union want to become more deeply involved in industrial decision making. The impact of communication and education have made routine employment unacceptable. At the same time management and ownership have evolved into a group less closely associated with operations and more separate from the daily functioning of the plant. Rivalry between the two groups has intensified and the destiny of the business enterprise will be deeply affected by the degree of mutual understanding developed.

The ability of economics to perform useful forecasting and interpretation of events cannot continue with the old tools of statistical relationships. At the same time as public opinion groups are expanding their effectiveness the old understandings and faiths are in doubt (Smith 1981).

Role of Federal Government

The federal government, whose great achievements include creating jobs in the 1930s, winning the war in the 1940s and leading the way to unprecedented prosperity and stability in the 1950s, and planning and carrying out space explorations in the 1960s, began to show its feet of clay in the 1970s. This was perhaps more visible in the economic area than in other fields. The depreciating dollar of the 1960s, rising deficits, and considerable unemployment were visible to everyone (Deaton 1977). The "wise" and "efficient" federal government kept promising these difficulties would be overcome. However, at this point in time it has proved incapable of carrying out any fundamental shifts in basic operational priorities and procedures (Muth 1961).

Rational Expectations

Failure of the economy to react in the 1970s from the introduction of Keynesian remedies as it had in the 1950s caught both economists and business and government policy makers by surprise. The generally accepted explanation goes under the label rational expectations (Deaton 1977). Decision makers reviewing past experience and examining the ingredients of current federal government programs concluded that their personal and business decisions could not be based on government-announced intentions. As a result they did not react to the situation as was generally true in the past.

Expansion of the money supply was no longer a stimulant because prices would climb more rapidly than wages. As a result profit margins would no longer increase and investment would not expand. The overall effect would not be the expected stimulated economy with higher employment, modest interest rates, and higher profits.

In the 1970s the rational expectationists saw money expansion to be the first step toward hyperinflation with reduced profits, as wages and raw materials combined to push costs up more rapidly than prices. The bite of the graduated income tax would increase, thereby reducing real savings, sales of automobiles and other durable consumer goods, and capital equipment. Under these conditions the rational expectationists purchased commodities such as gold and land and cut back on new industrial undertakings. Unemployment remained high and new undertakings minimal. Stagflation was the word coined to fit the situation, and perfect anticipation or rational expectations described the process by which conventional stimulants became impotent (Jump 1980).

Supply-Side Economics

Supply-side economics was another concept that took hold as an explanation of the Western industrial nations' failure to prosper in the

1970s. Supply-side generally refers to economic activity related to production of goods and services. Analysis of how this activity is organized and carried out is supply-side economics. The analyses emphasize that supply operates on its own and is not merely an activity stimulated by the purchase of goods and services for consumption (Stubblebine 1983).

Expanded Importance of Taxes

The tax reform analysis developed here is aimed at transforming the federal tax system from an economic process that weakens the impact of action aimed at stimulating the economy to one that is stimulative. For example, expansion of the money supply fails to stimulate investment through profit increases because the corporate income tax and the individual income tax take away much of any new profits generated. How this can be changed is obvious: simply reduce or eliminate graduated income taxes and direct taxes on corporate profits.

It is just as obvious that if these two major revenue sources are eliminated at the federal level, some new and substantial revenue source relying on taxes not assessed to a substantial degree on profits must be introduced. This, of course, is the expected role of the value-added tax (VAT) and the net wealth tax (NWT).

Concluding Remarks

Undoubtedly, the introduction of this major tax shift would be the source of great pain to many. The necessary adjustments could be made slowly, thereby giving everyone adjustment time. Or the change could be made quickly—in a year or two. European experience in a quick introduction of the VAT was generally good, and much less hardship arose than was expected. On the basis of European experience with a major portion of the tax shift contemplated, one must favor completing the changeover within a brief period (see Chapter 2).

FISCAL POLICY

Full consideration of the impacts of taxes on business and personal decisions has been largely neglected. For example, the impact of taxes on decisions to invest in a manner that takes advantage of tax shelters has not been carefully examined. As mentioned, the term tax expenditures has been coined to permit consideration of revenue losses arising from both tax shelters and the straightforward offer of reduced income taxes if investments are made in certain areas or to reach certain other goals.

Macroconsiderations

Fiscal policy, when included in macroeconomic analysis, bears down largely on the size of the deficit or surplus of government budget units. This leads to the examination of absorption of savings by government deficit financing and in some instances to the differing effect on savings levels of the use of different taxes. Fiscal policy impacts are examined relative to the impact of government finance operations on the aggregate demand and supply of savings. To a considerable extent both the emphasis and the analysis approach used rest on working out monetary pressures and relationships mainly within the private sector.

Efficiency Impacts

One area, for example, in which fiscal policy considerations are public sector oriented and not dominated by monetary policy relationships is the impact on the efficiency of government provision of services or the difficulties of reliance on revenue sources that fluctuate widely. A number of questions related to this and other economic relationships come to mind: Will the willingness and ability to use long- and medium-term debt to finance the use of most efficient methods be affected? Will the ability to meet needs in an efficient and comfortable manner be reduced? How can the costs of uncertain financing be minimized? How will personnel management efficiencies be maintained?

When taxation is considered along with the efficiency of the use of tax collections, a very important aspect of fiscal policy that is uniquely taxation-spending oriented is under consideration. This is also true when a property tax is considered in relation to services financed and in relation to its effect on land-use decisions (Pryor 1973a).

Decision Influence

Fiscal policy that would be real, not a description of tax collection sources and expenditure trends, would examine each government revenue relative to its influence on personal, business, and government decisions. Tax collection and expenditure trends as well as the changing balance between the two aggregates indicate only what is the likely quantity of new government borrowing and debt repayment. The impact is basically debt-management, monetary, and policy oriented. However, the activity under way affects availability of funds for productive private and public sector use. These impacts are typically given short shrift, and their monetary effects account for too much of fiscal policy analyses.

Tax Replacement

A very important aspect of fiscal policy concerns (1) how the economy and all of a society's social relationships would be affected by replacing one tax with another or (2) the decision-direction effects of significantly modifying a particular tax. For example, what decision changes would arise from the introduction of a negative income tax to replace a large portion of existing welfare-spending programs (Kurz 1978)?

Evolution of Change

Court decisions and legislation amending tax laws are making fiscal policy in bits and pieces. Analysis of these activities provides a base for judging the trend and direction of fiscal policy evolution. From the 1920s through the 1960s use of the income tax above all other taxes was favored at the federal level. During the past ten years the income tax has gained in popularity at the state level, while it has demonstrated a weakening hold on tax activity at the federal level (Bernard 1979).

More than likely many modifications of the federal income tax arise from its failure to bring about the expected redistribution of wealth and income. Filling up one income tax loophole seems only to cause more. The complications increase with each effort at making the law correspond to some concept of justice. Fiscal policy summed up in the words ability-to-pay has influenced most reform action in the field of tax legislation. It has been the basic tax principle. No other goal has been able to stand up to its charm and promise.

Intergovernmental Relations

Fiscal policy in the United States includes the way in which the national government through taxes will affect state and local governments' tax and spending decisions. By levying income and payroll taxes at substantial rates the federal government has forced states and local governments to levy at relatively low rates. Also, the heavy use of income as a tax base has substantially reduced income's power of inducement to work hard and at long hours. The effect has been to reduce both worker productivity and risk taking of enterprises.

Concluding Remarks

Recognition of fiscal policy's distinctive qualities should cause a shift in attitude toward changes in how the tax tool is used. The particular pattern of current taxation is partially responsible for both good and bad existing conditions. A society examining itself and wishing to improve its situation must consider the impact of its tax system. Fiscal policy's great potential for good or bad must be examined in detail. The breadth of fiscal policy cannot be limited to its relation to aggregate savings and the size of federal deficits.

FINANCING INCOME MAINTENANCE SPENDING

The relative international position of the United States in the use of general revenues to finance its social security program remains about as it was in 1960. Pressure for change really did not develop until 1970. Since then the nation's income security spending has increased sharply, but the financing procedures have not really changed.

In fiscal year 1980 the nation's military spending level was up about $30 billion above the 1979 level. In fiscal year 1981 spending jumped $12 billion more above the 1980 level to a total of $135,856 million. In fiscal year 1982 the expenditure increase was again substantial and the total reached $187,418 million. The projected level for fiscal year 1984 is about the same as for 1983.

These U.S. increases are much greater than those experienced in most industrial countries. Therefore, U.S. tax funds required for this area, both absolutely and relative to other nations, have expanded significantly. Yet, these substantial increases have not caused a basic shift in the nation's financing practice. Indirect taxes have not been increased to finance general expenditures, as is so clearly the European approach. Data developed in the following discussion will demonstrate this point.

Impact of Introducing the Value-Added Tax

The evolution of the revenue situation in Norway may be typical of the change arising when a value-added tax is introduced.

The retail sales tax was introduced in Norway on July 1, 1935, at a rate of 1 percent and was gradually increased so that by 1969 its effective rate was 13.64 percent. On January 1, 1970, a value-added tax at a 20 percent rate was introduced. The revenues from indirect taxes as a percentage of Norway's gross national product increased from 13.6 percent in 1969 to 16.3 percent in 1970 and 16.4 percent in 1971. During the same period income taxes other than payroll taxes decreased from 13.3 percent of national income in 1969 to 12.0 percent in 1970 and amounted to 12.8 percent in 1971.

A similar relationship is demonstrated by the revenue of West Germany. In 1968 direct taxes on corporations and households totaled DM54,980 million. In 1969 VAT equaled 18 percent of German revenues and totaled DM26,159 million. And in 1970 the VAT equaled DM66,010 million for a 20 percent increase from 1968. During the same two-year period (1968-70) indirect taxes, with about 50 percent collected from VAT, expanded from DM55,810 million to DM76,160 million, an increase of 36 percent. The German VAT rates were increased in 1971.

In France a comparable situation appears to have existed. In 1967 the taxe sur la valeur ajoutée provided 33 percent of the revenues of the general budget. In 1969 the figure was up to 41 percent.

Sweden's direct tax revenues did not increase in 1971. In that year indirect tax collections increased by 30 percent to represent 50 percent of total revenues. Indirect tax collections increased by another 10 percent in 1972. The Swedish VAT rates, like the German, were increased in 1971.

Increased use of VAT has permitted expanded government spending for general purposes while holding down income and profit taxes. Because VAT can be collected as border taxes on imports and can be refunded on exports, if not used directly as social welfare charges, its collections can expand without bringing about an upward pressure on export prices.

The Norwegian Royal Ministry of Finance and Customs has taken the position that VAT offers one possibility of helping a more neutral competitive situation both internally and internationally.

Growth of the Value-Added Tax

All of the European Community (EC) member states in 1983 were rather substantial users of general revenues to finance their social security programs. In the United States general revenues are not used.

Because interest received by social security funds is paid as a result of ownership of government securities, these amounts are also in a sense funds from general government revenues. Revenues from this source received by EC member states varied from 7.6 percent of social security revenues in Holland to 0.2 percent in France. In the United States about 3.5 percent of old age and survivor insurance trust-fund revenues formerly came from this source.

Income maintenance expenditures made by U.S. local and state governments from general revenue sources are rather large. On the other hand, this practice is largely nonexistent among EC member states and industrial nations generally. As a result, when nations are compared, the U.S. contribution from general revenues to support income maintenance programs is relatively understated.

Tax development in Western Europe and particularly in the European Community is proving VAT to be an indirect tax that admirably meets the economic and political fiscal needs of the times. In demonstrating this effectiveness VAT has within the past five years become a major revenue-raiser in Europe. The collections envisaged upon VAT adoption are always larger than the totals of taxes repealed upon VAT introduction. Also, VAT rates and coverage have tended to increase after adoption.

The very substantial additional revenues being provided by VAT to the nations using it are not used to directly finance social welfare benefits; this, however, can be the indirect effect. Social security benefits become indirectly financed with VAT expansions when income tax rates need not be raised, or they may actually be reduced despite expansion of government expenditure. This is possible because of the additional VAT revenues received. Under these conditions higher payroll taxes to finance social security become possible without increasing total tax withholdings from wages. In addition, general revenue funds can become available to cover general social benefit spending without increased direct tax collections. As income taxes become less important, that is, when a substantial VAT is used, several developments become possible. For example, social security benefits were increased in Germany when their inclusion in the income tax base was reduced. In this case the added collections from VAT for general revenue purposes have made possible higher after-tax benefit payments without an increase of direct taxes.

International Features of the Value-Added Tax

As mentioned previously, one of the desirable features of any indirect tax, including VAT, is that a nation may refund it on exports and apply it as a border tax on imports. This feature, which is based on the destination principle, is lost under General Agreement on Tariffs and Trade (GATT) understandings if VAT or any indirect tax is used directly to finance social welfare. Therefore, European users and potential users of VAT avoid directly identifying the general revenues it provides in financing social welfare expenditures. Of course, if a nation did not wish to refund the VAT applicable to all or particular exports, it need not do so. The same freedom applies to application of a border tax on imports.

It has long been recognized that a nation's ability to subsidize exports increases the extent to which it can follow an independent domestic economic policy. Enjoyment of a high degree of freedom from international economic restrictions is very attractive. Because subsidization of domestic export industries in order to gain this freedom easily becomes flagrant, and because the desired aim of increasing a nation's favorable balance of trade is neutralized if competitors in other nations are granted the same favors, international rules administered by both the International Monetary Fund (IMF) and the General Agreement on Tariffs and Trade exist to minimize these practices. The economic procedures adopted for generalization as permissible practices are based largely on the established practices of Western Europe. This is true in the treatment of exports and imports relative to domestic taxes.

An important portion of Western European interstate economic relations consists of a highly developed, general indirect tax system that grew into the very productive turnover or cascade tax after World War I. Since 1954 this European indirect tax system has evolved into the value-added tax. It is also true that nations with basically direct tax systems, like Great Britain and Ireland, have adopted legislation to introduce conventional subtractive VATs. The admittedly incomplete data reported above demonstrate that the portion of revenues being raised by VAT is increasing in nations having the tax and that VAT is being actively considered by more nations.

The development in Western Europe of both VAT and an expanding social security system is closely related to international competitiveness within the rules of the game as understood by the membership of GATT. These rules can be made clear by commenting briefly on some of the basic articles and amendments included in GATT, as found in the U.S. State Department's publication Basic Instruments and Related Documents.

Current Situation

Because flexibility in use of the destination principle does not adhere to taxes tied directly to the financing of income maintenance programs, it is not possible under GATT understandings to enjoy the advantages of the destination principle while using VAT to directly finance programs of this type.

Revenues from the use of VAT must go toward covering costs of general government programs. When this is done, VAT collections reduce the need for other tax revenues such as personal and corporate income taxes and estate and gift taxes, or they provide the revenues needed for expanded general social spending. Such a shift of emphasis makes room for additional payroll taxes without increasing direct tax payments or increasing direct taxes by a lesser amount as general social spending increases. Nations using VAT have this opportunity to protect their producers from a worsened international competitive position owing to higher social benefit costs. The United States and other nations that do not use VAT are unable to do so. This is an important, evolving fiscal situation possessing very basic, general economic implications.

WHO ENDS UP BEARING THE TAX BURDEN?

Tax incidence and justice have provided the basics of tax policy evaluation. These abstractions cry out for interpretation as society makes greater use of organized participants and taxes to provide the economy's expenditure support.

For example, in the United States increased costs partially owing to higher taxes are likely to rest much more heavily on the economic base of unorganized segments of the society than on the economic base of the organized. All taxes are levied directly or indirectly on the unorganized. As taxes are increased, the organized social segments increase prices paid by both the unorganized segments (which have lower real incomes) and those among the organized who have maintained their after-tax real incomes.

Tax Shifting

One portion of the society able to avoid after-tax real income losses from tax increases consists of workers with wage contracts providing for pay increases equal to price increases. Compensation under these contracts would increase just as surely from higher priced oil, for example, as from higher prices arising from increased taxes. However, if the new higher taxes were levied on those unable to pass the tax on to others, the cost of living would not be affected and organized workers would not become eligible for higher wages. Under these conditions cost-push inflation would not develop, despite the higher taxes.

Tax increases that do not result in higher prices reflect good tax policy. This approach supports heavy taxation of unorganized groups. The greater the portion of taxes falling in the first instance on the unorganized, the less will be the tax-caused pressures to increase prices and costs.

The Nonshifting Taxpayers

Those who are unable to avoid the economic burden of taxes are distributed over a broad spectrum of U.S. society. The unorganized segment includes, for example, many investors who may be required to pay a higher tax on a fixed level of interest and dividends established under prior long-term contracts. Workers for government and charitable organizations are also, at least partially, a portion of this unorganized group.

Tax increases aimed at avoiding inflation must be assessed on those who cannot increase the relative price of their service or product because of a weak market position. This basically means unorganized industry. Fundamentally, the inability to shift situation exists because supply cannot be reduced to clear the market if the tax is added to the old price, which was at the correct level to absorb supply. The result is higher taxes without higher prices. If inflation really is the worst of all taxes, then this approach (that is, taxing those unable to pass the tax on in higher prices, charges, or wages) is the best way to go.

Of course, one impact of a tax program aimed only at those unable to improve their income (in order to compensate for higher tax liabilities) would be to stimulate organizational development and new types of financial contracts to build up resistance. One approach to avoid income reduction (likely to be considered and actually drifted into or consciously adopted in some areas) would be to shift the tax backward. The retailer would put pressure on the wholesaler, the wholesaler on his supplier, and so on down the line. Theoretically, this backward tax shifting would continue until it encountered an area of supply that continued to be available when the price being offered for it had become practically zero.

Deadweight Loss

It is well to keep in mind when thinking about the tax burden that whatever type of tax is used, the collection itself will reduce the surplus of both consumers and producers. Some of the loss arises from the revenue transfer from private sector consumers to those who are able to enjoy additional satisfactions because of government-spending expansion. However, there is a deadweight loss in the transfer of spending power because the volume of trade is reduced.

The deadweight loss arises because taxes of all kinds, not just indirect or excise taxes, drive a wedge between the gross price faced by buyers and the net price or revenues after taxes effective for sellers. This is the popularized "Laffer wedge." Sales and production levels have been decreased because the cost- and revenue-curve intersections take place at a lower level of production. This occurs because tax collections have made the needed recoverable cost higher than the cost before the tax wedge was inserted. Consequently, private sector resources are reduced because of the need to bear this deadweight, or efficiency, loss (Reuss 1963).

Income Absorption Power of Land

When one considers what important economic product would continue to be available at a relatively constant quantity and quality when nearly free, one thinks of land. Undoubtedly, land offers some opportunity for the final absorption of backward shifting. In the economic functions it performs, however, it is far from a uniform product. For example, land provides space for buildings and houses, resources for extracting minerals, and fertile soil for growing crops. These are quite different sources of economic value.

All of the land uses mentioned and subgroups related to them are vital to the functioning of our economy. Also, the market value of land ranges from nearly worthless to literally thousands of dollars per square yard. In addition, land would not disappear if taxes were raised so high that its selling price approximated zero. Of course, it might not be completely utilized if most of the economic rents were taken as taxes, but the land and its basic locational characteristics (ranging from level of rainfall to closeness to the bus depot) are not affected by changes in net earnings (Schultze 1971).

Backward Shifting

Shifting a tax backward results in lower returns to those engaged in production and marketing activities occurring prior to the sale to a purchaser who does not resell the product or services directly or indirectly. The best example of backward shifting of a U.S. tax took place in the 1930s when the original Agricultural Adjustment Act of 1933 provided for the levy of a processing tax on meat-packers and flour millers in order to provide revenues to pay subsidies to wheat- and hog-raising farmers. This tax was declared unconstitutional in 1935 (United States v. Butler 1935).

The wheat- and pork-processing tax was levied on sales of pork and flour, and it resulted in a lower pretax price for both. The tax was shifted backward to the farmers, resulting in lower earnings from farming and no change in the price of pork and flour.

The lower farm earnings were capitalized into lower land prices. Shifting of a land tax through capitalization to a fixed investment and/or to land means that the market value of the capital good or land used in the economic process is reduced to correspond with the capitalized value of the new earnings level.

Capitalization of Tax

In a sense a tax shifted through capitalization of a reduced income is borne entirely by the owner of a slowly depreciating capital good or land at the time cost was increased through taxation or some other manner (Schultze 1971). When this happens, the tax is shifted backward onto a physical good, not onto the user of the capital good or land, after the original adjustment has taken place through capitalization of the new level of earnings. The after-adjustment rate of return on the investment in land would return to the old level as the lower cost of land is adjusted to the higher tax and the resulting reduced income. Under these new conditions a smaller portion of the cost of operation would consist of land costs. This would be true of agriculture and, to a degree, of all industries.

Concluding Remarks

The levy of taxes on those unable to pass the taxes forward in higher prices and incomes sets up a condition suitable to lower after-tax incomes. This pressure is reduced by the opportunity for backward shifting until the price at which land is offered is reached. Reduction of land-use cost can compensate for much of the pressure for higher prices arising from higher taxes. Taxes on those unable to increase prices and income would, however, possess considerable backward-shifting ability because of the size of their economic activity. Therefore, higher taxes on unorganized savers will result in lower land prices. The real income from production lost through higher taxes not compensated through higher incomes is partially regained through lower economic rent payments for use of land.

FEDERAL AND STATE TAX CORELATIONSHIPS

A common example of the many tax-determined investment policies is the treatment under federal income tax of interest received from ownership of state and local government securities. This has become a very complex area, as is so common when attempts to widen a loophole encounter efforts to reduce it. For example, the Economic Recovery Tax Act of 1981 contains a number of favors for business and investors. Sylvia Porter reported in her column on August 11, 1981, that "so befuddling did the original clean legislation become in the end that tax lawyers and accountants will make fortunes in coming years." Certainly there must be some way to make more productive use of these highly trained and intelligent professionals.

Municipals

The current federal tax system provides a substantial inducement to hold securities issued by state and local governments and their agencies. These securities, called municipals, benefit from tax exemption of the interest paid to holders of the debt obligations. Interest paid on this debt is not taxable as income of individuals, businesses, or institutions under federal income taxes.

The quantity of securities has expanded as one impact of higher income tax rates, which result from taxpayers entering higher tax brackets when incomes attempt to keep up with the inflation rate. Prevailing inflation, without broadening the tax rate brackets or initiating some other adjustment, expands the demand for tax-exempt securities. The expanded demand has been partially satisfied through growth of borrowing areas that meet the requirements to be tax exempt.

Buyers

The growth of so-called industrial bonds illustrates the increased use of tax-exempt securities. Industrial bonds are used for an agreed-upon business investment. The business firm accepts responsibility for paying the interest and retiring the bonds. The sponsoring governmental jurisdiction also accepts responsibility for that obligation and will step in if the business firm falls short. If purpose, offering, and guarantees meet federal requirements, the bonds will benefit from interest exemption on the federal income tax.

The market interest rate for industrial bonds is usually 20 to 30 percent below the market for similar securities with taxable interest payments. These bonds are particularly attractive to individuals who were subject to the former 70 percent income tax rate. This occurs because the interest rate level is basically set by the top, federal, corporate income tax rate, which was 46 percent. Reduction of the top federal income tax rate to 50 percent decreased the attractiveness of municipals. The ability under the law for banks to deduct interest costs of financing a purchase of tax-exempt securities has caused municipals to continue to be very attractive to banks.

Suppliers

Most municipals are issued by school districts to finance new schools or by cities to build improved sewer systems. The bonds are clear obligations of the issuing government. They enjoy the full faith and credit of the local government. The property base located in the area is pledged to meet interest and retirement requirements. The risk is very low, even lower than that for industrial bonds.

The interest rate in 1983 on long-term state and local government debt was about 9 percent. It was around 11 percent on long-term federal government bonds. The amount of borrowing by state and local governments through issue of long-term bonds is substantial. State and local governments have been borrowing new funds at close to $50 billion a year. The amount of borrowing repayments currently approximates the new borrowing. The most productive state and local borrowing is done to finance capital expenditures. Borrowing is a method of leveling out payments over a period of years. The debt has many characteristics of business and individual borrowing.

More Productive Use of Capital

The borrowing activities described above are often financed by persons who receive substantial incomes from other investments. They are the ones who can afford to invest in new and risky business undertakings. However, the existing tax system and the treatment of interest paid to owners of municipals pushes the high-net-wealth holder toward the predominantly nonrisk municipals. The special tax treatment enjoyed on the interest arising from the ownership of municipals encourages no-risk and nonbusiness investment, while stimulating state and local government borrowing.

Development of the replacement tax system of VAT and NWT and repeal of income and estate-gift tax systems would provide pressures for more active use of the savings of the rich. A tax on net wealth discourages safe and low-income-earning investments. It also discourages holding wealth in commodities such as gold and land, both unproductive absorbers of wealth. Under NWT the wealth-holder must pay a tax based on market value. This value is about the same whether or not the current owner efficiently and completely utilizes the asset.

Under the fiscal system considered here state and local governments will find themselves competing for funds on the same interest-earning level as that of businesses. This will decrease the attractiveness of municipal-owned utilities and will generally increase the cost of state and local government investments. These somewhat undesirable economic impacts arise from the removal of a subsidy that is difficult to justify. The existing tax advantages of investing in tax-free and safe municipals reduce the quantity of risk capital available.

Federal Tax Modifications

Although the federal government allows tax exemption of the interest from state and local securities, it has not removed all state and local economic activity from its taxing power. The courts have declared in a number of cases that income from sales to state and local governments must be taxable. Therefore, a federal NWT may include as a portion of its taxable base its holdings of state and local government debt.

Current expansion of interest exemption on municipals to include financing of industrial development and housing has become sufficiently important to justify serious consideration of a constitutional amendment guaranteeing the federal government's right to tax the interest paid by state and local governments. The growing difficulties so clear under the present system would be eliminated under the proposed new federal tax system.

Concluding Remarks

The new federal tax system proposed in this book will treat all securities with fixed interest rates just as municipals are treated now. This will place the interest received by owners of state and local government debt in the same fiscal situation as other interest received by those who purchased municipals at lower prevailing rates than nonmunicipals. This shift in the market for fixed-return investments will push up the capital value of regular, taxable fixed-return investments and will push down the market value of municipals.

The bull market in regular bonds resulting from the changed tax situation will exert downward pressure on interest rates. Of course, this will be somewhat modified by the bear market developing in municipals because tax exemption will become generalized. The overall financial impact, however, will be toward lower interest rates and capital gains to owners of taxable securities. The bond market will be substantially strengthened. Lower interest rates on private enterprise securities will stimulate the industrial securities market and will decrease the federal budgetary cost of the national debt. This is certainly an impressive list of "goodies." And they are basically produced by putting municipals in the same tax pocket with all other securities.

Several important, economically favorable results can be expected from the impacts mentioned above. First, the reduced general interest cost will bring the federal budget closer to balance without cutting operating budgets or increasing tax collections. Second, state and local governments will lose their ability to stimulate housing and industry development through the offer of below-market interest rates to borrowers meeting the requirements established. Also, state and local government budgets will be somewhat increased because federal tax-free interest will be available to all borrowers. Third, lower interest rates will reduce financing costs generally; this will stimulate investment and economic growth because of the multiplier impact of expanded investment.

EARLY AMERICAN POLITICS
OF DIRECT TAXATION

Article 1, section 2, clause 3 of the United States Constitution states that

> representatives and direct Taxes shall be apportioned
> among the several States which may be included within
> this Union, according to their respective Numbers.

This reference to apportionment is repeated in section 9, clause 4 of the same article.

> No Capitation, or other direct, Tax shall be laid, unless
> in Proportion to the Census of Enumeration herein before
> directed to be taken.

Although clause 3 of Article 1, section 2 was altered by the second section of the Fourteenth Amendment, the general rule of apportionment "in proportion to the census of enumeration" still stands in 1983. By this rule the total revenue of a direct tax is first specified by Congress, then the sum is divided among several states according to population, and then it is levied upon the objects of the tax by the several states. A direct tax was seen to be uniform but was administered by the states.

A definition of <u>direct tax</u> is not supplied within the Constitution itself, and although its nature has always been, and continues to be, a matter of academic controversy, the Supreme Court has settled on a practical definition. A direct tax is either a capitation tax or a tax on real or personal property because of ownership. There are two balancing qualifications of this definition. First, a tax upon the subject of property is direct, but a tax upon another subject and merely measured by the value of property is not necessarily direct. Second, a tax is direct only if it is so in practical application; conversely, a tax having the same result as a direct tax, when practically applied, is in fact a direct tax no matter what Congress or the government may declare it to be.

Taxes and Representation

The Court did not derive the definition and set of qualifications simply or quickly. The question, What is a direct tax? has rung in the halls of Congress and the judiciary since the forming of the federation. During the Constitutional Convention itself there was some controversy over just what made a tax direct. James Madison recorded in his notes of the convention that "Mr. King asked what was the precise meaning of direct taxation? No one answered." (See Chapter 9 for additional discussion of the constitutionality of a tax.)

The direct tax rule was primarily a compromise between the issues of representation and taxation. It was argued variously that representation should be proportional to taxation, to wealth, or to population, and that taxation should be proportional to representation or wealth. Direct taxation was thus an important issue for it would help set the methods of selecting representatives and of gathering revenues in the new union.

At first glance the issue in 1774 seems only to be about representation, but this view forgets the cause of the American Revolution itself. It was largely a war of taxes and representation. The English government had begun to levy taxes upon the highly independent colonies, and the latter were enraged that they were given no say in either the amount or method of such taxes.

Tax Efforts

Article VIII of the Articles of Confederation established a tax quota system whereby all expenses of the federal government would be paid "by the several States, in proportion to the value of all land within each State, . . . and such land and the buildings and improvements thereon shall be established according to such mode as the United States in Congress assembled shall from time to time direct and appoint." The method of individual payment of taxes was reserved for the individual states to guarantee their independence (Madison 1927).

The immediate response to this system of taxation was mixed, and by 1786 the quota system had broken down. The tax quotas were not enforceable by the Confederation, and there was controversy over whether the states were paying their fair shares and over the justness of taxes based only on the value of land (especially among farmers unable to meet their land tax burdens). Some farmers even revolted in Massachusetts, and this in part forced the calling of the Constitutional Convention of 1787.

When the members of the Constitutional Convention met, they eventually concluded that limiting federal taxation to a quota system based on land would be insufficient to finance the new government. They were expected to base most future taxes on commerce, imports, and consumption. The issue persisted of linking representation to taxation and/or population and/or wealth, and rules to govern their relationship under the Constitution were proposed early. The difficulty came in finding a simple standard by which to measure all these factors, and though various arguments were made to fix representation permanently at a set number, the search for a simple multipurpose standard continued.

Wealth and Population

After finding the conflict between wealth and population to be unsolvable, the Constitutional Convention at first sought to find a ratio of wealth to inhabitants. But this immediately reintroduced contention over the proper classification of slaves—as it had in the convention to draft the Articles of Confederation—and over the proper enumeration of inhabitants through establishment of a national census. Summarizing the debates to that point, James Madison stated that "the value of labour, might be considered as the principal criterion of wealth and ability to support taxes," and thus population itself was a suitable measure of wealth. Though the debates continued as before, Madison's idea indeed became the standard measure for both taxation and representation. To ensure that both taxes and representation would remain linked together, an addition was made to the drafted constitutional clause on representation in a proviso that taxation shall be in proportion to representation. On consideration that this wording might unnecessarily force the new government to apportion all types of taxes, the clause was again altered to provide that direct taxation ought to be proportioned to representation. After some minor adjustments this clause resulted in the final wording of Article 1, clause 3 of the Federal Constitution (Madison 1927).

Meaning of Direct Taxation

What was meant by direct taxation? The question returns again and again. When Gouverneur Morris of Pennsylvania made the motion on direct taxation in 1787, he made reference more to indirect than direct taxes, and like most politicians since, he found it easiest to define direct taxes by exception. He stated that indirect taxes (such as those levied on imports, exports, and consumption) would be inapplicable under the rule, these being nearly equal among the states anyway. By this he meant that objects of indirect taxes were distributed more or less in proportion to population and wealth in the states. These indirect taxes were believed to be more convenient to collect than direct ones, and they were to become the major source of revenue for the new government. Still, this observation on indirect taxes did not explain clearly what direct taxes were. A more understandable meaning of direct taxation, then, must be drawn from the general debates on the topic.

As to the meaning of direct taxation itself, Morris, a member of the original Constitutional Convention, clearly distinguished it from the other types of taxation mentioned in the Constitution. He saw direct taxes to be collected directly by the new government upon the wealth of the people. In his words, "Let it not be said that direct taxation is to be proportioned to representation. It is idle to suppose that the Genl. Govt. [sic] can stretch its hand directly into the pockets of the people scattered over so vast a Country." It was seen that for a long time the people of America would not have money to pay direct taxes. Therefore, the collection of direct taxes would push them into revolt.

Apportionment

Late in the Constitutional Convention an addition was made to the reference on capitation taxes in section 9 of Article I. It stated that capitation and "other direct taxes" must be apportioned, and it was intended to prevent any pretext whereby Congress might take liberty with the rule of apportionment. It reinforced the idea that taxes on wealth and population distribution were to go together. Convention members realized that using population as the standard for both taxes and representation would not always be equitable and might even prove inapplicable, but they also believed they must set some standard to restrict the new legislature from developing taxes oppressive to the states or people.

Thus, we can conclude that the Constitutional Convention members referred to taxes levied on objects of wealth or property when using the phrase direct taxation and that by inserting it into the Constitution they intended to secure the states against central government threats to their wealth and independence. This conclusion is strengthened by comparing the tax quotas of the Articles of Confederation with direct taxes under the Constitution. Both tax systems concerned levies on measures of wealth; both were designed to ensure equitable burden of taxation among the states; and both required apportionment, the first by the value of land and the second by the population of the states. The direct tax rule appears to be a modified extension of the older quota system and to have been instituted to ensure that the central government would treat the states and citizenry equitably.

The Remaining Difficulty

Still, although a meaning of direct taxation can be drawn from the debates of the Constitutional Convention, no clear definition was set to paper. The question of constitutional limit on direct taxation was left open and was forced upon the Supreme Court in 1796, just eight years after the Constitution's ratification. This was the case of Hylton v. United States, and at issue was the constitutionality of an unapportioned tax on carriages used for the conveyance of persons. It was argued that the tax was a direct tax on property and thus was unconstitutional unless apportioned. The Court, however, argued that only taxes that could be easily apportioned should be classified as direct because there was no set definition of a direct tax. Since a tax on carriages could not be easily apportioned, it need not be.

The Sixteenth Amendment was ratified in 1913. It empowered Congress "to lay and collect taxes on incomes, from whatever source derived, without apportionment among the several States, and without regard to any census or enumeration." After repeated tries Congress had finally acted on the Court's suggestion in the Pollock v. Farmers' Loan and Trust Company case of 1894.

Concluding Remarks

It was felt by some that the Sixteenth Amendment would entirely get rid of nice questions as to what might be direct taxes, but this was not to be. In the first cases after ratification the Court held that the Sixteenth Amendment was obviously intended to simplify and make clear the limitations of the taxing power of Congress and not to create radical and destructive changes in our constitutional system. The amendment had not purported to confer power to levy income taxes in a generic sense, as that authority was already possessed, but its purpose was to relieve all income taxes from consideration of the source from which the income was derived. Thus, notwithstanding the Sixteenth Amendment, the constitutional restriction on direct taxes still held, although the Court's problems now shifted from classification of direct taxes to discerning what constituted income under the new amendment.

FEDERATED TAX SYSTEM

Abolition of federal income taxes would allow several fundamental changes in the character of economic decisions and tax opportunities available to state and local governments. These opportunities can be usefully divided into four groups.

Taxable income: There would be an expansion of taxable income because the federal income tax would no longer be available as a deduction from it. Several states limit taxable income reduction from this source to some maximum figure. Obviously, limiting the availability of federal income tax payments as an income reduction expense treats income tax costs more harshly than other costs. This injustice will no longer be practiced after federal income taxes are repealed.

Tax legislation: Pressure on state and local governments to conform with federal practice will be eliminated. States in particular have been constantly victimized by pressures to adjust to federal practices. With the elimination of federal income taxes states will enjoy more freedom in operating income tax systems that fit their individual needs.

Tax rates: State and local income tax rates will be able to increase because income will no longer have to bear substantial federal individual and corporate income tax rates. These higher rates applied to higher available taxable income will substantially increase tax revenues. However, because states compete with each other to attract industries and capital, the exploitation will be considerably less than that currently practiced by the federal government.

Local government: As a result of their increased potential for tax collection, states will be able to finance an expanded portion of local government activities. This potential will in turn reduce the local government's need for high property taxes. Decreased need for property taxes and abolition of federal estate taxes will somewhat compensate for the federal government's entrance into the taxation of net wealth.

Enforcement of Income Tax Legislation

Elimination of federal income taxes will take away from state income tax enforcement efforts the information the Internal Revenue

Service (IRS) has been making available to them. These services are substantial and both increase income tax collections and reduce income tax enforcement and administration costs.

When the federal government collects income taxes, every state gains access to all IRS files on each taxpayer who has filed a federal return, claimed dependents, reported a gross income, and the like. The IRS will also report the current address of any former payer of state income taxes. Every state may also benefit from any audit adjustments made by the IRS on a taxpayer reporting that state as his or her address. Corporate income tax returns may also be requested from the IRS of any corporation reporting a situs for its business within the state. In addition, the IRS may request from the states any information gathered in their audit reports.

Federal Assistance

The usefulness for the states of the cooperative effort described above was estimated at $267 million in 1977 out of total state and local individual and corporate income tax collections of about $38,400 million. The added collections directly attributable to federal assistance constitute around 1 percent (Penniman 1980). Collection additions that arose indirectly because of knowledge of federal cooperation with state income tax departments are not known, but they must be several times the directly attributable additional collections.

Multi-State Tax Commission

It is sometimes stated that without federal cooperation the states could not manage an income tax on individuals and certainly not an income tax on corporations. This position flies in the face of two basic facts. First, states were collecting income taxes in a very satisfactory manner before cooperation with the IRS was made available and before it was utilized by most states. The use has become widespread within the last ten years. Second, states are active in expanding the operation of the Multi-State Tax Commission (MTC). The commission assigns auditors from different states to combine their efforts at auditing the returns of corporations operating in a number of states. In this way the tendency of corporations to locate their profits in a state either not using the corporate income tax or having low rates is avoided. The term <u>unitary</u> is applied to the approach now used by 45 states to allocate domestic profits to source states. Some 24 states require that U.S. subsidiaries be lumped together with the main company for tax purposes. Twelve also include foreign subsidiaries. The federal government and most foreign countries do not use the unitary approach. Instead, they use arm's-length calculations.

Elimination of federal income taxes and the expected somewhat higher rates of state income taxes will stimulate use of the MTC. The Supreme Court has given the green light to efforts of over 20 states to cooperatively determine through the MTC the location of taxable profits of multistate corporations. This remains an area where opinions differ, however, and in the international area it may be affected by additional Court action.

One cannot help but be optimistic when evaluating the likelihood of states being able to administer their income taxes alone. State tax administration has enjoyed constant improvement during the past 20 years. It shows an upward curve of efficiency that is over and above the added assistance of computer operations and federal cooperation. Finally, the pressures for more complete and effective use of land, labor, and capital arising from the new federal tax approach will increase the size of the private sector's economic base available to support governments.

Death Taxes

Returning to the states their former monopoly over death taxes will be another and final step in the federal government's reduced use of death taxes. An increasingly smaller portion of decedents owe any federal death taxes. By 1985 the minimum level of a taxable estate will be up to $600,000 from $60,000 in 1942. It is estimated that the 1981 amendments will reduce federal death and gift tax collections from $6 billion to $3 billion. The beginning tax rate would be 37 percent; the top rate, 50 percent.

With death and gift taxes entirely in the hands of states, various approaches to charitable deductions are likely to arise. In addition, states can be expected to move toward greater use of inheritance and gift taxes. The interest will be more in collecting revenues than in reallocating ownership of wealth. Also, unlimited charitable deductions can be expected if gifts were made to institutions within the state. States would compete to induce legal donation of estates within their boundaries. This effort would be concentrated in attempts to attract charitable deductions.

Concluding Remarks

The fundamental change in the federal tax system described in this book will result in substantial shifts in administrative procedures and legislation for state and local taxes. For example, states will

shift their taxes toward the income, profit, and estate tax bases.
Also, the administration of local government's property tax will benefit from the federal government's use of a net wealth tax.

THE VALUE-ADDED TAX AND INTERNATIONAL TRADE

Border taxes are placed on imports to make the tax burden on
them equal to that carried on goods produced within a country. Tax
rebates are given on exports so that the tax burden they bear after imposition of border taxes by the importing country will approximate
the taxes included in the price of competing goods. This practice,
combined with European tax developments, continues to weaken the
U. S. balance-of-payments position. The situation is not self-correct-
ing and will require positive U.S. measures. Tariffs are separate
from border taxes, and negotiations setting tariff levels do not affect
border tax rates. Rather, border tax limits arise from domestic tax
levels.

Destination Principle

Under the destination principle the burden of taxation allocated
to a good in the nation of production is an irrelevant consideration.
The fact of tax payment by the ultimate user is the focus of attention.
A product highly taxed in the area of production but exempted from
local consumer taxes in the nation of use is a good that permits the
purchaser to avoid taxes he or she could pay (Sullivan 1963).

The destination principle is applied in the case of sales taxes
by refunding or exempting from the sales tax goods to be utilized or
sold outside the nation of production. This relief from VAT liability
on exports is called zero rating. The approach is uniformly applied
by all nations and has been included as appropriate under the General
Agreement on Tariffs and Trade (see Chapter 8).

The destination principle and zero rating are applied much less
to income taxes. In order for them to be applied to goods the portion
of domestic cost consisting of income taxes would have to be refunded
to exporters. The importing nation would then apply to imported goods
a rate equivalent to income taxes allocable to similar goods produced
domestically. In theory this sort of procedure is possible; in practice
it would be very difficult and it is seldom attempted. For example,
variations in profitability of different activities and production processes would have to be calculated.

Origin Principle

The origin principle calls for payment of the tax where the taxable activity takes place. The tax base is the economic activity, and it is assumed that the jurisdiction in which this activity is located has a right to enjoy the taxes levied. Therefore, the tax is not refunded if goods are exported, nor is a border tax at the same level applied on imported goods to make up for domestic taxes allocated to similar goods or to make up for taxes refunded by a government on exports. The European Economic Community (EEC), by developing very similar VAT taxes, has also moved toward the origin principle. But the switch has been very slow because VAT rates still vary substantially.

The origin principle is basic to taxation at the source. The source of a tax base is production activity under the origin concept. Taxation of income at source is an application of the origin principle. When income is controlled by owners outside the country, the owners' nation usually permits deduction from tax liability of the income tax paid in the country of the source. This treatment of taxes paid at source on income distributed to owners outside the nation of source is considered to be avoidance of double taxation, not taxation on both the origin principle and the destination principle.

If it is assumed that every firm benefits from government expenditures to the extent it pays taxes, then the collection of commodity taxes under the origin principle keeps the situation in equilibrium. Application of the destination principle, particularly under conditions approaching a common market, would disturb the cost-price relationship. If taxes were relatively high in a country exporting to a country with relatively low taxes, and if the destination principle were applied, the exports of the high-tax country would be subsidized by the amount of tax difference. This is essentially the situation enjoyed now by Belgium in the EEC.

Tax Harmonization in the European
Economic Community

When commodity taxation becomes possible between EEC member states on the origin principle, one member state will be able to vary rates without creating conditions requiring retaliation in another member state. This gives each member state considerably greater freedom to vary commodity tax rates in order to meet its local economic requirements and its international economic goals.

The international commercial relations of nations outside the EEC continue to be profoundly affected by the adoption of a relatively uniform, high-rate VAT by EEC member states. In effect, the EEC, in regard to general indirect taxes, is keeping the destination principle in dealing with non-EEC nations while adopting the origin principle in dealings with members. This constitutes the development of a tariff wall around the EEC.

Economic Impact of Development of Common Value-Added Tax

How does this development affect the international trade activity of business firms? The answer seems to be clear-cut. All EEC businesses try to expand exports to countries outside EEC. This eases somewhat the foreign competition U.S. businesses would face in EEC member states but intensifies the competition faced in non-EEC countries.

Potential Development

Payment of border taxes only by firms outside EEC adds to the advantage already provided by the EEC customs union of producing within EEC for sale to EEC member-state buyers. The tax revenues of an EEC member state will be increased most if exports are made within the EEC and imports are received from outside the EEC. With EEC indirect tax harmonization accomplished, rebates would not have to be paid on exports within the EEC and border taxes could be collected only on non-EEC imports. The EEC member states having large third country markets and large EEC-source imports would be in an unfortunate internal revenue position. This tends to develop individual member-state foreign trade goals that might be counter to the foreign trade goals of EEC as a whole. The business concerns of the EEC find the tax rebate from international sales to non-EEC countries helpful in meeting profit targets. The lack of tax rebates on exports to EEC member states tends to reduce emphasis on this trade area of EEC firms (Sandford 1981).

Concluding Remarks

What will happen to U.S. export industries if the tax situation in the United States remains basically unchanged?

Briefly, there will be greater difficulty for U.S. products to enter the market of EEC member states and intensified competition from EEC exporters in markets outside the EEC, including the U.S. domestic market. The development will decrease U.S. sales within the EEC and will stimulate U.S. investment in the EEC. Also, elimination of tax frontiers between EEC member states will stimulate greater fiscal innovation within the EEC (Lindholm 1980).

4

BUSINESS
TAXATION
CONSIDERATIONS

CORPORATE INCOME TAX

The breadth of the corporate income tax base has always been limited to businesses organized as corporations. Also, the tax rate has been applied only to legally defined profits. Finally, U.S. corporate profits realized in foreign nations are not included unless they are brought home; then the corporate income taxes paid abroad are credited against the federal corporate income taxes owed.

Basic rates of the corporate income tax have remained high with some substantial reductions of the rate applicable to the legally defined profits of small corporations. Nevertheless, under conditions of high nominal profits the corporate income tax collections, even in nominal dollars, have demonstrated a tendency to decline. For example, collections in fiscal year 1983 were down about $30 billion from the level in fiscal year 1979. In the same period nominal gross national product (GNP) went up by $700 billion and social security contributions by $70 billion. The corporate income tax has had a declining revenue-raising potency. This is owing largely to loss of breadth of the base.

Historical Background

The concept of taxing a business operation on the basis of its corporate franchise was initiated during the nineteenth century by states on the eastern seaboard. The corporate franchise was seen to extend valuable privileges such as limited liability and the rights of a separate entity in perpetuity.

As industrial development continued, more and more business managers made use of the limited liability and perpetual life advantages of operating as a corporation. The first expansion of use of the corporation in organizing manufacturing occurred in the textile industry. Corporations were most popular among transportation, banking, and insurance businesses. Until the twentieth century most states established corporations by adopting special legislation for each incorporation. Gradually, state after state established general legislation providing for chartering of a corporation if certain conditions were met. The chartering of corporations remains basically a state function.

In 1909 the federal government jumped into the use of a special tax applicable only to businesses organized as corporations. The action was taken primarily as the result of western and southern political pressure for an individual income tax, a tax that had been declared illegal in the Pollock cases of the United States Supreme Court, decided after the 1894 federal income tax legislation. The new income tax was limited to corporations and was enacted as an excise tax measured by income. The law was declared legal by the Supreme Court, and a new area was opened in business taxation. This action largely defined the meaning of direct tax prohibition in the federal Constitution.

The 1894 income tax legislation had included undistributed corporate profits, along with other profits, as a portion of the individual income tax base. This was not possible after the Pollock v. Farmers' Loan and Trust Company cases, so the device of separating corporate profits from other profits was adopted. These profits were subject to an excise tax measured by the profits. The tax was declared not to be an income tax. Therefore, it was not a direct tax and was not under the constitutional provision requiring apportionment according to representation.

Lack of Plan

As is clear, the current corporate income tax arose from a series of accidents and legal mistakes and misinterpretations. The legislative results of these conditions have been allowed to continue up to the present time. The legislation was not adopted because it was a just tax or because it was the best way to raise a given quantity of revenues without hurting the economic decision-making process. Rather, it was a procedure to circumvent the Constitution as it was then interpreted. After the Sixteenth Amendment was adopted in 1913, there was no longer any need for this subterfuge. But the corporate income tax has not been repealed.

To a degree, the corporate income tax is inevitable when government makes use of an individual income tax. When this is done and the business enterprise is treated as an artificial individual, some procedure is needed to make the legally created creature subject to taxes at a level comparable to that carried by single proprietors and partnerships of one type or another. The levy of a corporate income tax is a procedure to do this.

One must conclude, therefore, that the adoption of individual income taxes around the world is an important explanation for the popularity of the corporate income tax, despite all its bad characteristics. If the logic of this statement is followed, one must propose the removal of both the corporate income tax and the individual income tax as the best approach for federal tax reform in this area.

Birth of U.S. Corporate Income Tax

The corporate income tax had an interesting birth. It was as much a child of the U.S. populist movement and the desire to control giant trusts as a procedure to collect needed tax revenues. An internal revenue need existed, but the introduction of the individual income tax or a national land tax encountered strong constitutional hurdles, making them unlikely revenue sources.

In 1909 President Taft signed legislation providing for an excise tax measured by corporate income. The rate recommended was 2 percent, the rate adopted was 1 percent, and the tax worked well.

President Taft pointed out that the tax would give the government, the stockholders, and the public knowledge of the real business transactions and the gains and the profits of every corporation in the country. He intimated that as a result, intelligent and realistic national control of corporations by the federal government could be realized and reliance on state regulation would no longer be necessary. These justifications no longer play a role.

State Development

The states, not the federal government, were the creators of corporations. They saw the original use of the corporate franchise by the federal government as a taxation handle to be used by the federal government to facilitate moving onto their turf. One way to retard the use of corporate profits as a federal revenue source was for the states to move vigorously into this taxation vacuum. This they did—but always under wraps—as each state must consider its competitive tax position in the attraction of industry. Abandonment of the corporate income tax by the federal government will lead to expanded use of this tax by states. However, interstate competitions can be expected to keep the expansion reasonable.

European Corporate Tax Reform

The European Economic Community (EEC) countries have never been as dependent upon corporate income taxes as the United States. One impact of this less-committed position has been more action toward solving the double taxation problem, that is, income taxed to corporations and taxed again to the stockholder when dividends are received. The EEC appears ready to establish a scheme that would have each member country grant its own stockholders full credit for taxes paid on profits distributed as dividends from any corporation operating in any EEC member country. To make the procedure work, each country would give credit for taxes collected on dividends distributed in another member nation.

The reform procedure under consideration is very complex, even when only EEC countries with their similar economies are included. The nations of the world with their budget deficits find it very difficult to give up any functioning tax—even one as generally bad as the corporate income tax (Break 1977).

One must keep in mind that the corporation is a creation of the states and that under the program developed in this book all income and death taxes are returned to the states. Such action will reduce the difficulties encountered by previous efforts at tax reform in this area. A job of eradication and new plantings, not pruning, is required; actually, this is a much more manageable job.

The Economic Recovery Tax Act of 1981 is the latest example of how impossible it is to reform the federal income and death taxes. A simple proposal becomes a "Christmas tree" and a tax-expert enrichment act (Wall Street Journal 1983b).

The Economic Concept of Profits

On the face of it, the generalization that high taxes on income reduce the scope of profitable investment is acceptable. If a new investment produces profits of $100,000, equity-capital-attraction cost of $100,000 can be covered with earnings. If a corporate income tax then taxes away $40,000 of this $100,000 in earnings, then only equity-attraction costs of $60,000 can be covered. If this $60,000 rate is insufficient to attract new capital to the area or to pay the cost of holding old capital, growth of the industry will cease and old capital will not be replaced as it wears out or becomes inefficient (Knight 1933).

This seems to be a fairly straightforward proposition, but the special character of profits causes the relationship of profits to investment to be considerably less than straightforward. Profits have not been satisfactorily defined in economic theory. The best definition on which there is agreement is that pure profits is a payment for risk and that profits needed to hold equity (ownership) are partially a payment for risk and partially a payment of interest (Samuelson 1958).

The original justification given by economists for such an approach to business taxation rested on the definition of this income as monopoly income. The taking of monopoly income by government was seen in the 1930s, and still is today, to be a very favorable approach to government financing. The difficulty in using monopoly earnings as a tax base is that not only are profits difficult to isolate, but the portion, if any, of these amounts that are the return gained through exercise of monopoly control is too complex to be attempted by a tax collection agency.

Analysis of Profit Taxation

We have all heard it said, "Profit is not a dirty word." We have also heard it said in a derogatory manner, "He is only interested in profit." Uncertainty over the role of profit is deeply rooted in economic writings. The classical position is that profit does not arise when truly competitive conditions exist. When profit does exist, therefore, monopoly powers are being enjoyed (Samuelson 1958). If profit is high, the monopoly is strong. It is, of course, only a short step from this position to one advocating high taxes on profit, that is, taxing away the monopoly gains.

The base of the corporate profits tax is supposed to be the income remaining to be allocated to equity capital after all other claims have been met. Recent inflation and the failure to fully provide for inflated replacement costs of goods and capital have meant that profits are nominal and not real. They have not been true after-cost profits (Fabozzi and Fonpueder 1981).

Taxable Profits

The legal definition of profits is the base to which the corporate income tax is applied. This definition may permit losses to be deducted or carried forward. It may provide for a deduction of depreciation at a rapid rate or at a normal life-expectancy level. Taxes paid in foreign countries may be deducted from domestic taxes due on profits returned to the United States. And the list continues. Some deductions are important only to certain companies and under unusual conditions.

There are a number of ways to treat profits retained by the corporation and the portion paid out to stockholders, that is, distributed profits. Countries also vary in how they handle taxes paid by corporations. Most of the different approaches being used and one or two that have not been implemented are summarized below.

1. All corporate profits are taxed at a uniform rate.
2. Only corporate undistributed profits are taxed.
3. Only corporate distributed profits are taxed.
4. All corporate profits are treated as if distributed to stockholders and the total becomes a part of individual taxable income.
5. Corporate income taxes paid on dividends paid out are treated as prepaid individual income taxes.
6. All corporate income taxes are treated as prepaid individual income taxes.

The U.S. tax on corporate profits is called a corporate income tax. This gives the impression that income taxes paid by corporations use roughly the same base as individual income taxes. This, of course, is not true.

In arriving at its tax base, a corporation can deduct all of its costs plus a depreciation figure. An individual cannot deduct food or unspecialized clothes. A corporation is not restricted in this fashion, and energy costs, structures, and the like are all deducted before the corporation's profit tax base is reached.

Originally, the personal exemption allowed an individual to eliminate basic living costs from the individual income tax base. This relationship has long since been abandoned, and today's $1,000 exemption does not even pretend to cover living costs for one year.

Investment Generation

The corporate income tax reduces the availability of investment funds to the very business management teams that have proved to be particularly efficient. Profits, the economic concept basically taxed by the corporate income tax, is a measurement of efficiency. Corporations that are efficient, lucky, and operating in expanding areas make profits. Also, the small business operating in a new and expanding area has a particular need for profits to finance expansion. The taxing away of these profits forces management to look for an external source of new funds. The results are inevitably slower growth of the most efficient providers of goods and services, sellouts to large corporations, and a relatively low tax burden on those unable to function at a high level of efficiency. This, of course, is not a tax system that nurtures the profitable (that is, efficient) enterprises.

New and as yet unprofitable businesses operating under a fiscal system emphasizing the corporate income tax are able to avoid paying as much of the costs of government as would be the case if they functioned under a government financing approach that relied largely on payroll, sales, and property taxes. This is obvious. It is also clear that once a new business has reached the profitable level, the corporate income tax places a cap of a sort on further rapid growth. The corporate income tax also reduces the ability of a proved entrepreneur to put his abilities to work in another new and risky undertaking.

In the case of an unprofitable business operating in a corporate income tax environment, the tax paid is insufficient to cover costs of government services utilized. Therefore, under a corporate income tax environment the successful enterprise is discouraged and the failure is subsidized. The result is, of course, retarded economic development and reduced efficiency with which resources are utilized. This is bad economics.

Weakening of Corporate Income Tax Supports

At one time the concept of the cyclically balanced federal budget enjoyed wide acceptance. The fiscal policy supported large deficits during a recession and substantial surpluses during prosperity. The success of this approach in the 1950s caused the U.S. business group called the Committee for Economic Development (CED) to support it as a built-in, desirable, compensatory fiscal policy. Later experience has demonstrated that during prosperity most democratic governments are unable to develop surpluses for use in retiring debt accumulated during the previous downturn. With its sharp revenue increases during prosperity and declines during recession, the corporate income tax fitted well with a built-in compensatory economic policy (see Table 4. 1). When the concept proved to be unworkable, this basically Keynesian support for the corporate income tax was eliminated.

Another support formerly available to the corporate income tax arose from the economic experience of the 1930s. Observers generally concluded the depression was partially the result of oversaving. The corporate income tax was seen to rest on profits received largely by big savers. Therefore, a substantial corporate income tax would help to prevent another depression by decreasing savings through taxation of profits. Today, and as far as we can see into the future, it is a shortage of savings rather than overabundance that is seen to be the economic difficulty. Therefore, the relationship of corporate income tax to level of savings has become a minus rather than a plus.

Collections

The data in Table 4. 1 do not show the fluctuation in corporate tax collections that existed in the 1950s and 1960s. For example,

TABLE 4.1

Federal Corporate Income Tax Collections 1971-82,
Estimates 1983-84
(in millions of dollars)

1971	1972	1973	1974	1975	1976	1977	1978
26,785	32,166	36,153	38,620	40,621	41,409	44,892	59,952

1979	1980	1981	1982			1983	1984
65,677	64,600	61,137	49,207	estimates ➤		35,286	51,770

Source: Council of Economic Advisers, Economic Report of the President, 1983 (Washington, D.C.: U.S. Government Printing Office, 1983), p. 247.

between fiscal years 1967 and 1968 corporate income tax collections fell from $33,971 million to $28,665 million. In 1969 the collections were up again to $36,678 million, but in 1971 they were below the 1968 level. The collections in 1971 were $26,785 million. The 1983 collections were down to the 1973 level.

These collection fluctuations did not have the economic stabilizing effect postulated by compensatory economic policy. Rather, when tax collections were down, the government's borrowing activity reduced capital available for private use to revive the economy. When tax collections were high, new government programs were initiated. The additional revenues were absorbed in this way, rather than being used to repay government debt. Thus, investment and productivity were stimulated by lowered interest rates.

Aspects Inherent in Corporate Income Tax Reform

A basic fiscal-justice hurdle is created if repeal of the individual income tax does not accompany repeal of the corporate income tax. The difficulty arises because the corporation is treated as a legal entity separate from the stockholders. That means the corporation can hold income, and the income is not taxed if it is not distributed to the stockholders. A tax gain from a repealed corporate income tax is eliminated when personal income is also untaxed. This approach completely avoids all problems associated with taxing income allocated to stockholders and income retained by the corporation. In other words, exemption of income at both the corporate and individual levels avoids all the problems now associated with location of the income tax liability when a corporate entity is the earner or receiver of the income.

Corporations should not have untaxed income if income to individuals and partnerships is taxed. That is obvious. One alternative that tax economists have discussed for dozens of years is to allocate corporate income not distributed to stockholders as though it had been distributed. When this is done, all corporate income is taxed at the tax rate level of the different holders of the corporation's stock.

Special Treatment

One obvious weakness of the approach described above is that special treatment must be given to welfare and other nontaxable stockholding organizations. What rate would be applied to the earnings allocated to these stockholders? To date their share of corporate earnings is subject to the corporate income tax—and that is all.

Sometimes these organizations have argued that because they are tax exempt, corporate income tax paid on their portion of the earnings should be refunded. So far their pleading has fallen on deaf ears. But the tax position taken by tax-exempt organizations is really on the side of justice. In this case, however, justice is directly expensive, perhaps involving $10 billion of lost federal tax receipts. Indirectly, the cost could be much greater.

Action to give welfare institutions tax exemption of earnings related to their stockholdings could lead to a general demand that double taxation of dividends be eliminated. After all, there are undoubtedly many low-income receivers and people with little net wealth whose earnings from small stockholdings are taxed at the corporate income tax rate. If the corporation is large, the rate is 46 percent. That is pretty harsh treatment, but it is necessary. Corporate income tax collections must be maintained. After all, the annual federal deficit continues at record levels.

Source of Popularity

When considering the strengths and shortcomings of the corporate income tax, one must conclude that the famous British statement "We went where the money was at" just about sums up the justification for using the corporate income tax. For the tax surely decreases investment both through lower savings and through the need for a higher gross return before an investment decision can be made. It is also surely true that the tax increases prices and therefore is regressive.

The explanation for the success of the U.S. drive for the corporate income tax—and it was the prestige of the United States that pushed the corporate income tax around the world—lies to a considerable degree in the confused picture of where the tax's economic burden lies. The incidence uncertainty is so high that the tax assumes some of the characteristics of a miraculous event—a no-burden tax. Investors demand a return level based on after-tax profits. Workers' wages are not reduced and an additional percentage is not added on to what they purchase. Consumers do not pay an additional charge on the houses they occupy or the automobiles they drive. On and on it goes. Economists interested in taxation have decided, as would be expected, that the corporate income tax must leave an economic burden someplace. But they do not know exactly where, which is generally true of tax burden analysis, so they usually divide the corporate income tax burden equally between wages, prices, and profits.

Concluding Remarks

It is true that some tillers in the field of tax incidence have not given up on the corporate income tax. One of these is Harberger (1962). He concluded in 1962 that the corporate income tax acted to reduce savings. This caused the cost of savings to go up, thereby reducing the areas of profitable investment. He concluded the analysis must stop here. This makes the corporate income tax a tax on capital. It reduces the active seed corn.

This discussion has drifted away from the main topic, namely, why the corporate income tax cannot be eliminated in a program that retains the individual income tax. The corporation with its limited liability is a useful device to gather and manage all kinds of undertakings. It is also a necessary handle for raising revenues when individual incomes are used as a tax base. In addition, the tax has political appeal because its economic burden is difficult to identify. Undoubtedly, the practical political and economic supports come from the fact the tax goes "where the money was at."

ESTATE AND GIFT TAXES

The estate and inheritance taxes arose largely because in more primitive times it was one of the few approaches that could be used to shake loose some taxes from the wealthy. Assurance of the right to pass on property at death requires a government guarantee. It was therefore an area where taxes could be levied (Andrews 1973; Brannon 1973).

Today, the transfer of title to property at death is not needed to collect taxes. From the beginning estate transfer has been used as a tax base because it worked, not because it was right. Obviously, a reexamination of death taxes is appropriate in today's climate where taxes do not require the unique situation of transfer of title to property at death to be administered. Both Adam Smith and David Ricardo developed analyses demonstrating that death taxes decreased wealth and checked economic growth. Both of these fathers of free private enterprise were great believers in expanding wealth and investment. Today, economic growth is needed to keep unemployment under control. In 1776, the year Adam Smith's Wealth of Nations was published, economic growth was needed to avoid starvation.

The French were the earliest users of inheritance taxes. The roots of this tax approach go back to the ancient Egyptians and Romans and adoption of the Roman vicessina hereditalium in early sixteenth-century western Europe.

Colonial revolutionary leaders in the United States regarded the inheritance tax as a necessary part of preserving democracy. Thomas Jefferson supported an extreme position relative to the right of inheritance in a letter to James Madison.

> The earth belongs in usufruct to the living. The dead have neither powers nor rights over it. The portion occupied by any individual ceases to be his when he himself ceases to be, and reverts to society.

Legislative History

The present federal estate tax was enacted in 1916 and was modified in 1942 and again in 1976. This was not the first time the federal government had looked to estates for a peacetime tax base. It first ventured into the use of estates as a tax base during the period 1797–1802, then again during the Civil War. An estate tax was enacted in 1862 and stayed on the books until 1870. It was brought back in 1898 and lasted until 1902. The estate tax legislation of 1916 was apparently little affected by previous experience and legislative provisions. The tax enacted in 1916 was considered a war tax, as it had been in 1797 and 1862. In 1920 the federal estate tax was very nearly repealed. World War I had been concluded and the states wanted exclusive use of estate and inheritance taxes.

The states had been levying various death taxes since the 1890s. In order to keep the estate tax in 1920, the federal government had to placate the states by giving them a credit against the federal tax. This credit was originally set at 25 percent in 1924, and within two years it was up to 80 percent. The states continue to pressure for more credit because it is still calculated on the 1926 rates (Advisory Commission on Intergovernmental Relations 1981).

In the 1930s rates were raised and exemptions were reduced. This was a period when the real value of the dollar was increasing. The exempted estate went from $100,000 in 1926 down to $40,000 in 1935. At the same time rates jumped from a top 20 percent rate in 1926 to 70 percent of portion over $50 million in 1935. In 1932 the gift tax was introduced.

As all this rate-increasing and taxable-base-decreasing was going on, the states were left at the 1926 legislative gate. Stability came to the federal death and gift taxes in 1941 and 1942, respectively. From being among the least legislatively stable federal taxes, death taxes became the most stable. Collections during the period 1979–83 have remained at about 1 percent of total federal budget receipts and about 2 percent of total state government tax revenues (see Table 4.2).

TABLE 4.2

Actual and Estimated Estate and Gift Taxes, Fiscal Years 1977–85
(in billions of dollars)

Year	Federal Receipts	State Receipts
1977	7.3	1.8
1978	5.3	1.8
1979	5.4	2.0[b]
1980	6.4	2.1[a]
1981	6.8	—
1982	8.0	—
1983	6.1[a]	—
1984	5.4[a]	—
1985	5.1[a]	—

[a]Estimated figures.
[b]Preliminary figures.

Sources: Council of Economic Advisers, Economic Report of the President, 1983 (Washington, D.C.: U.S. Government Printing Office, 1983), p. 315; and Advisory Commission on Intergovernmental Relations, Significant Features of Fiscal Federalism, 1979–80 (Washington, D.C.: ACIR, 1981), p. 60.

Recent Modifications

The death and gift tax hearings held in 1976 resulted in the first major amendment of legislation in this area since 1942. The aims of the amendments, as of so much tax legislation, were to simplify the law, to close major loopholes, and to modify taxable wealth levels subject to the graduated rates. Very little testimony represented David Ricardo's opinion that such a tax was a burden on capital and should be avoided. Also, popular discussion did not take into consideration the point of view that "the federal government in using death taxes was invading a field that much more properly should be reserved to the states"—"properly" meaning that the transfer of title to property upon death is a function of the state, not of the federal government. As was mentioned previously, however, the federal government does provide the environment required for easily conducting title transfers when interstate considerations are involved.

Impact

The collections from federal estate and gift taxes are apparently capable of having a much greater impact than their size would lead one to expect. For example, testimony at the 1976 hearings of the Ways and Means Committee pointed out that family businesses were destroyed, that capital accumulation was reduced, and that inefficiencies in managing wealth were stimulated by the estate and gift taxes. Tax revenue benefits from all these troubles were estimated at $7.6 billion for fiscal year 1982. This is about 12 percent of corporate income tax collections and about 1 percent of total federal revenues.

One must wonder if a tax as complex as the federal estate tax and having so many bad impacts is worth all the trouble. Of course, political and economic support for the estate tax exists because of what are seen to be its good effects. One good effect in these days of $200 billion annual deficits is the money the tax provides, even if it is only 1 percent of the federal government's budget collections—every little bit helps. More than likely a reasonably detailed estimate of estate tax collection costs at the combined taxpayer and government levels would come close to the tax collection level.

Wealth Redistribution and Other Effects

The complexity and its cost find justification above and beyond the revenues provided. Through its collections the estate tax also works to reduce the concentration of wealth and, in doing this, provides an important service toward the preservation of democracy.

Several questions come to mind when this wealth-equalization impact is mentioned. First, one wonders if there could not be a better way to bring it about. For example, would a net wealth tax be capable of doing a better job at a reduced level of hysteria and tension that are inevitable with a death tax? The next obvious question is how the collection of 0.07 percent of 1 percent of GNP can be very effective in reducing the concentration of wealth. In addition, data show that only the wealthiest 6 to 7 percent of all decedents actually pay any estate tax. Therefore, the tax burden is very limited in terms of numbers making up the total taxpaying population. Location of the economic burden of the limited payments actually made under death tax legislation is in itself very uncertain. For example, can the decedent bear a tax incidence? Are inheritances windfalls? How are decisions on capital use affected by the tax?

Estate Tax Legislation

An interesting federal death tax skirmish has been going on since 1976 and continues unabated although action has shifted. It was 200 years after the declaration of U.S. independence and the peak of revolutionary spirit that a real effort was made to reduce the income tax advantage enjoyed by undistributed and unrealized income.

Congress declared that the heir who sells inherited property must count it as capital gains and then bear the appropriate tax upon the difference in value since purchase, rather than upon the increase in value since the owner's death (which the original tax had involved). The change was to become effective in 1977, but rich and fairly rich people and their attorneys raised such a fuss that the effective date was postponed until 1980. In 1979 the effort was abandoned and the 1976 legislation was repealed. The so-called carry-over basis (meaning deducting from the selling price of property only the original purchase price) was dead. Unrealized income from estates now avoids taxation it would have borne if realized prior to the owner's death. The repeal also ended the most significant liberal reform in the federal tax reform act of 1976. It was estimated that the reform would have increased U.S. Treasury annual receipts by about $1 billion by the year 2000 (Wall Street Journal 1979).

The skirmish currently is active in another section of federal death taxes. This time the drive comes from taxpayers. Success would cut federal estate and gift taxes in half, which would mean a direct loss of $3 billion in tax revenues by 1985. The package enacted in 1981 reduced the number of taxable estates by about 95 percent. Indeed, this action is more than a skirmish. It justifies the title battle. The tax-exempt estate increases from $192,000 to $600,000 and taxation of estates passing between spouses is eliminated. Legislation combining these two efforts makes more sense than either one singly. Maybe the tax base should be indexed to avoid the upward float of the rate applicable to the true value of the estate. And around and around it goes.

Need for a New Approach

The basic problem in federal tax legislation, which is really insolvable and which causes continued increase in tax legislation complications and in injustice claims, arises from the need to mesh all tax laws with the graduated individual income tax and the corporate income tax. Real tax reform, simplification, and stable government revenues are not possible until the two income taxes are eliminated. It is becoming very apparent that the turn to income as the major national government tax base was the wrong turn. A government requiring one-third of GNP must be very careful to preserve adequate revenue stability plus appropriate private-savings and investment levels.

Brief Look at an Alternative

The value-added tax has been used as a major tax in Europe since France moved its production tax to the broader-based VAT format. It has proved to be a good stable revenue provider and European business people report the tax to have a neutral impact on business decision making (General Accounting Office 1980, 1981).

Table 8.1 in Chapter 8 provides aggregate VAT collections as percent of gross domestic product (GDP) and of total tax collections for the eight member states of the EEC and Brazil.* The calculations were made from 1976 and 1977 data. The VAT is a major revenue source in 15 nations in addition to the EEC group and Brazil. With the possible exception of West Germany, the EEC countries are much more centralized in their revenue-raising activity than the United States. In addition, these nations raise as total taxes about one-third more of the GDP than the United States. Nevertheless, the VAT provides a formidable portion of the revenues raised by EEC nations and other users of VAT.

---

*The GDP is perhaps a better base to use in measuring tax effort than the GNP. It differs basically from the GNP in that only domestically produced goods are counted and the foreign goods used are deducted.

Capital-Use Impact of Death Taxes

There exists a generally accepted idea that death taxes (estate, inheritance, and gift taxes) are levied not to provide revenues but to redistribute net worth upon death and/or to adjust assets to minimize taxes upon death (Collie 1973). However, at least in the case of gift taxes and their lower rates, the legislation is also aimed at moving wealth into the hands of younger and more vigorous owners. Congress wanted wealth to be used more productively by encouraging transfer of property ownership prior to death and even in advance of old age.

The idea of encouraging vigorous use of capital is a good one. However, to limit it to somewhat lower rates on gifts up to a legislated maximum amount is not going to accomplish very much. There is no doubt but that the economic soundness of the U. S. economy depends on vigorous use of capital as well as on a stimulated and educated work force. This is obvious, of course, but all too little realized in practice. This is clearly the case in federal tax policy with respect to wealth and income taxation. The tax laws lower savings levels while also retarding risk taking.

If the goal in taxing wealth is to put wealth to work as productive capital while providing tax revenues to the federal government, then the legislation in place cannot even reach the target. In fact, through its encouragement of inactive trust accounts as a safe haven for capital, the estate tax discourages vigorous use of capital.

So how can vigorous use of capital and the concept of ability-to-pay be made a part of the federal tax system? The answer is in the use of a substantial annual tax on net worth. The whole idea of a tax liability accruing at death is inappropriate in a modern society.

NEED FOR LOW TAX RATES

Occasionally in the past, and with some greater frequency currently, it has been said that tax reform proposals must break away from technical studies and recommendations and move toward serious in-depth reviews of long-run tax impacts (Ture 1972). One of the basic elements in current federal income tax trends has been toward a narrower tax base and higher rates. During the past ten years the tax-revenue productivity of the results of this trend have not been high enough to balance the budget—or even to come very close in most years. This deficit and its impact must be included in any study of the results of using an ever-narrowing tax base and high rates, which are partially the result of upward bracket creep.

When one considers the narrowing tax base, it becomes impossible to say without doubt that the narrow base arose from high rates or that high rates arose from it. Certainly, one must conclude, however, that the ever-narrowing tax base prevented real rate reductions, which in turn were a major cause (on the revenue-supply side) of revenue shortfalls and rising deficits.

Inflation and the Federal Debt

Ten years ago the total interest-bearing public debt was about $400 billion. During the past ten years it has risen to three times that amount. During the same period the consumer price index has somewhat more than doubled. So what has actually happened on the direct-government-debt side is that the government has slightly more than used up the reduction in real debt that arose through price increases.

Again, the analysis becomes involved in the temptation of circularity and the confusion of cause with effect and spurious correlation. Did the debt increase because of inflation, or did inflation cause the debt increase? More than likely neither did the job alone. They reacted on each other. But the question remains as to how it all got started. Shortage of oil? Maybe. Keynesian economics? Maybe. Inappropriate tax system? Maybe. Whatever the true explanation is, there can be little doubt but that emphasis on the inappropriateness of the tax system has been minimal. Tax analysis that has been carried out has rested too much on technical issues and not enough on long-term goals.

The existing high tax rates are apparently necessary to make federal tax collections approach expenditure levels. Or maybe lower rates, even without broadening the tax base, will increase collections.

High Rates and Tax Shelters

High tax rates develop continuous, heavy pressures to develop and use tax shelters. High tax rates also strongly affect decisions about organizational approach and management decisions. The impact leads to location of profit centers, use of investment funds, and uncertainty over the type of financing to be used. For example, when interest payments as an expense are deductible from taxable income and tax rates are high, debt financing is encouraged. In addition, high income tax rates discourage savings, as the return from investing savings is subject to a high tax rate. As a result of these two pressures, interest rates are pushed up and the return needed on new investments reaches a level that forces many new investment opportunities to be cast aside. The return after taxes required to compensate for risks and the like is not sufficient.

Usefulness of Low Tax Rates

An economy relying on private funds for investment requires a tax system that does not discourage the use and creation of savings. The use of low tax rates with a broad base fits the basic requirements for the job.

High tax rates make it worthwhile to allocate the best manpower to the task of reducing the tax base. Under conditions of high tax rates good management cannot make decisions without including tax rates as an important portion of the analysis.

When tax rates are low and the base is broad, any effort to substantially reduce taxes requires a massive shift in operations. For example, a 15 percent VAT places the same tax rate on profits as on wages. The decision to use capital or labor is not affected by a difference in tax burden carried by capital and labor. A tax on net wealth actually encourages risk taking so that the realized income from savings or capital permits payment of the tax out of earnings rather than out of net wealth. Also, because the net wealth base is huge (as is true of the production base as well), revenues realized from the two taxes using these bases can be substantial without need for confiscatory rates. As a result, the attractions of a federal deficit should be substantially reduced.

Replacement Taxes

The political difficulty of developing two federal taxes, one on total production and another on total net wealth, arises of course, from the fact that everything and therefore every citizen is a source of tax revenues. The tax game that has been played so vigorously during recent years to get out from under the tax payment base loses its attraction. Yet to include all of production and all of net wealth would mean that everyone is included in the tax bite. Everyone therefore becomes to a degree a contributor in meeting the costs of government. This in turn means that taxes cannot be avoided in any meaningful way.

One cannot expect old ways and attitudes developed under high-rate, narrow-base taxes to die immediately. Rather, what can be expected with some assurance is that the payoff from efforts to shelter oneself from the law will not be large enough, in light of the vastness of the shifts needed, to justify the effort. Tax stability with a minimum of tax-determined economic decisions will result. And it will be good for our democratic capitalistic society.

BUSINESS TAXES AND PRICES

Traditional economic theory teaches that direct taxes are not included in prices of goods sold but result in a reduction of the after-tax return of those subject to the tax. Income taxes, including corporate, individual, and social security taxes, are generally considered to make up the list of direct taxes. The economic burden of these direct taxes rests on those receiving incomes as a result of the sale of goods and services produced by a firm. The after-tax income is assumed to be reduced from the before-tax level. It is also taken for granted that the before-tax income level is not changed by the imposition of additional direct taxes.

Traditional economic theory teaches that indirect taxes, which include all types of excise, turnover, and sales taxes, do not increase prices by the amount of the tax if the taxes are general; that is, if they cover all products and services. The theory concludes that special excises increase the prices of products taxed. It follows that prices of products exempted from the special excise taxes tend to fall. Again, general prices have not been increased by the indirect taxes. Established theory concludes, therefore, that taxes only increase prices if they cause a shift of resources to less efficient use.

Property taxes, death taxes, and wealth taxes generally do not fit easily into the direct and indirect tax classification. John Stewart Mill was uncertain about property taxes but seems to have considered them to be direct taxes. The United States Constitution, as interpreted, considers property taxes to be direct taxes.

Tax Developments

With the theoretical preliminaries taken care of, we are ready to dip into the institutional world of taxes and prices. The value-added tax (VAT) is a general business tax that was first adopted by France (taxe sur la valeur ajoutée [TVA]). In Europe the VAT has been adopted by France, Germany, Holland, Denmark, Norway, Sweden, Belgium, Ireland, the United Kingdom, Luxembourg, Austria, and Italy. (See Table 7.5 in Chapter 7 for data on VAT's impact on prices in selected countries.) It is administered as a net-turnover tax. The amount of tax liability is calculated on each invoice or sales slip. The tax due is reduced by tax included on invoices of purchases. This is called the subtractive method of calculation. When the VAT paid upon capital goods is deductible immediately and in full, it also becomes a consumption VAT.

The VAT fits the definition of an indirect tax that is also a general business tax. An important element of VAT's popularity arises from the international treatment it enjoys under the General Agreement on Tariffs and Trade (GATT) because of its classification as an indirect tax and an ad rem tax and not a personal tax.

Because VAT is a type of general indirect tax, the traditional incidence conclusion is that VAT is not shifted forward and cannot cause an increase in the general after-tax price level. Experience with VAT in the United States seems to support the no-price-impact conclusion of theory.

Michigan Experience

The Michigan Business Activity Tax (BAT) was a VAT legislated as a subtractive VAT, but it was administered largely as an additive VAT. For this reason it was declared to be a direct tax by the Michigan Supreme Court. The court found BAT to be a direct tax because it was actually administered as an adjusted gross income tax. This suggests another consideration—the method of administration affects a tax's categorization as direct or indirect.

Although the Michigan BAT was an incomplete value-added tax, it did provide significant revenues and was administered in an open economy. Manufacturers in Michigan were in competition with producers from states using a state corporate income tax. The record does not show that Michigan producers were put at a price disadvantage. This was the situation even though BAT caused the total state tax taken from state manufacturing activities to increase. Today, Michigan has a somewhat different VAT, the Single Business Tax (SBT). It is an additive consumption VAT and is being so administered. (See Figure 1 in Chapter 1 for a computation outline of this tax.)

The VAT, levied on the additive basis with the base made up of amounts earned in wages, profits, interest, and rents, definitely possesses important characteristics of a flat-rate, gross business income tax that is withheld at the source. When VAT is levied as a net-turnover tax, as it is in Europe, the taxable base has not really changed. It is just another method of arriving at the value added by the firm. The subtractive procedure also makes it possible to avoid the problem of appropriate depreciation rates.

European Experience

When VAT is calculated on each invoice, the tax is being administered on the subtractive basis. When the subtractive procedure is used, the amount of tax tied to that particular purchase can be seen by the purchaser. He sees that a tax payment is added to the price.

The additive method makes VAT more like the payroll or corporate profits tax in that the amount of tax included in the price is unknown by the buyer. How this difference affects the incidence of a business tax or the total cost of an acquisition is difficult to determine.

The TVA of France was under development over a long period. Its impact on prices during its introduction was blurred by the 1958 devaluation of the French franc. The original adoption of TVA took place in 1954; it had been introduced to a limited extent as early as 1949. The impact seems to have been deflationary. Perhaps this was because it reduced the likelihood of budget imbalance and expanding central bank credit.

On January 1, 1968, Germany introduced the Mehrwesteurer, a value-added tax. During 1968 German prices were apparently more stable than those of any other major industrial nation except Italy. In the late spring of 1968 the U.S. corporate income tax was increased. During the six months after this action industrial prices increased at a more rapid rate than during the same six-month period of the previous year. In both nations many factors were influencing prices other than tax shifts. Nevertheless, the price level changes in the two nations with quite different tax-legislation shifts must be considered significant. The price shifts also confirm what theory teaches us to expect.

International Treatment of Tax Costs

The General Agreement on Tariffs and Trade permits taxes categorized as indirect a quite different international treatment from those categorized as direct. Direct taxes are not refundable but indirect taxes are. Also, border taxes may not be levied on imports to compensate for domestic direct-tax collections.

Indirect taxes on exports can be refunded and border taxes of an equal level can be assessed on imports. The VAT is accorded the same treatment as special excise taxes or gross turnover taxes. The GATT assumes that all indirect tax collections are reflected entirely in higher prices; it does not differentiate between general and specific indirect taxes. This approach flies in the face of accepted, indirect tax theory and also, of course, indirectly accepts the idea that the way a tax is administered affects its impact on prices.

Basically, GATT's tax rebate on exports rests upon two assumptions: (1) that in some way the general price level can increase through the imposition of a general excise tax and (2) that the levy of direct taxes depresses the return to factors of production and does not result in price increases to permit maintenance of after-tax income levels.

Concluding Remarks

It is doubtful whether sufficiently definitive quantitative studies or theoretical developments will be forthcoming during the upcoming tax debate to establish how different taxes paid by business affect prices. Growth of the use of VAT and its current application in Europe as a tax tied to sales have fostered GATT's treatment of a general tax with GNP as its ultimate base like a special excise tax. The manner of VAT's use in Michigan demonstrates the practicality of the additive VAT. If the federal government should follow Michigan's lead, the world will learn much more of the difference in effect on costs and prices of a tax levied on wages, interest, profits, and rent from a tax levied on income received from the sale of value added. In addition, GATT will be faced with a difficult decision.

5

INDIVIDUAL
INCOME TAX
CHARACTERISTICS

INTRODUCTION

For the moment it is helpful to examine enforcement provisions in excess of those needed to assess a flat rate on some readily identified base such as gross expenditures or net wealth. In our system of government finance this amounts to comparing the costs required to administer a tax on individual and corporate incomes and those required to collect the same total with taxes on gross expenditures and net worth.

Income, which appears to be such a simple concept, is now nearly impossible to define (Kaldor 1955). Income tax codes of the world's industrial nations use a legal definition that evolved from legislation and court decisions during the past 100 years or so. The result is a concept that requires arduous study and costly research even to define.

These shortcomings of the taxation of individual and corporate income have grown as society has attempted to compensate for the system's failure to accomplish its original goals of a steady revenue source and a more equal distribution of income. Instead of switching to a different tax base to reach these generally accepted aims, Congress attempts to modify the existing system to overcome the growing problems. The result, measured in any reasonable manner, is a continually worsening situation. By becoming more complex the law is also reducing, not increasing, its correspondence with generally accepted notions of equity and stability.

It should be mentioned in passing that any relation of taxable income to economic income must be put down as largely coincidental. It has little relationship to the generally acceptable definition that includes both realized and unrealized increases in spending power (Simons 1938).

Moving the U. S. federal tax system away from progressive personal income taxes, estate taxes, and taxes on business profits to taxes on sales of production and annual net wealth would go beyond a major tax reform. It would require a fundamental change. It questions the basic concepts of tax justice and how to raise taxes, while encouraging an efficient and growing private sector.

As this discussion develops, particular attention will be given to how elements of the fundamental tax reform under consideration affect the tax movers of society. For example, how will the administrative problems of both federal and state revenue departments be affected? How will the wage earners, 50 percent of the total population, be affected? What will be the effects on new saving and investment? Would the pressure on income and wages of a tax system using these different economic quantities be so great that social demoralization would set in? Do high income and profit taxes create stagflation? Will the revenue demands of a highly developed welfare and defense state be so large that all old, as well as new, revenue approaches need to be developed to preserve a capitalistic democracy?

Taxing individual income encounters all the problems inherent in developing acceptable deductions for an ability-to-pay tax. The corporate income tax utilizes this legal organization as a basis for tax liability and largely avoids any ability-to-pay considerations in establishing the tax base. Despite this apparently basic difference the two income taxes are tied together in so many ways that abolition of one seriously weakens the other. Therefore, this study must—and does—conclude that both taxes be repealed.

INDIVIDUAL INCOME TAX:
HISTORICAL PERSPECTIVE

A little history of the individual income tax with emphasis divided between domestic and worldwide developments helps one to understand what exists today in the United States.

Writers of the United States Constitution were anxious to limit the national government's taxation power, while establishing a strong central government. These two aims are basically inconsistent because taxing power is a large portion of government power. This was only partially realized by Madison, Jefferson, and other influential political leaders.

The basic weakness of the concept of strong national government with limited taxing power was not fully realized until the Civil War with its immense national-government financing needs. Political support for increasing the national government's taxing power was found to lie in an expansion of ability-to-pay taxation at the national level, perhaps of the type that had developed in the United Kingdom. This was the individual income tax. But it was also a direct tax that could not be used by the U. S. national government because of the constitutional requirement that collections from a direct tax be allocated on the basis of population. A constitutional amendment was required.

Income Tax Roots

The idea of levying an income tax on individuals is often regarded as a modern phenomenon associated with the development of commerce and industry, emergence of a money economy, and new pools of private wealth. This is not quite the case. The rudiments of income taxation may actually be discerned in primitive societies when public necessities such as the common defense began to be felt. At first the chief of the clan or tribe was supported by gifts, either of service or of property. These voluntary commitments were in time transformed into a legal obligation and their performance was brutally enforced. The merchant's profits or the annual increase of a farmer's flocks and herds were taxed, as was the Jewish tithe paid to the Levites. The complex fiscal theory of taxation rising in step-by-step gradations appears in the writing of the Indian sage Manu, a pre-Christian tax reformer who criticized arithmetical-proportion tax rates because, as he pointed out, the man taxed 10 out of 100 rupees is actually struck more severely than the man who pays the same fixed sum on 1,000 rupees. He reported that the poor man is taxed with prodigiously greater severity than the man who can earn and receive 10,000 rupees in a year.

The Old Testament contains references to levies measured by some version of personal income. Regular direct taxation of Roman citizens measured by their income began shortly after establishment of the Roman Empire. Rome gave us the word tax from taxatio, meaning an estimate or appraisal. Tithing was used at the time of the republic. Under the later empire a whole web of taxes made the task of the Praetorians (civilian magistrates) so complex that they found it necessary to retain a large staff of accountants, or scriniarii. Sound familiar? Maybe this is what crushed the Roman Empire, and not the fabled Gauls.

Information on western European tax practices of the post-Roman era to the end of feudal times is scanty. In the early Middle Ages the rulers enjoyed prerogatives that entitled them to exact personal services (such as road building and fighting) and levies on agricultural commodities that were collected by public officers. Tithe barns for storing the payments made in commodities still stand in Sieburg, Germany, and for sheltering the dîme royale in Angiers, France. Later during the Renaissance, with the expansion of trade and the formation of substantial amounts of private capital, these obligations were commuted into money payments—like the taille personnelle in France, which applied to personal property, and the taille réelle on ownership of hearth and land. Rudimentary elements of graduated income taxation have also been identified in the English history of the fifteenth century. In England, as on the continent, there were also numerous charges or excises such as customs dues, market fees, and tolls at roads, bridges, ferries, and city gates. In the Florentine Republic in Italy, particularly when it was a flourishing democratic and commercial center, a graduated income tax was imposed. At one time it reached 50 percent, the current top federal rate. It was known as the graziosa, or gracious tax, because it fell lightly on those with low incomes.

During the time of the Third Crusade both England and France levied an income tax known as the Saladin Tithe to finance recovery of the Holy Land from the Muslim sultan Saladin. The income tax was considered temporary and was aimed at war finance.

Development in the United States

In America, as early as 1643, the colony of New Plimoth passed a statute taxing the colonists "according to their estates or facilities." Although the act did not specify how a person's faculties should be measured, it did differentiate faculty and personal ability from tangible property.

In 1646 the Massachusetts Bay Colony adopted a tax law extending to the "return and gains" of laborers, artificers, and handicraftsmen as well as to personal and real estates. A number of American colonies adopted the faculty tax prior to the Revolutionary War and used it during the war to meet the exceptional needs for revenue. As soon as the war was over, the faculty tax fell into disuse.

The modern income tax in the United States and around the world dates from the Napoleonic Wars. In 1799 the British turned to the income tax to finance the struggle against France when Napoleon I was at large in Europe and constituted a direct threat to England. Under the leadership of William Pitt Parliament approved the income tax law that set the pattern for later income tax legislation by other nations.

The British law taxed residents of Great Britain on their entire income from any source. Nonresident British subjects were required to pay on their income from property in Great Britain. Tax abatements were allowed for children according to a legislated schedule.

A national income tax was imposed in three different periods of U.S. history. The first time it was a temporary Civil War finance expedient. The tax was nevertheless retained for 12 years, 1867–79. The second time it was hoped it would be a permanent tax, but this was not to be. It was declared unconstitutional after the first collection in 1895. The third time was after the ratification of the Sixteenth Amendment in 1913. However, the decisive political fight, which led to establishment of the general income tax principle, was actually fought in 1909, when the corporate income tax was adopted.

The income tax in the United States was the symbol of a protest of poorer groups against wealthier groups. The labor, agricultural, consumer, and debtor groups, particularly those of the West and South, were unduly burdened by the tariff and other legislation favored by the wealthier eastern manufacturing and financial interests. The income tax was considered more equitable, an offset to unfair national taxes, and a means of redistributing instead of increasing the concentration of income and wealth (Goode 1976).

Civil War Income Tax Provisions

The first federal income tax was proposed by Representative Schuyler Colfax (Rep. Ind.) as a substitute for a land tax in the special session of Congress called by President Lincoln. One cannot help but wonder how U.S. history would have changed if the federal government had kept the land tax. The federal land tax adopted (and later repealed) was to raise $30 million, apportioned among states on the basis of population. Until that time the low expenditures of the federal government had, for the most part, been met by tariff receipts. Direct federal taxes were unknown to the pre-Civil War generation. Not even tobacco and liquor were taxed. The war levies of 1815 had been allowed to expire some 40 years previously.

The amendment providing for an income tax was not passed the first time it was introduced. Nevertheless, the committee bill was recommitted and when it was again reported out, it provided for a 3 percent tax on income in excess of a personal exemption of $600.

This first federal income tax law was not put into operation because the administrative procedures were vague and because the Treasury hesitated to send federal officers into the states. Fiscal needs were so great, however, that the income tax was retained in the amended law of 1862 and numerous other taxes were imposed, such as those on gross receipts of many corporations, excises on articles of consumption, and licenses on professionals, vocations, and occupations. Also, along came the Bureau of Internal Revenue in 1862 to administer the new taxes. Only after much debate was a federal administrative system adopted.

In the first months after the outbreak of the Civil War, neither Congress nor the secretary of the Treasury had much courage when it came to imposing taxes. It is difficult for us to appreciate the psychology of a people totally unaccustomed to paying for support of the national government except indirectly through the tariff. Aside from borrowing, three new expedients were devised to finance the war: (1) fiat money (greenbacks); (2) the internal revenue system, that is, excise on liquor, tobacco, and other consumption goods, licenses on business, and gross-receipts taxes on certain corporations; and (3) taxes on incomes of individuals.

The first income tax law, that of 1861, was very simple and short; in fact, it did not specify whether the tax was on gross or net income, nor did it enumerate any allowable deductions other than taxes. It was not dissimilar to the currently proposed flat-rate income tax. Before it went into effect Congress drafted another measure. This law of 1862 provided for the first national income tax to be levied in the United States.

The concept of taxable net income evolved gradually. In drafting the first two laws, members of Congress were not sure whether gross or net income should be taxed. They were afraid to designate net income for fear taxpayers would take out too many personal expenses. In the laws of 1861 and 1862 the only specified deductions were "national, state, and local taxes." The law of 1864 allowed deductions for business expenses, interest, taxes, and rent—even rent paid for homes—but did not mention depletion of natural resources, although this matter was debated.

The law of 1866 and succeeding measures permitted the allowance of (1) losses actually sustained during the year arising from fires or shipwreck or incurred in trade and (2) debts ascertained to be worthless. Depreciation was not included as a deduction. Much of the phraseology of the Civil War laws was carried over into laws written after the adoption of the Sixteenth Amendment.

Taxable Income

Members of Congress in the Civil War period were as puzzled as those in recent times over the taxation of profits from sales of capital assets. The law of 1864 taxed net profits realized from sales of real estate purchased within the year for which income was estimated. In 1867 an amendment was made to tax net profits from sales of real estate purchased within two years previous to the year for which income was estimated. Efforts to extend this provision to personal property were unsuccessful.

In 1913 the income tax was no longer considered a temporary wartime expedient. Each of the acts passed in 1864, 1865, 1866, and 1867 contained a provision that the law was to be in force until

1870 and no longer. In 1870, therefore, the question had to be settled. It was then voted by a close margin that the tax should be collected for 1870 and 1871 and no longer.

Objections to the Civil War income taxes emphasized four com-
plaints: (1) the revenue was not needed after the war, (2) the law was
inequitable in many of its provisions, (3) the administrative methods
were inquisitional, and (4) the administration was inefficient and subject to political influence. These were all good, reliable objections
to using income as a tax base and to applying graduated rates to an
ill-defined base established, for all practical purposes, largely by
Internal Revenue Service (IRS) regulations.

INDIVIDUAL INCOME TAX: MODERN PERSPECTIVE

Taxation of income is a means of acquiring revenues from those
receiving bloated war profits or possessing a profitable monopoly.
When ability-to-pay was related to these two income explanations,
the collections amounted to reduction of incomes not arising from
either mental or physical effort. In the case of war profits and monopoly profits, the income arose out of harmful activities and controls.
Amount and timing of these income sources would not be affected by
the introduction of income taxes. Both sources of the income bearing
additional taxes under an income tax were largely outside of the allocation of awards owing to efficient and imaginative business or personal operation procedures.

Profit in classical economic theory was a surplus in excess of
the funds required for continuing operation. The costs of capital,
labor, energy, and raw materials were all covered prior to the emergence of profits (Samuelson 1958).

Competitive Costs

Under the economic system envisaged when income taxes were
introduced in Britain to finance the Napoleonic Wars, the wages received as well as the pure cost of capital (that is, market interest)
would be only enough to purchase needed labor and capital services.
These payments, called wages and capital earnings, were set at the
necessary level to make costs and efforts required worthwhile. The
amount received amounted to the cost of producing the activity purchased.

The income tax envisaged as an ability-to-pay tax was not seen
as a tax that increased the cost of producing goods and services. It

was regarded as a tax limited to government capturing in an administratively acceptable way a portion of war-created and monopoly-sourced profits. When the tax is paid by income earners in a competitive market where costs and payments are in balance, the inexorable effect is to increase costs. This in turn reduces the quantity of goods and services that can be enjoyed and purchased from the private sector.

Ability-to-Pay Defined

The concept of taxation according to ability-to-pay has never been easy to identify. In 1915 the federal income tax coverage included only about 1 percent of the people, those possessing an ability-to-pay. The ideas of equal sacrifice and declining utility have often been called upon to support the justice of an income tax with graduated rates. Extreme use of the utilitarian concept of tax justice was set down in the United States by T. N. Carver in 1904. He based his justification of an income tax, which was levied at graduated rates and commenced at a minimum income level, on the British utilitarian writers starting with John Stuart Mill (in his On the Principles of Political Economy and Taxation [1817]).

Mill regarded a graduated income tax as a necessary, major element in any modern tax system. He accepted this because he believed in the concept of decreasing marginal returns, that is, satisfactions per last unit decreases as the available quantities increase. There has always been some general belief in the psychological relationship between satisfaction per unit and number of units consumed. However, it has been less generally accepted when the units are monetary and many diverse goods and services are available for purchase and enjoyment, and when the power of wealth can be put to a variety of uses. Finally, of course, this approach necessarily assumes that costs of private sector goods and services will not be changed by the levy of an income tax on the earnings from capital and the wages of workers.

It is necessary for a graduated income tax either to rest upon some measured concept of disutility realized from various rates applied to a uniformly defined income base or to take 100 percent of income above an established level in order to bring in adequate revenues. C. F. Bastable, the public finance guru of the nineteenth century, argued that income tax rates could not be set that would equate sacrifice and therefore create tax justice. In fact, an effort to do so would increase injustice.

The justice of a particular pattern of taxes must, from the very nature of the situation, utilize some theory of the distribution of the economic burden of taxation. The term incidence is used to identify the economic burden of a tax.

Incidence

The incidence of direct taxes, that is, income and wealth, is generally assumed at first to rest on the possessor of the income and/or wealth. As I will show later on, this may not be the situation. Whether it is the true situation depends on the economic and political power of the possessor of wealth and/or income (Phares 1980).

On the other hand, a tax levied on food may increase its selling price and, therefore, the cost of living. However, the incidence of the tax may not rest on workers belonging to a strong union. The union may use the increase in cost of living to increase wages. The higher wages may increase prices again. And so it goes.

Really, what we have here is a demonstration that taxes of all kinds act pretty much the same as other costs and prices. All prices include a tax cost used to finance citizen-identified services provided in part or totally by government. The portion of price that is not taxes pays for private sector goods and services.

Business-Cycle Moderation and Growth
of Federal Government Debt

One of the more interesting supports for the income tax has grown directly out of economic business-cycle policy. The economy, it was theorized with the help of some supporting data, could enjoy increased stability at high levels of action if the tax collections increased substantially during prosperity and declined sharply during recession. Of course, this is a basic characteristic of corporate profit taxes and to a lesser degree of the graduated income tax—at least if some very large loopholes are eliminated.

For this theory to work the following conditions are required: when a good boom is raging, the government would run a big surplus that would be used to retire a government debt accumulated when the economy was weak. Of course, as we have all learned during the past 45 years, the U.S. social-political-economic system does not work that way.

The idea of using the additional revenues a graduated income and profits tax system produces during a boom to retire the government's debt does not appeal to many decision makers. Rather, they opt for additional spending programs and/or reduced taxes.

Consequently, when the economy arrives at the next recession, it finds itself burdened with more debt than it had at the start of the boom period. Under those conditions the accumulation of debt at an even faster pace seems to be irresponsible—at the very least. Of more concern, however, is the onset of inflationary conditions and savings shortages for private business uses, resulting in an increase in severity of the economic problem.

Finally, it is becoming clear that the best tax is one that provides relatively stable revenues. The concept of the wildly fluctuating revenue-productive tax has lost its support—or most of it. It is also becoming clear that government, through its spending of tax dollars, provides many basic, needed resources and services. The need for these services and the cost of providing them continue through good and bad times. In fact, unemployment compensation and other spending areas tend to grow during a recession. As a result the federal government's deficit grows to such a level that financing of additional programs to stimulate the economy becomes nearly impossible. The cyclically balanced budget becomes a monster fueled by the basic revenue-raising characteristics of the graduated income and profit taxes.

Tax Effect on Work and Vacation Decisions

The typical skilled laborer or professional person now pays an average income tax of 40 percent and a 13 percent payroll tax. This tax level has a much greater impact on personal economic decisions than was the case in the 1950s and 1960s, when the same people were taxed at a 20-to-30-percent total rate. The findings of basic studies by George Break (1957), Robin Barlow, Harvey Brazer, and James Morgan (1966), and others no longer depict the true situation. Their conclusions that the income tax does not materially affect individual work decisions are no longer useful. Real tax rates are too high.

Today the individual income tax reduces the professional and skilled effort that produces taxable income. This reduced effort is being replaced by a less productive effort in areas where high taxes can be avoided. The opportunities range from operating a sheep ranch to managing an apartment building and then giving preferred treatment to tenants who understand the situation and offer cash for services received. Al Ullman, the former chairman of the House Ways and Means Committee, frequently notes the harmful impact of the individual income tax on living and working decisions of the country's great middle class.

Just a few years ago Charles Lindblom (1977) could say that skilled people and property owners thought of their earnings on a pre-income tax level. It was the "scores" they made, not the disposable income, that counted. Those days are gone. Everyone, from the person who mows your grass to the purchaser of stocks and bonds, talks and makes decisions on the basis of after-tax earnings. The income tax is a deduction or payment of such importance that every economic decision is affected—often toward wastes of all kinds. These wastes range from vacationing at a less desirable place and time to investing in risky oil and gas development partnerships.

The impact of taxes resulting in a productivity reduction is an additional collection burden beyond the burden of the tax payment itself. This is often called the deadweight loss. The deadweight loss equals the difference between an individual's before-tax and after-tax wealth minus the revenue raised by the tax. Current estimates place the average deadweight loss for husbands as a group, as a proportion of income taxes collected, at about 29 percent (Hausman 1982).

Personal Exemption

The personal exemption is an aspect of the ability-to-pay concept that is essential throughout the income tax's history and central to its current reform changes. The personal exemption can also have an important role in the development of net wealth and value-added taxes, the two tax replacements to be used in the new tax system.

In the original individual income tax theory the personal exemption was considered to be high enough to cover basic cost-of-living requirements. Certainly this is no longer the way the tax works, but it was true in the 1930s. Currently, the personal exemption of the federal individual income tax is $1,000. This is the same dollar amount exempted that prevailed between 1932 and 1939, when the all-items consumer price index went from 38.8 to 41.6. Currently, the index is at 290, about seven times as high as in 1939.

With the personal exemption remaining around the current amount, the individual income tax is levied on income required to purchase basic necessities. A person with income equal to twice the personal exemption, for example, is apt to be paying income taxes while being eligible for welfare assistance. This taxpayer has no ability-to-pay as it is usually defined, yet he or she is subject to the federal individual income tax. Under a flat-rate, value-added tax and a flat-rate, net wealth tax the concept of personal exemption is quite different. The taxes are the cost of government collected as a percentage of production sold in the market plus a percentage of wealth. No attempt is made to use taxes to adjust individual welfare.

Adjustments under the Value-Added Tax

Under the value-added tax (VAT) the concepts of personal exemption and ability-to-pay can be reached by exempting transactions concentrated in the lower income brackets. For example, rents paid by those occupying subsidized housing could be excluded from the VAT base. Also, food purchased for home consumption could be taxed at a lower rate than other purchases. Of course, it is quite possible that poor people will buy restaurant meals and that rich people will purchase food for home consumption. The VAT, however, may actually come closer to being a real ability-to-pay tax than does the combination of corporate and individual income taxes.

To say the least, the incidence of the corporate income tax (CIT) is very uncertain. There exists the possibility of forward shifting in the prices of goods and services produced and sold. In many ways the CIT is really nothing more than an incomplete VAT. The CIT is a tax on that portion of the firm's value added that consists of taxable corporate income as defined by the CIT legislation (Harberger 1962).

Current reliance on the corporate and individual income taxes fails in many ways to levy taxes according to ability-to-pay of the poor and the people in the lower-middle-income bracket. It is, of course, the assumed ability of income taxes to allocate tax burdens according to ability-to-pay at lower income levels that justifies the use of such taxes. This largely unproved advantage promotes the use of taxes that (1) are very difficult to administer, (2) reduce investment and savings, and (3) discourage exercise of initiative and additional income-producing effort.

Loss of Support

Much of the previous political support for the individual income tax, as well as the current loss of political support, can be traced to a switch in belief that in practice the graduated income tax is the most honest and just approach. The individual income tax not only fails to bring about a more equal distribution of income and to soak the rich, but it also treats the low-income family unfairly and causes over 90 percent of the taxpayers to doubt that it should remain as the nation's central revenue-raiser (Field 1981).

The income tax cannot increase the well-being of the very poorest portion of the population because it does not pay the income tax directly. To help the poor under the income tax system requires a negative income tax with all its built-in inefficiencies (Tobin et al. 1967). And, of course, the poorest will have their welfare most directly affected by the government's expenditure policy, not by its tax policy.

When a system consisting of income taxes and an estate tax is compared with a system consisting of VAT and the net wealth tax, two general influences come to mind. First, net wealth is a more stable source of income than income earned daily by bearing risks or conducting income-earning activities. Second, the business value-added base can be identified with greater ease than the individual income tax base.

Taxing Capital Income

Several recent studies have concluded that untaxing capital income can have a much more exhilarating effect on employment and production than had been suggested by previous analyses of the welfare cost of taxation of income attributed to capital productivity. One area of new research involves the variation in marginal tax rates of the corporate income tax depending on both the industry in which the taxpayers operate and the method of financing adopted (Summers 1981). The general conclusion of current research in the murky area of economic effects of capital-income taxation strengthens the position of those who rest their opinions on that taken by the founding fathers of the private enterprise system: that is, that wise tax policy should encourage capital accumulation and its use as dictated by a free market.

Income Tax Burden

The United States Constitution sharply distinguishes between direct (income and capital) taxes and indirect (tariff and transaction) taxes. However, it does not clearly distinguish the characteristics of a direct tax from those of an indirect tax. Economists writing in the eighteenth century generally placed property and income taxes in the direct tax category and sales taxes and tariff duties in the indirect tax classification. As C. J. Bullock (1900) and others writing about this problem at the end of the eighteenth century concluded, the distinction was not useful either economically or legally.

Economists defending the distinction between direct and indirect taxes turned to the allocation of the burden of these taxes (that is, incidence) as a place to hang their coats. It is stated, never with much proof, that direct taxes were not shifted but rested where collected. On the other hand, indirect taxes were shifted forward and the burden did not rest on the original taxpayer or on the producer of raw material. Economists did not go much beyond this declaration, and they still have not. In May 1981, as a matter of fact, the U.S. Treasury, in the person of Undersecretary Norman B. Ture, announced that data did not show the graduated income tax resulted in a reduction of concentration of income receipts even though the rates were highly graduated. This situation indicates either (1) that economic pressures to increase the concentration of incomes are so strong that a graduated income tax working in the opposite direction can only hold the fort or (2) that the graduated income tax does not remain where levied but is actually shifted. As a result the rate schedule does not change the allocation of income that should be taking place (Blakey and Blakey 1941).

During the Civil War the North levied an individual income tax, which remained as a statute from 1861 to 1872. The Blakeys' report showed the tax to be the most unpopular of all revenue measures used by the North. It was regarded as legal partially because it was an emergency war tax. In 1894 a federal income tax law was passed again. This law was speedily declared unconstitutional in the two 5-to-4 Pollock v. Farmers' Loan and Trust Company decisions of 1895. At the time observers felt that the court's decisions were not determined by the Constitution. Rather, it was felt the five judges voting for constitutional prohibition of direct taxes were actually voting their economic, not their legal, opinions.

Because the courts work with narrow vision, they can be at least partially excused for staying within the direct and indirect tax framework provided by the Constitution. Later discussions in this book will examine more carefully the trend of court decisions in this area.

Prices and Taxes: Effect on Each Other

The different treatment of taxes and prices has created the concept of the just tax. In a way the just tax has replaced the just price of medieval days (Sullivan 1963).

If we could eliminate the old direct and indirect tax dichotomy, it would be easier to gain a fruitful understanding of how taxes affect prices.

If taxes were increased to provide more free consumer goods (for example, medical services), prices of the remaining market-provided goods and services would go up to permit the resource transfer. However, consumers would have more money to cover the higher prices because medical services would be free. Prices would be up but inflation, as an increase in the cost of living, would not have taken place. This anomaly of government taxing and spending is often neglected.

It is true, of course, that the higher prices would bring about a reallocation of consumer satisfactions. Those not using medical services would have a reduced scale of living. The large users of medical services would have an expanded scale of living.

Taxes are prices. Every consumer purchase includes a tie-in purchase of taxes. Many common-sense economic generalities perpetuate the idea that depreciation costs and indirect business taxes affect prices more directly than other costs (that is, income taxes and raw materials). The more appropriate stance at this point in our understanding of the economic process is that all costs and payments are equally represented in prices (Dernberg 1974).

Concluding Remarks

Any prevailing tax system affects the relative willingness of people to work, take risks, and cooperate with government in its economic stabilization policies. In the past the use of a graduated personal income tax combined with a separate tax on corporate profits and estates was generally assumed to possess very desirable externalities. Current performance belies these expectations. Taxes on incomes and profits and a one-time tax on wealth were acceptable when government spending could be financed by income and payroll taxes with combined rates of 19 to 20 percent. But this is not today's environment. A new dominant tax system is required.

INCOME TAX ADJUSTMENTS

Current debates over tax policy continue a heavy emphasis on income and profits as the tax base. They are treated as sacred cows; tax reformers have not dared disturb them in any substantial way. It is now appropriate to explain why this is the situation and why it cannot be tolerated when ways are sought to eliminate taxation as a contributor to stagflation.

This section analyzes the generally assumed (but seldom discussed) basic characteristics of taxation of income and profits. After these federal tax basics are presented, a much more rational tax approach arises.

First, the income tax and its ability-to-pay justification must be examined in some detail. Because they are strongly entrenched, it must be a no-holds-barred examination.

The federal government's collection of corporate and individual income taxes at substantial rates is mirrored in a reduced fashion at the state and local government levels. Also, taxes paid at state and local government levels are deductible as business expenses in calculating the taxable income of business firms. Federal tax legislation also permits the deduction of state and local property taxes, income taxes, and retail sales taxes in establishing taxable income.

Regressivity Impact

One result of the tax arrangement described above is that $1,000 of the state and local taxes deductible from taxable federal income is a saving of $500 for the person in the top 50 percent bracket. For the taxpayer in the 20 percent bracket the tax saving is only $200. Thus, all types of state and local taxes are regressive. To overcome this regressivity push, these taxes must be removed from the list of deductions (Freeman 1973). The other approach is to set limits on the amount of federal taxes deductible from the state and local government tax base.

Coordination of Income Taxes

The usefulness of setting a deduction maximum is being recognized in state tax legislation that sets an upper limit on the deductibility of federal income taxes in arriving at taxable income. The procedure outlined above results in unfair taxation. Taxes paid to the federal government that are above the allowable deduction bear double taxation.

Deduction of state and local income taxes from federal taxable income, and vice versa, have tended to increase the acceptance of the income tax. State income taxes can be adopted at progressive rates, yet they may be proportional as well as progressive in collection impact. Thus, their political and economic acceptance has increased.

Income Tax Interrelationships

Endless discussions have taken place about the relationship between the federal government's income and estate taxes and those of the states. The nub of the problem is that they are personal taxes and their payment directly affects the size of personal income loss. The special characteristics of this relationship come to the surface in a number of ways.

One example is the favoritism developed when interest and property tax payments are allowed as deductions in arriving at federal taxable personal income while rent payments are not given similar treatment. From one point of view the renter also benefits from the treatment of interest and property taxes because real estate owners are permitted to offer their quarters at reduced rates. Going further, it can be argued that if rents charged do not take this tax saving into account, the higher profitability of owning rentals increases; this stimulates a supply increase that results in lower rents to eliminate vacancies under the new supply situation. But for this to work, income taxes on profits must not discourage risk taking and property taxes must encourage the building of structures by falling largely on land values (Gaffney 1969).

In this situation the deductions allowed in calculated, federal taxable income have become a federal housing program that affects land use and urban planning throughout the nation. Pressures to adjust to the situation result in expanded condominium development. The condominium is a prime example of how the federal income tax causes less-than-best use of investment resources. At least this is the situation if flexibility in housing use is one of the major satisfactions available at a lower-cost, before-tax deduction in rentals than in condominiums.

Tax Overlap

Procedures to eliminate important difficulties of federal-state overlap would undoubtedly make even more complicated an already complex federal-state tax relationship. Also, one does not have to possess the power to see the future to conclude that we have only started to allow for special income situations. Evidence of this is all around us in the federal tax legislation of the last several years, particularly in the Economic Recovery Tax Act of 1981. Again, the only reasonable answer is for the federal government to abandon its income and estate taxes in favor of a substantial VAT and a modest net wealth tax.

In a speech before the National Conference of State Legislatures on July 30, 1981, President Reagan pledged support for what might be called his second stage of decentralization of U.S. government functions. The second stage provides for returning to the states their traditional revenue-raising authority so they can finance a substantial increase in the financing required under block grant programs envisaged by the Reagan administration. This, of course, is a basic aspect of the new model envisaged in the federal fiscal program considered in this book.

Income Tax Justice and Complexities

The term tax expenditures is a fancy name for tax loopholes. They are enacted to encourage a particular economic activity through tax reductions. They are often used to recognize special circumstances. To a degree they incorporate the concept that all income belongs first to the government.

Of course the concept is fraught with such unanswered questions as, Why should the treatment of depreciation be different for a homeowner than for a business? and If depreciation is a deductible expense for a business, why not also for a homeowner?

These two questions cut much more deeply into the fabric of the justification for taxing the base of the individual income tax than is apparent. They lead to the question asked when Congress first adopted the income tax in 1862: How gross should the personal income tax base be?

For example, why should the household—the trainer and provider of labor—not be able to deduct from taxable income the total cost of raising, training, and providing for survival of "the laborer" when aged? Certainly, equality of treatment between households and businesses can be readily justified. Sometimes it is pointed out that the imputed income from occupying an owned home should be included in taxable income. If all expenses are deductible, this would be an appropriate adjustment.

In effect, one is saying that taxes and interest paid by a business are considered deductible costs but that tax expenditures extended to housing are different. The taxable income of a business is net income, while the taxable income of a household is gross income. Why should this be? Is this not another example that income constitutes a poor tax base?

Table 5.1 summarizes the income tax base lost through provisions in the federal tax code that reduce the base or the rate that would be applied if the normal tax structure had prevailed.

The revenues lost, in the U.S. Treasury's estimation, are very substantial. Each tax expenditure is supported by special interest groups who strive for the expansion of particular tax expenditures. Each new or expanded tax expenditure increases the technical difficulties of the tax code and decreases the available revenues to meet budgetary commitments. The Treasury's description of retirement tax credit provides a good example of how the provision of a relatively simple loophole adds to administrative difficulties and costs.

> The retirement credit for the elderly allows individuals who are 65 years of age or older to take a tax credit equal to 15% of earned and retirement income up to $2,500 for single individuals and married couples filing a joint return where only one spouse is 65 years of age or older, and up to $3,750 for joint returns where both spouses are 65 years of age or older. The $2,500/$3,750 base is reduced by tax exempt retirement income, e.g., social security payments, and by one-half of the taxpayer's adjusted gross income over $7,500 for single individuals and $10,000 for

TABLE 5.1

Combined Effect of Income Tax Expenditures
(in millions of dollars)

Description	Fiscal Years					
	Corporations			Individuals		
	1980	1981	1982	1980	1981	1982
Capital gains	1,175	1,455	1,600	22,295	23,645	26,975
Exclusion of interest on state and local debt	7,150	9,025	10,020	3,565	4,340	5,195
Deductibility of state and local nonbusiness taxes				20,495	25,480	31,680
Deductibility of charitable contributions	870	890	885	7,860	9,510	11,505
Itemized deductions[a]				40,915	50,955	62,315
Deductibility of mortgage interest and property tax on owner-occupied homes				22,170	28,065	35,465
Benefits for the elderly[b]				10,320	12,965	15,760
Fringe benefits[c]				35,010	41,335	48,550
Government benefits and payments[d]				18,280	23,765	26,450
Total	9,150	11,370	12,505	188,910	220,060	263,895

[a]Interest on consumer loans; mortgage interest and property taxes on owner-occupied homes; charitable contributions; medical expenses; casualty losses; nonbusiness state and local taxes other than on owner-occupied homes.

[b]Exclusion of social security and railroad retirement plus the additional exemption and tax credit for the elderly.

[c]Employer contributions for medical insurance, medical care, pensions, and earnings plus premiums on group life, accident, and disability insurance.

[d]Exclusion of military benefits, allowances, and disability pensions; OASDI disability insurance; OASI for retirees, dependents and survivors; railroad retirement; workman's compensation benefits for disabled coal miners; untaxed unemployment benefits; public assistance benefits; veterans disability compensation, pensions, and GI bill benefits.

Source: U.S., Office of the Budget, Special Analysis, U.S. 1981 Budget (Washington, D.C.: Government Printing Office, 1981), p. 230.

married couples filing a joint return. [U. S. Government Regulations 1981]

International Complexities

The very complex procedures that have evolved as the income tax has been modified in the international area will be largely eliminated from tax administration at the federal level when the proposed new model is introduced. This will be very helpful in increasing basic economic efficiency.

Currently, the transnational corporations doing business in the United States are subject to a federal corporate income tax and to state and even city corporate income taxes. Through the years the states have rightfully and successfully opposed all federal legislation to reduce their business-taxation powers and, to about the same vociferous degree, federal limitation on taxation of foreign-controlled personal income.

Under these circumstances the best that can result from legislative proposals such as House Resolution 5076 of 1980 and treaty arrangement efforts such as the U. K. treaty of February 1980 is a stalemate (Ainsworth 1980). (See the discussion in Chapter 3 of cooperation between federal and state government.)

State tax administrators oppose any federal restrictions on constitutional state-taxation authority. Multinational corporations regard the U. S. tax position as an exercise in double taxation. Congress, for its part, considers the granting of tax credit for foreign taxes and royalties to be too generous already and is not about to increase these tax credits against taxes due on income earned abroad and returned to the United States.

Use of corporate and personal income taxes as the major revenue source in the United States has provided an economic inducement to developing tax havens that increase real economic costs. The four countries reported to have the lowest corporate income taxes are Bermuda, Liberia, Panama, and Switzerland. Corporations from the United States organize subsidiaries in these countries, allocate profits earned elsewhere to the subsidiaries, and locate operations such as international transportation under the flags of the tax-haven nations.

The nub of the problem comes into focus as these details are considered. What is double taxation? Where and how often can personal and corporate income be taxed as it moves from sales at prices above costs to claimants of a portion of the earnings?

Maybe this relationship should be stated in terms of the necessary sales prices to allow income claimants to receive the funds required to make their resource contributions. Taxes levied on these payments influence the price level necessary to make available the resources required in carrying out the operation.

The growth of tax expenditures acts (1) to modify the impact of a change in legislation to fill another loophole or (2) to reduce an unfair burden that developed when new legislation was enacted to stimulate another business activity. Around and around the appeals and changes go.

Because income tax rates are high and progressive, and because they are not closely tied to an actual sale and purchase, they breed complexities. These characteristics cannot be removed through further amendments and modifications. As the United States has learned the hard way, simplifying legislation leads to more complications. A new federal tax system is needed.

Concluding Remarks

The most significant changes made since the original income tax act in 1913 are as follows: a credit for dependents and a deduction for charitable contributions, introduced in 1917; collection at source, eliminated in 1916 and reenacted for wages and salaries in 1943; preferential rates on long-term capital gains, adopted in 1921; exemption of salaries of state and local government employees, eliminated in 1939; sale of tax-exempt federal bonds, discontinued in 1941; the standard deduction, adopted in 1944; income splitting for married couples, enacted in 1948; and an averaging system and minimum standard deduction, introduced in 1964. The 1969 act included replacement of the minimum standard deduction by a low-income allowance, adoption of a minimum tax on selected-preference incomes, and a top marginal rate on earned income of 50 percent (Peckman 1971).

THE UNDERGROUND ECONOMY

Like the wind, the underground economy is not readily visible but its impact is apparent and can be measured to a degree. Like so many economic terms in common use, the exact meaning of underground economy is not consistent and therefore measurements of it vary widely.

Sometimes, underground refers only to illegal economic activities leading to income that is illegally not reported as taxable income. Often the term is used to refer only to income that is not reported for taxation. The source of the income could be legal or illegal, and perhaps both.

The underground economy has not generally included illegal reduction of any tax other than the income tax, although of course, sales and property taxes are also reduced illegally.

If the underground economy includes all taxes illegally withheld and all illegally sourced value or income, our understanding increases. No estimates of this total exist. The underground economy is minimized when limited to illegally sourced income, which is not reported in the income tax return because to do so would lead to arrest. This limits tax evasion to only illegal income.

Actually, tax evasion arises largely from wage income that cannot be readily checked. Often the tax saving is divided between the payer and the payee. Collusion results in a lower payment and a higher after-tax receipt of funds.

Information gathered and analyzed about the underground economy largely supports the conclusions developed through normative analyses. That is to say, when tax rates are high and the tax base is narrow, the portion of total possible tax revenues actually collected declines. Another important determinant of the size of the underground economy should not be forgotten: that tax-providing data useful in reducing taxes also possess a built-in tax collection improvement factor.

The underground economy reduces the effectiveness of public sector and private sector policy actions through its reduction of the accuracy of macroeconomic data such as the following: number employed, level of gross national product, income distribution, size of the public sector and price shifts, and the reporting of these basic data. If unreported economic activity is approximately 10 percent of the total, the possibility of inappropriate policy decisions is indeed large. One can therefore conclude that the use of taxes with a low proclivity for evasion is an important fiscal characteristic that needs to be taken into account in any tax legislation consideration.

Currency Use

The underground economy's size and changes in size are frequently related to monetary policy. Change in the quantity of currency outside of banks is often used as an indicator of shifts in underground economic activity. The expansion of private currency holdings in turn reduces the reserves available to the banking system. This situation reduces the economy's responsiveness to monetary actions.

The relationship of currency in circulation to underground activity is often used to estimate the size of the underground economy. This relationship in turn can be used to estimate the change that has occurred in the underground economy and, therefore, the adjustment to be made in reported economic aggregates.

Detailed studies by Vito Tanzi and George Iden of the International Monetary Fund define the activity of the U. S. underground economy as the incomes generated through the excessive use of currency (1980). It is presumed that excessive use of currency to generate incomes is not reported to the tax authorities. Although these incomes may be from illegal activities, this approach to measuring the profitability of the underground economy does not measure illegal income.

Expansion

Vito Tanzi, who has been working in this area for many years, is very disturbed by what he finds to be a currently strong upturn in the underground economy since the mid-1970s. Most likely this increase is closely associated with the substantial increase in marginal tax rates, which arose from inflation and very small decreases in tax rates applicable to money-income levels.

ADMINISTRATION COSTS

Any effort to estimate the direct, or so-called out-of-pocket, costs of the federal income taxes must be incomplete until a national study is concluded that would provide an estimate of the time spent by taxpayers in developing their returns to meet Internal Revenue Service requirements. The continued expansion of opportunities for everyone from the multinational corporation to the college professor to lessen taxes has forced additional private time to be devoted to developing tax returns that minimize tax liability.

In the case of the large firm the tax department has often blossomed into a department reporting directly to the president, while previously it was a portion of the finance department. A similar blossoming of tax provisions facing the typical small business and professional person has stimulated the rise of tax return specialists.

An exploratory study was completed by the Division of Research of the College of Business Administration at the University of Oregon during the summer of 1981. A brief questionnaire was sent to a national sample of all practicing lawyers who were members of independent law firms and of all practicing certified public accountant (CPA) members of independent CPA offices.

The base for this study obviously did not include all practicing accountants and lawyers. The executive offices of companies employ substantial numbers of both CPAs and lawyers. In addition, these professionals find employment in such tax-form completion offices as H&R Block, to mention the largest.

Accountants

Questionnaires sent to the national sample elicited replies from accountants ranging from the self-employed to members of national accounting firms. All regions of the country replied very nearly at the same level as CPAs are distributed, with one exception. As would be expected, CPAs practicing in the Pacific area responded more heavily.

The time spent in carrying out income tax responsibilities for their clients consumed 34.6 percent of total time devoted to their profession. Tax activity of CPAs amounted to 127 million hours, or 16 million days per year.

Using the Department of Labor's average yearly salary for accountant professionals ($19,113), the direct salary cost of independent CPA expertise required to administer the income tax amounts to $1.1 billion.* The profession estimates that about 40 percent (in addition to the salary costs of accountants) is required to meet office expense. This gives a total of $1.5 billion as the estimated, independent CPA cost of administering the income tax.

Lawyers

The survey of practicing lawyers who were members of independent law firms was based on the listing in Martindale-Hubble (113th Annual Edition, 1981, volumes 1 through 8). The basic finding was that lawyers belonging to law firms spend 21 percent of their working time on tax law.

There are 13,402 law firms in the country that deal with taxation. They average 14 attorneys each. The 187,628 lawyers dealing with tax law earn an average yearly salary of $35,588; 21 percent of their time is spent on tax law. Tax-law work, therefore, absorbs $1.4 billion of lawyer time. The legal profession, as does the accounting profession, estimates that the cost of maintaining the office and other expenses are about equal to 40 percent of the remuneration of the professional. This works out to be a tax-law cost of services of about $2.0 billion annually (U.S., Department of Labor, Bureau of Labor Statistics 1980).

Internal Revenue Service

The 1982 Special Analysis Budget of the U.S. government reports the allocation of funds for collection of taxes at $2.6 billion.

---

*The sample was random but not scientific.

This figure includes retirement, office space, and so forth, as well as salary payments.

Findings

Total estimated costs of the services of the government, law-yers, and accountants in income tax administration add up to the amounts presented below (U.S., Department of Labor, Bureau of Labor Statistics 1980).

Income Tax Administration Annual Cost	Billions of Dollars
Federal government	2.6
Lawyers in law firms	2.0
Independent CPAs	1.5
Total	6.1

An educated guess of the administrative costs of taxpayers' structured time allocated to calculating personal and corporate income taxes, plus costs of in-house specialists for businesses, would be at least equal to costs gathered in the surveys. That puts direct admin-istrative costs of the income tax at $12.2 billion for $371 billion of collections, or about 3.3 percent of collections.

If time is valued at $6 per hour, and 600 million hours are spent at the income tax-preparation task, as we estimated, then the cost of preparing income tax returns is $3.6 billion to the taxpayer.

Concluding Remarks

Administrative costs of the existing federal tax system appear to be growing exponentially. A change made today affects directly or indirectly a large portion of the huge tax and related economic de-cisions.

The complexity of administration required by the federal tax system has spawned specialists by the thousand who possess the un-derstandings required to lower income and estate tax liabilities. The situation is reaching the point where management to minimize taxes constitutes a large portion of management responsibilities. This, of course, is unproductive in the traditional sense.

High tax-management costs reduce the ability of U.S. firms to compete in international markets. A tax system so complex that the average professional or small-business person must employ special-ists is a tax system that needs replacing.

6

SOCIAL
SECURITY
FINANCE

PAYROLL TAXES

Federal payroll taxes are used entirely to meet the administrative and benefit costs of social security. The payroll tax is assessed 50 percent on employees and 50 percent on employers. The combined rate of the two taxes started out in 1937 at 2 percent and has now reached 13.3 percent. During the same period the salary tax base has increased from $3,000 to $29,700. Total annual collections have increased from $12.3 billion in 1958 to $226.3 billion in 1982.

Growth of Program

Program revenues have expanded at a very rapid rate but the expenditure responsibilities have increased even more rapidly. Through the years the social security trust fund has in effect been lending to the general Treasury by its investment in federal government bonds. During the current period of adjustment it would appear to be appropriate for the general Treasury to lend to the social security trust fund, but only under a strong pledge to repay within a 10-to-20-year period.

Of course, the Treasury is in deep deficit and has no funds to lend. However, currently a substantial portion of federal debt obligations arise from off-budget lending. Certainly the social security fund would be as appropriate a borrower as many of those currently financed with Federal Financing Bank guarantees. The bank's actions make funds available now for use by the Federal Housing Administration, Farm Credit Banks, the Student Loan Marketing Association, and the like.

Payroll Tax Financing

The financing of social security pension payments with tax levies on wages and commissions paid and received is appropriate. By equating current tax collections with current benefit payments, such a program puts into effect a pay-as-you-go system of retirement payments for the vast majority of income earners. Modifications in the system, particularly during the past 20 years, have broken away from the direct relationship of benefit potential and tax payment. The folly of this policy switch is being realized now. My recommendation for a continuation of the social security tax to finance retirement and certain limited additional family benefits is based on a belief that the welfare portion not associated with tax payment will be cut back. This is already happening. The political strength of those benefiting by a tax-benefit-type social security system will make itself felt.

Private or Public Sector

The payroll tax has been frequently found wanting in the past because the collections, as a percentage of earned and unearned income, were regressive. That is, social security tax payments directly paid out of income received constituted a larger portion of the incomes of lower income receivers than of higher. Of course, the closer benefits are to total employee and employer payroll tax payments, the less appropriate is the regressivity argument. The payroll tax becomes a purchase of a benefit. The size of this benefit considered appropriate in our society requires a larger proportionate payment from the lower income receivers than the higher. They both pay the price needed to finance the benefits they receive.

It is like the purchase of a loaf of bread. The loaf costs a larger portion of the income of the low earner than of the high earner. This approach to establishing the justice of flat-rate social security taxes leads one to ask, Why not have the system in the private sector? The answer issues directly from an important difference in the gathering of funds by government or by a business firm. The difference is that government can use its police power and its broad coverage to bring nearly everyone into the system. The private sector does not possess this power.

Under a private sector system the very ones that will need the support of social-security-type payments the most will have failed to keep up their payments. If a private sector system is used, or if benefits correspond exactly to payments plus interest, the beneficial influence of government in this very legitimate functional area is being needlessly cast aside.

Social Security Concept

All the social security systems of the world have social weight-
ing as one of their features. It means that some reliance is placed on
general government revenues. The temptation to expand this portion
of the system always exists, as it looks like a "free lunch." The attractiveness of using general revenues to finance social security has
been only partially resisted in the United States, but more here than
in other industrial nations. Along these lines a change in financing
of the Supplemental Security Income (SSI) would be appropriate (Break
1977).

Financing of SSI with general revenues helps to maintain the
closeness of the relationships between dedicated tax payments and
benefits. The SSI program's substantial skew toward benefits in relation to payments justifies payment financing with general revenue
funds rather than with payroll taxes. This procedure would avoid introduction of a means test into the social security program.

Economic Impact

A wrong turn was taken when the nation's health insurance, or
Medicare, program was initiated with financing from payroll tax revenues. It has acted to reduce the correspondence between payments
and benefits. Payroll tax financing of Medicare is basically inappropriate, as the benefit distribution is inherently very uneven.

The continued use of a payroll tax divided between employee and
employer except for the unemployment insurance, which is paid entirely by the employer, acts somewhat to stimulate business procedures
using less labor and more capital. This disadvantage is outweighed
by the desirability of keeping the basic social security benefits tied
to payments. A large portion of the current financing difficulty has
arisen from benefit eligibility expansions that are largely unrelated
to payroll tax payments (Vedder 1982).

The burden of the payroll tax has been increasing as costs of
social security benefits have increased. A substantial portion of income taxed under the payroll tax is also included in the base subject
to federal, state, and local individual income taxes. These income
taxes have graduated rates, particularly at the federal level, and have
therefore realized higher rates on the same level of real income as
inflation has continued.

This situation has undoubtedly affected the willingness of producers to sacrifice in order to increase earnings. The substantial,
combined payment rates on earnings promote the working out of payment procedures that are less efficient before taxes but more efficient

after taxes. In the case of the payroll tax, where tax collections are made to finance social security and where individual pension benefits are closely tied to lifetime tax payments, the expanding real collections of the individual income tax cause serious crowding-out problems (Carver 1904).

Incidence of Payroll Taxes

Efforts to measure the incidence of payroll taxes have not been very useful (Peckman 1974). If it is assumed payroll taxes are paid by employers, then they are a type of indirect business tax. If it is assumed they are paid by employees, they are a direct personal income tax. If it is assumed they are forced savings of employees, then payroll taxes cause an increase in the portion of disposable income saved and in the portion of income in the future arising from interest. If the payroll tax is an indirect business tax and all indirect business taxes are shifted forward, the payroll taxes are paid by purchasers of goods and services. If all indirect business taxes are shifted backward by business, then those factors with the least elastic supplies will bear the tax incidence (Schultze 1971).

The General Agreement on Tariffs and Trade (GATT) treats payroll taxes as a portion of the wages of employees or as a direct income tax (U.S., Department of State 1961). For this reason payroll taxes or any tax levied to finance social security cannot directly benefit from the destination principle. Therefore, the use of indirect taxes to directly finance social security does not under GATT pave the way to the refund of taxes on exports or to the levy of border taxes on imports. The word directly is important here, for financial support is being provided very indirectly through reduced use of income taxes to meet general budget needs.

In the national economic accounts both payroll tax paid by employers prior to wage payment and the portion paid along with wages and deducted from contracted wages are treated as if borne by the employee. The taxes result in a reduced contribution of wages to disposable personal income and in no reduction of the contribution of profits or rents (Okner 1975).

Under the existing, national economic-account procedures the finance of social security with indirect taxes would decrease national income, from which all payments to factors of production are made. The reduction of amounts received by each productive factor as a result of the new indirect tax replacing the payroll taxes would be indeterminate. The change would, however, eliminate the deductions of employer and employee payroll taxes from payments made to labor as a factor of production.

As was mentioned above, GATT does not permit equivalent border taxes or refund on exports of taxes used to finance social security (GATT 1961). Therefore, indirect taxes used to directly finance social security could not benefit from destination-principle treatment.

Social Security Costs

To go one step further in determining (1) the nature of direct and indirect taxes and (2) the allocation given to social security taxes in international understandings, we must consider the effort of the Organization of the European Economic Community (OEEC) at standardization. In 1960 the OEEC defined the term direct taxes to include "all income taxes, estate and gift taxes, personal capital taxes and all social security contributions" (Stone 1979).

The definition makes the property taxes paid by commercial enterprises indirect taxes, and it makes the property taxes paid by individuals direct taxes. This is approximately the breakdown followed in the U.S. national economic accounts. However, because a considerable portion of U.S. property taxes are "set aside to finance worker benefits," the United States could encounter difficulties if it assessed as countervailing duties on imported steel, for example, an allocation of the property taxes of the steel industry. Nevertheless, it could be a first step toward harmonization of U.S. and European taxation of goods in international commerce (Munnell 1977).

The continuing efforts to develop a just tax have brought forth studies aimed at locating where the economic burden of different taxes rests. As the studies multiply, the end result of their findings becomes less satisfying and more complex.

The tax approach proposed in this book provides for the repeal of federal individual and corporate income taxes. When this change is put into effect, the tax base available to the payroll tax will expand substantially. Income earned will be taxed at the federal level only by the payroll tax.

Wage-sourced income is generally taxed at a marginal rate of 30 percent of taxable income. The payroll tax rate is applied to earnings before individual income taxes are deducted. Under the tax approach considered here, the base to which the payroll tax is applied does not change, but it is no longer subject to another income tax with marginal rates between 30 and 40 percent. Therefore, one result of eliminating the federal individual income tax will be a much sounder, and in an after-tax sense, a much larger payroll tax base.

Revenue Collections

As Table 6.1 demonstrates, the collections from federal payroll taxes have increased steadily year by year. The projected level of collections for 1984 at $243 billion approximates the federal government's individual income tax collections in 1980. Of course, the value of the dollar has decreased during the past two years and is forecast to decline at around 6 percent per year during the period 1982–84.

TABLE 6.1

Federal Social Insurance Taxes and Contributions 1973–82,
Estimates 1983–84
(in millions of dollars)

1973	1974	1975	1976	1977	1978	1979
63,115	75,071	84,534	90,769	106,485	120,967	138,939

1980	1981	1982			1983	1984
157,803	183,720	201,498	estimates	➤	210,313	242,937

Source: Council of Economic Advisers, Economic Report of the President, 1983 (Washington, D.C.: U.S. Government Printing Office, 1983), pp. 246–47.

Concluding Remarks

There is considerable justification for assuming that both the individual income tax and the social insurance taxes are assessed on income. Taking this position, we find that $538,526 million out of total federal budget receipts of $659,702 million estimated for 1984 are acquired by levying taxes on income as defined in the tax code. In addition, of course, nearly all states and some cities levy an individual income tax. Finally, the corporate income tax is forecast to provide $52 billion of federal revenues in addition to state and local collections. It is high time for income, however it is defined, to be relieved from this horrendous burden.

RELATION OF THE VALUE-ADDED TAX
TO SOCIAL SECURITY FINANCE

The advantages of having the financing of the social security program related directly to benefits outweigh the disadvantages of using a payroll tax at a rate high enough to cover costs. When the personal income tax is eliminated, many covered employees will find their income tax reductions more than sufficient to cover the full amount due from social insurance taxes and contributions.

Social insurance taxes and contributions reached the $215 billion level for fiscal year 1982. When the federal individual income tax is repealed, the increased disposable income (both individual and business) that is expected to be retained will total about one-third more than this amount. It is assumed that payroll taxes will remain the same after the individual income tax is repealed. Collections from a new value-added tax (VAT) would replace much of the revenues lost through repeal of the federal corporate and individual income taxes.

The financing of social security has created a major need for large federal tax collections. Payroll taxes that finance social security costs place a heavy burden on U.S. exports and improve the international competitive position of Western European producers of export goods and services (General Accounting Office 1980). Use of countervailing duties until the U.S. tax system is harmonized with Western Europe's is a step within the general spirit of GATT. However, the United States continues to attempt the economic adjustments required to rectify the adverse economic situation without making a major shift in tax-collection procedures. This just will not work; 15 years should be enough time in trying (Munnell 1977).

Introduction

At this point in time it looks as though the United States and other free-world industrial nations will continue to support with taxes one-third to over one-half of the income used to finance production outside the immediate family. This situation is often called the welfare state, and it is seen as undesirable (Break 1977).

The discussion here does not judge whether big government spending is bad or good. Rather, the analysis is entirely concerned with the economic impact of the tax program utilized to transfer a huge amount of purchasing power to government control.

The federal tax system places great emphasis on profits and wages as the economic base to which tax rates will be applied. Production, sales, and capital are not used as major tax bases. Why this is so can be partially found in the provisions of the Constitution and its emphasis on financing federalism. Another basic explanation seems to be that development of the tax system took place largely during periods of war and deep depression.

To be realistic, reform of the federal tax system must meet five goals. First, the number of general taxes in use cannot be increased. Second, the complexity of compliance must be substantially reduced. Third, the rich and the powerful must bear relatively heavy taxes. Fourth, the tax base must be as stable or more stable than the general economy. Fifth, the tax system cannot make a higher net return necessary if an investment is to be made.

Tax Reform Framework

The new tax system briefly outlined in Table 1.1 meets the five requirements. The number of taxes is reduced by one. The revenues to be expected are relatively stable. The ordinary individual and business firm would not have to struggle with a complex tax return. The truly wealthy person would be subject to a tax that uses wealth as its base and that would stimulate more complete use of wealth's potential productivity. The U.S. international competitive position would be improved because of the favorable international treatment accorded to indirect taxes such as the value-added tax (Munnell 1977).

A Few Specific Effects

The nation's major fiscal problem is generally agreed to be the financing of the federal social security program. The reform suggested in this book would allow the release of substantial funds as reduced income tax liabilities. Wage earners would no longer have income taxes withheld from their paychecks. The released funds could be picked up by social security as needed. The social security system would have the potential of providing substantial additional funds to finance its operations without going beyond a payroll tax with reasonable rates. The social security system could continue to be financed completely from its own payroll tax.

There is much to be said for financing social security from collections of a payroll tax. Perhaps the principal advantage is that the worker, and of course a large portion of the voters, are made directly aware of the program's costs. More than likely the unemployment assistance program would be less burdensome if its financing came from wage earners, not from employers as a percentage of wages and from general federal revenues when state funds dry up.

Also, use of payroll taxes to finance social security reflects a general finance approach used around the world. Prior to continued high unemployment, the taxes provided by a payroll base were relatively stable. They remain more stable than graduated personal income taxes or corporate income taxes with all of their tax-expenditure and international economic baggage.

Concluding Remarks

Income has proved to be a much weaker tax base than has been assumed by U. S. tax engineers throughout the years. The time has come for the federal government to sharply reduce its reliance on income as a tax base; it should limit its use to the payroll tax. Both capital and transactions can constitute the base for substantial taxes while capitalism and the market are preserved as the principal bases for allocating resources.

This analysis of social security financing assumes that the advantages of directly relating the financing of the social security program to benefits outweigh the disadvantages of using a payroll tax at a rate high enough to cover costs. It is also true that VAT can indirectly finance social security benefits while replacing income tax collections.

Social insurance taxes and contributions are estimated to reach the $243 billion level for fiscal year 1984. This is about $50 billion less than the expected individual income tax collections for the same year.

7

THE
VALUE-ADDED
TAX

CONSIDERATIONS IN A SHIFT FROM INCOME
TO TRANSACTIONS AS A TAX BASE

Few would deny that it is an important plus for a tax to assist
in making international adjustments. When a general tax measured
by value of product does this better than a general tax measured by
income, product taxation possesses an advantage justifying its consideration for adoption. Support must stop here if the enjoyment of international tax strengths requires the surrender of important good
and useful domestic attributes possessed by the current tax system.
Domestic tax effectiveness cannot be surrendered to gain international advantages. The tail cannot be permitted to wag the dog.

Prices

Uncertainty exists as to the effect on prices of a movement toward general rebatable excise (GRE) taxes (rebatable on exports under rules of the General Agreement on Tariffs and Trade [GATT]) and
away from income, net wealth, property (IWP) taxes (nonrebatable on
exports under rules of GATT). The analysts assume, of course, that
aggregate tax collections would remain constant. Many theorists have
considered these tax-price relationships and the findings to be incon-
clusive.

The relative prices of goods and services produced in different
nations entering into international trade are affected by the international exchange rates established for each currency. Establishment
of an equilibrium group of exchange rates would include the different
tax systems and tax rates as a part of the determination. In addition,

the efficiency of government expenditures of tax collections would affect relative prices of internationally traded goods and services.

It seems impossible to measure a variation in domestic prices of internationally traded goods and services that arises from a difference in the portion of total taxes from GRE and IWP sources. In addition, the difference that has existed historically has been included in current international exchange rates. If the effect on export prices of a nation's shift from GRE to IWP taxes (or from IWP to GRE taxes) is substantial, other nations must be willing to make the types of adjustments identified above. An improvement in international competitiveness by a change to GRE taxes is only measurable as the change (1) permits additional tax rebates on exports and additional compensatory taxes on imports and (2) relates to domestic prices of goods entering into international commerce.

Taxes and Ability-to-Pay

The control of governments by popular majorities is tied to taxation based on ability-to-pay. The aim of such taxation is to collect a larger portion of the incomes and (maybe) wealth of middle-income and rich groups than of the poor. Because the number of poor has been much larger than the middle-income groups or the rich in all societies until the modern affluent ones, popular support for ability-to-pay taxation has been dominant. Taxation based on income with progressive tax rates possesses the apparent ability to collect taxes according to ability-to-pay, while this is not an obvious characteristic of taxes based on product (Morgan 1962).

The position that IWP tax emphasis and democracy go together possesses a strong historical basis for acceptance. However, the position does not seem to lend itself to current economic conditions where productivity potentials within the industrial nations are sufficient to eliminate poverty. The IWP taxes are adaptable to relatively high tax collections from the rich. Emphasis on taxes of this type had redistribution of income as an important goal. It was a democratic goal aimed at increasing the well-being of the poor by reducing the well-being of the middle class and the rich.

In the United States the goal of income redistribution has been pushed more actively than in most other countries, especially since the 1930s. Despite high individual and corporate income tax rates and the inclusion of capital gains in taxable income (as well as what must be the best income tax enforcement organization), progress toward the goal of more equal income distribution through tax collections has been disappointing. In recognition of the shortcomings of progressive income tax rates in redistributing income, their use has been nearly abandoned in Germany.

The democratic method to help the poor is rapidly shifting from taxing policy to spending policy. The size of the economic pie has increased rapidly and continuously since World War II. This new economic level and expanding productivity point toward a future in which democratic governments will spend to maintain citizens' income throughout life and will provide support to increase citizens' education and productivity.

Under the circumstances of the present and the visible future, the role of taxation in a democracy will be to provide stable revenues while encouraging economic growth within a framework of close international interaction. Such a tax goal does not require that democratic governments continue their previous tax attitudes (Heclo 1974).

By deciding to have governments spend for this and that the voter determines the interim size of debt and the ultimate level of tax collections. The decision to spend as a consumer is intimately associated with a money payment. In the case of a decision to have government spend, the spending and the money payment are not as closely associated. The result is a weakened ability of income receivers to weigh benefits with costs in making public spending decisions and to realize the relation to costs of public sector spending decisions.

This highly tenuous but logically appealing set of speculations does not appear to have caused differences in the aggregate or in the allocation of public sector spending. Governments buy about the same services and goods when they are GRE tax countries as when they are IWP tax countries. Also, the private sectors of high GRE tax countries do not appear to have become less efficient in resource use or in satisfying income earners' desires than those of high IWP tax nations.

Expenditure Variations

The expenditure of tax collections other than social security taxes varies considerably from nation to nation. The United States, for example, spends a larger portion of its tax collections for armaments and armament development than the other capitalist industrial nations.

Differences in the allocation of tax collections surely affect costs of producing and selling. However, the difference is not reflected in treatment permitted under GATT in granting subsidies to exporters or in allowing collection of surcharges on imports.

Efficiency or business orientation of public expenditures do not seem to bear any close relation to type of tax base or measure used. There is no indication that France and Germany, large GRE tax users, spend their tax receipts any less efficiently than the United States. Emphasis on general excise taxes does not seem to have pushed tax collections to higher levels than emphasis on income taxes. For example, the low level of Japanese government expenditures seems to be largely explained by very low armament costs arising directly out of World War II and by low highway and social expenditures directly related to the Japanese way of life and not to a rather heavy reliance on IWP taxes (Myrdal 1953).

Concluding Remarks

Tax change is certain to affect the size of the check that different taxpayers send to the U. S. Treasury. It is also certain that a larger check will develop more adverse voter response than a reduced check. A reduction in direct tax payments affects voter attitudes favorably. Therefore, it is politically desirable for a large number of taxpayers to enjoy reduced tax payments. If this situation is accompanied with capital efficiency stimulants, an increased level of investments, and reduced bureaucratic harassment, the tax change combines a high degree of economic acceptability with political desirableness. This would be the result expected from introducing a VAT that replaces personal income taxes, estate and gift taxes, and some corporate taxes based on income.

INTRODUCTION AND DEVELOPMENT OF THE VALUE-ADDED TAX

The U. S. federal government makes less use of production and sales as a tax base than any other industrial nation or, for that matter, any sovereign nation including South Africa and the communist nations. Not until the 1930s did states actively develop retail sales taxes to partially utilize this fiscal opportunity. Action was sparked by the sharp decline in real estate values and the related decline in property tax collections. The retail sales tax worked so well as a state revenue-raiser that its use was expanded when the birth bulge of the post-World War II years hit the schools.

Undoubtedly, the state development of retail sales taxes retarded federal development of taxes of all kinds that are levied when the sale of production takes place. However, the federal government had also found the income and payroll taxes to be very good revenue-raisers. As a result, instead of looking for new federal revenue sources, it was constantly considering procedures for redistributing federal tax collections to local governments. Since 1975 the fiscal situation of the federal government has reversed itself. Currently, the federal government is running huge annual deficits, such as $200 billion in 1983.

TABLE 7.1

Summary Evaluation of Income Taxes and the Value–Added Tax

Characteristics	Income Taxes	Value–Added Tax
Ability-to-pay		Perhaps better, certainly no worse
Resource allocation	Loopholes have destroyed strengths	Acclaimed as neutral
	Encourages tax-minimization–determined decisions	
Foreign activities	Discourages profits and encourages export of savings	Profits used same as if no tax—makes United States a more competitive production center
Foreign trade	Places greater burden on U.S. exporters than typically carried by foreign exporters	Encourages exports and discourages imports
Revenue potential	Large revenue provider but erratic and allows many special favors	Proved to be both stable and very strong revenue–raiser in Western Europe—greater than income taxes
Administrative cost	Very high when private costs are included with government outlays	Little at private level; about 1.5 percent to 2 percent at government level
Inflationary effect	Becomes a part of costs like any other outlay, but also reduces innovative developments through reduction of available savings	The amount due is a constant portion of the costs of all economic units; by encouraging savings and reducing consumption, helps maintain price stability
Level of government spending	Tends to stimulate government spending because tax per unit of consumption is not visible	A decision to spend includes a clear tax cost burden and therefore tends to keep spending down

As mentioned previously, expenditures at the federal level as a percentage of gross national product (GNP) have been expanding slowly. Actually, as the deficits have grown, real tax collections have been slipping somewhat. The data suggest that it is not the quantity of revenues collected by the federal government, but rather the types of revenue sources used and the failure to keep revenues at a level approximating a balanced federal budget that constitute the nub of the economic problem called stagflation.

The taxes collected by all levels of government in the United States are just a bit less than one-third of the GNP. This is considerably below the level in major industrial nations of Europe. In fact, only in Japan are tax collections as a percentage of GNP substantially below the U.S. level.

Serious federal fiscal difficulties exist despite the relatively modest level of tax collections. The difficulties are closely associated with the shortcomings of the federal tax program, for example, failure to use a value-added tax (VAT); inefficiencies of federalism; and resulting state, local, and federal government duplication. It is also true that heavy, basically nonproductive, defense commitments reduce the goods and services available in the U.S. private sector. However, when all is said and done, the conclusion still must be that the U.S. federal tax system is not appropriate for existing economic and social conditions, both domestic and foreign (see Table 7.1).

The VAT is a major tax used in a large portion of the industrial free world, but not in the United States, with the single exception of Michigan and its Single Business Tax (SBT). The VAT has proved to be a good tax collector and its use must be given considerable credit for the stability of Western nations and the improved revenue collections of a number of developing nations.

Roots of the Value-Added Tax

The United States has been a big importer of taxes. The income tax came from England. The inheritance tax was a French import. The sales tax was a Dutch-Spanish invention. Property taxation goes back to the breakup of feudalism in China and Europe. The value-added tax will not be an imported tax if adopted by the federal government. The roots of the VAT concept and its original theoretical exploration occurred in the United States. German attention was considerable in the early stages of VAT development, but German tax scholars were not attracted to VAT as were those in the United States.

The interest in VAT by U.S. tax economists arose from a desire to generate an economically neutral tax that would provide substantial revenues without reducing the effectiveness and efficiency of the market system. Because the United States was (and remains) the great free-market nation, it was very appropriate that the early examining, explaining, and advocating of VAT take place in this country (Sinai 1972).

The birth of VAT as a legislative proposal occurred during U.S. tax discussions after World War I. The VAT was considered as a possible replacement for numerous World War I excise taxes and the excess profits tax. The heritage of VAT is forgotten, or neglected, when VAT is called a foreign tax. The VAT is as American as apple pie (Fiedler 1965).

There is another reason, in addition to U.S. belief in the economic desirability of the free market, for expecting VAT to be considered first by U.S. economists. The VAT is sound economics; as sound today as it was at the turn of the century when it was conceptualized within the stimulating intellectual climate of the University of Chicago. Thorstein Veblen and his students (particularly the brilliant Wesley Claire Mitchell, founder of the National Bureau of Economic Research) developed the statistics that made possible the calculation of the GNP. And VAT, of course, is conceptually a tax on the GNP (the market value of production activity). Once the total current production became measurable, its use as the base for a general business tax was a natural development (Hulton 1981; Fisher 1942).

The Value-Added Tax and Economic Research

It was in the United States that economics had broken away from armchair philosophizing. Economists in the United States started economics on the long road of becoming a real social science. One of the steps involved development of the VAT, a tax on total production, a tax that becomes part of the cost of all consumption. Another step aimed at quantifying the expenditure shortfalls that caused depressed economic conditions. In both cases the early U.S. development was grasped and utilized more effectively in Europe.

Research Efforts

In 1932 and 1933 the Brookings Institution recommended adoption of VAT in Alabama and Iowa. In 1964, a little over 30 years later, the same Brookings Institution published the proceedings of a conference entitled The Role of Direct and Indirect Taxes in the Federal Revenue System. The conclusion of this conference was that VAT would not be helpful to the United States in developing sound domestic fiscal policy or an improved international economic balance (Mork 1975).

Gerhard Colm, a German-trained fiscal expert who became a leading tax specialist in the U.S. federal government and in the American Planning Association, published in Social Research in 1934 the article "The Ideal Tax System." It was an article recommending and describing VAT.

In 1940 Paul Studensky, a U.S. tax researcher, concluded VAT was the ideal business tax. His ethical-philosophical foundation for VAT bears the short title "Cost of Services Variant." He saw VAT to be a neutral tax because wages; rent; interest and profits; the return to factors of production, labor, land, capital, and entrepreneurship—each bore the same direct tax burden. This is called the income or additive VAT. The VAT used in Europe and other countries (but not in Michigan) is a transaction or consumption VAT. Studensky believed that government services benefited each of the factors of production largely in proportion to income received. Payment of VAT became a collection for government services enjoyed by both the public and the private sectors.

The very earliest origins of VAT, again occurring in the United States, can be traced to the writings of Professor T. S. Adams, father of the 1913 individual income tax legislation. An article of his in the Quarterly Journal of Economics supported VAT as the best approach to the taxation of businesses (Adams 1921). He had previously supported the basic concept of VAT in 1911, ten years earlier.

Value-Added Tax Legislation

Awareness of VAT in the United States led to the introduction of Senate Bill 3560 on March 11, 1940, in the 16th Congress, second session, by Senator C. Joseph O'Mahoney. It was a legislative proposal for the introduction of VAT by the U.S. federal government.

In 1970 the federal government through the report of the president's task force on the taxation of business voted 13 to 2 "that should the need ever arise for substantial additional federal revenues, the government should turn to the value-added tax or some other form of indirect taxation rather than to an increase in rates (indexing assumed) of the corporate or personal income tax." The same task force voted 2 to 13 for the immediate adoption of VAT.

In 1979 House Resolution (HR) 5665 was offered in the Committee on Ways and Means of the U.S. House of Representatives. Hearings were held on November 8, 14, and 15, 1979. The bill did not go to the floor of the House. A modified VAT bill (HR 7015) was introduced by the ways and means chairman, Ullman, on April 2, 1980. Hearings were not held on this proposed legislation. The VAT tax rate of both bills was 10 percent and they both provided base exemptions and lower rates on certain sales. The expected revenues of HR 5665 were $130 billion. The collection estimates were for 1980 and 1981. The new VAT taxes were not accompanied by sharp reductions in or elimination of existing taxes.

Value-Added Tax Collections

The annual rate of personal consumption expenditures of the United States during the first quarter of 1983 totaled $2.2 trillion. Applying a 15 percent VAT to this base, collections could be about $330 billion. If the total of GNP were included in the base, the level of collections of a 15 percent VAT would be over $450 billion. Actual tax collections available from a national VAT would be $450 billion less $30 billion through exclusion of most government undertakings included in the GNP total (Ture 1973).

In Europe, where VAT does not replace income and estate taxes, the collections are about 10 percent of national final consumption. There can be no doubt but that the tax base available to a no-exemption, flat-rate VAT at the federal level in the United States could, with the help of a net wealth tax, readily provide needed replacement revenues under the tax reform program envisaged in this book.

French Leadership

The French led the way in introducing a national VAT. It was introduced originally to replace their production taxes. However, in order to enjoy the GATT advantages of application of the destination principle rather than the origin principle, the French labeled their VAT a consumption tax. Under the destination principle taxes paid can be refunded to exporters. In the case of VAT this means zero rating. Under the origin principle, which GATT applies to income and capital taxes, taxes may not be refunded on exports.

U.S. Proposals

The major difference between the U.S. VAT (HR 5665) and VAT (HR 7015) is the following: areas where a low 5 percent rate applied under HR 5665 were zero rated under HR 7015. In addition, the 1980 VAT legislative proposal establishes special rules for real property, interest transactions, and insurance companies, and it provides for the exemption from VAT of businesses with taxable transactions that do not exceed $20,000. A number of the complicating provisions in HR 7015 arise because of the continued existence of individual and corporate income taxes at the federal level (GATT 1961).

Concluding Remarks

Widespread use of the retail sales tax at the state government level has undoubtedly reduced the federal government's willingness to introduce either VAT or a gross turnover tax. The Sixteenth Amendment to the federal Constitution in 1913 and the clarification of the federal government's right to levy a personal income tax also reduced federal interest in a tax oriented toward either gross or net transactions.

The allocation of government responsibilities did not require a large expansion of federal revenues except during periods of active warfare. Revenue demands of the post-World War I period were readily carried by the new personal income tax, the somewhat older corporate income tax, and a reformed death tax system. A similar situation also evolved after World War II. Then, however, the rates required were much higher. The problems inherent in the high rates were not quickly recognized. In addition, the expanding social security fund needs were heaped on top of the already expanded, older requirements. The result was the crisis that we explore in these discussions.

The data presented in Table 7.2 were gathered by the Advisory Commission on Intergovernmental Relations on the basis of interviews

TABLE 7.2

Tax Approval Level of Federal Use of Sales or Income Taxes
(in percent)

Region	Income Tax	Sales Tax (value-added tax)
Entire United States	24	52
Northeast	31	40
North central	21	58
South	21	55
West	24	52

Source: Advisory Commission on Intergovernmental Relations, S-12, 1983, p. 2.

TABLE 7.3

Comparison of Different Methods of Calculating the Value–Added Tax

	Tax Exclusive Price (in dollars)	Tax Rate (in percent)	Additive Method[a]	Direct Subtractive Method[b]	Indirect Subtractive Method[c] (invoices)
Inputs[d]			Calculated on the basis of the value added by the firm ($3,500: 15 percent of $3,500)	Calculated on the basis of the tax–exclusive prices of inputs and outputs. Outputs are $6,500, inputs are $3,000, $6,500 minus $3,000: 15 percent of $3,500	Calculated on the basis of the tax applied to outputs and inputs tax. Tax applied to outputs is $975 ($6,500 x 15 percent) and tax applied to inputs is $300 ($2,000 x 15 percent). There is no tax applied to inputs of fuel: $975 minus $300
Materials	2,000	15			
Fuel	1,000	0			
Value Added					
Wages and profits	3,500	15			
Outputs					
Finished goods	6,500	15			
			$525	$525	$675
Net tax due			$525	$525	$675

aThe additive method is the best approach in applying VAT where inputs and outputs are difficult to measure, for example, banking, insurance, real estate, and the like. Because profits, if any, become a portion of the tax base, the difficult problem of defining profits remains (for example, what level of depreciation should be allowed). Also, because this approach is not closely associated with sales, but rather, with profits, interest, and wages, it may have difficulty being treated as a rebate on exports under VAT.

bThe direct subtractive method is more closely associated with sales, as it is calculated by subtracting total inputs from total outputs.

cThe indirect subtractive invoicing method permits precise calculation of the tax content of a sale. It is used by Western European nations.

dThe tax due through use of the additive and direct subtractive approaches is increased to the $675 level at the next stage of the production and marketing process.

Source: C. T. Sandford, Costs and Benefits of VAT (London: HEB, 1981), p. 169.

of a scientific sample of the population. The data, which have been gathered since 1972, demonstrate a growing interest in replacing the federal government's use of taxes based on income (however defined) with a sales tax, that is, popularization of VAT in the United States. The following question was asked: Suppose the federal government must raise taxes; which should be adopted—income tax increase or VAT introduction? The answer as summarized in Table 7.2 is a resounding victory for VAT as the desired source of additional revenues.

There are a number of ways of calculating the VAT. However, all of the users of VAT, with the exception of Michigan, have adopted the indirect subtractive method. See Table 7.3 for a summary of possible ways of administering the VAT.

IMPACT OF THE VALUE-ADDED TAX ON PRICES

Although VAT is now used by 31 nations and each year new national governments shift to it, a consensus on its impact on prices does not exist. The traditional approach to indirect taxes concludes that VAT is shifted forward and prices increase by the amount of the tax. Worldwide economic conditions of the late 1960s and the 1970s were so price disruptive that it is very difficult to determine the VAT's impact.

Data for Table 7.4 were prepared by the fiscal affairs department of the International Monetary Fund (IMF). The table divides nations using VAT into four groups based on price impact from the introduction of VAT. The difficulty of separating VAT's effect on prices from all other influences explains why definitive research in this very important area of fiscal policy has not been completed (Tait 1981).

By far the largest number of nations introducing a national VAT since 1967 fall into the fourth category, where the introduction of VAT had little measurable effect on inflation as measured by changes in cost of living. The nations range from West Germany and Brazil to Senegal and Nicaragua. The number of nations in this category very nearly doubles when circumstances are examined in more detail than when the allocation is based on data alone (Smith 1981).

Price Adjustments

The only possible conclusion from the data in Table 7.4 is that VAT does not readily lend itself to upward price adjustments, even though the administrators frequently assume forward shifting and give examples of how it can be done. This is as accurate a generalization as can be made from the numerous and complex elements entering the price determination arena during the first round of adjustments to a new VAT.

TABLE 7.4

Countries Allocated to Categories for Effect on Consumer Price
Index of Introducing the Value-Added Tax

	Allocation on Data Alone	Allocation after Considering Circumstances in More Detail
Shift case	Denmark	Denmark
	Uruguay	Uruguay
	Netherlands	Netherlands
	Ecuador	Ecuador
	Bolivia	Panama
	Panama	
Shift plus acceleration case	Norway	Norway
	Honduras	
Acceleration case	Morocco	Italy
	France	Israel
	Sweden	Peru
	Ireland	
	Italy	
	United Kingdom	
	Chile	
	Argentina	
	Israel	
	Peru	
Little or no effect case	Ivory Coast	Ivory Coast
	Senegal	Senegal
	Brazil	Brazil
	Federal Republic of Germany	Morocco
	Madagascar	France
	Luxembourg	Federal Republic of Germany
	Belgium	Madagascar
	Austria	Sweden
	Colombia	Luxembourg
	Costa Rica	Belgium
	Nicaragua	Ireland
	Korea	Austria
		United Kingdom
		Bolivia
		Argentina
		Colombia
		Costa Rica
		Nicaragua
		Chile
		Honduras
		Korea
Unknown*	Mexico	Mexico

*Introduction of the value-added tax too recent to categorize.

Source: Compiled by the author from International Monetary Fund data.

126

A VAT that does not directly increase prices based on first-round analysis but that does not result in lower prices may, when credit trends are taken into account, be a major cause of lower prices. Table 7.4 identifies ten nations raising additional revenues because of VAT introduction. If VAT did not directly increase the level of government expenditures by the amount of collections, it did decrease deficits and the expansion of the money supply. This would stimulate price decreases.

If VAT does not increase prices (and this was largely the case in 26 of the 31 nations introducing VAT since 1967), then the GATT position on how indirect taxes (including VAT) can be treated on products entering international commerce adversely affects nations making little use of VAT and other indirect taxes. Approval by GATT of the refunding of VAT on exports gives exporters from nations using VAT a competitive advantage. Also, condonement by GATT of a border tax on imports equal to VAT rates gives the nations using VAT additional protection of their domestic production.

Economic theoreticians frequently argue that prices increase when VAT is introduced so that international trade advantages do not develop from its use. The IMF findings, summarized in Table 7.5, basically destroy the theoretical positions frequently propounded by supporters of GATT. Using VAT and taking advantage of the GATT position relative to indirect taxes increase employment and the strength of domestic industries. This, in turn, assists government efforts to implement noninflationary policies.

Concluding Remarks

The IMF studies must put to rest the position that there is something inherently inflationary about the introduction of VAT. In fact, the situation is just the reverse when credit expansion pressures and the international strength of the currency are taken into consideration.

VALUE-ADDED TAX: STILL THE BEST?

When the value-added tax is declared to be the best of taxes, it must meet some tests. First, is it really neutral? And what is so good about neutrality? Second, the base is broad and resists exclusion pressures. Are these two characteristics acceptable as good without doubt? Next, do the above attributes truly exist?

It is easier, perhaps, to prove they exist as desirable attributes of VAT than to prove general agreement exists over desirable tax qualities. A tax with collections sensitive to shifts in the economic climate was considered to be desirable because of this characteristic

TABLE 7.5

Summary Table Showing Impact of Introduction of Value-Added Tax on Prices

Country	VAT Introduced	Designed Effect on Revenue	Percentage CPI Change in Quarters before and after VAT		Other Concurrent Tax Changes	Any Other Concurrent Changes	Price Controls	Taxes Mainly Replaced[c]	New VAT Rates[d] (percent)
			General[a]	Attributed to VAT[b]					
Argentina	Jan. 1975	Equal yield	37.2	Minor	Provincial tax changes	Utility rates increased, devaluation	Yes, but relaxed	Wholesale sales tax	16
Austria	Jan. 1973	Equal yield	2.4	Nil	Lower income taxes	Strict credit control	Yes	Cascade wholesale tax	8,16
Belgium	Jan. 1971	Equal yield	2.6	Nil	—	Increased wages	Monitored and some control	Cascade wholesale tax	6, 14, 18, 25
Bolivia	Oct. 1973	Equal yield or increase	9.5	Nil	New luxury tax rates, increased excises	—	No	Multistage ring system	5, 10, 15, 20
Brazil	Jan. 1967	Equal yield	15.8	Nil	—	—	No	State sales taxes and municipal industrial taxes	12
Chile	Mar. 1975	Increase	146.7	Minor	Taxes on gasoline incomes and property raised	Utility rates increased and rent controls relaxed	No	Cascade turnover tax	20
Colombia	Jan. 1975	Increase	12.9	Nil	Income, property, capital-gains taxes changed	Many incentives abolished	No	Simpler VAT	4, 6, 10, 15, 35
Costa Rica	Jan. 1975	Increase	e	Nil	Increased excises	—	No	Multistage ring system	.8
Denmark	July 1967	Increase	8.0	5.0	Lower income tax	Increased transfers and increased wages	No	Wholesale tax	10
Ecuador	July 1970	Increase	8.7	(7.1)	Mining taxes reduced	Devaluation	No	VAT was a new tax, some turnover taxes on mining and manufacturing replaced	4
France	Jan. 1968	Equal yield	2.1	1.0	Tax exemptions abolished and income tax adjustments	Increased wages	Yes, after VAT introduced	Simpler VAT	6, 4, 13.6, 20, 25
Federal Republic of Germany	Jan. 1968	Equal yield	1.5	0.6	—	—	Monitored	Cascade retail tax	5, 10
Honduras	Jan. 1976	Increase	1.0	Nil	—	Rapidly expanded credit	No	Multistage ring system	3
Ireland	Nov. 1972	Equal yield	5.5	Nil	Some tariff reductions	—	Monitored	Wholesale and retail sales tax	5, 26, 16, 37, 30, 26

128

Country	Date	Revenue objective	CPI change[a]	(b)	Other tax measures	Wage and allowance measures	Increased wages and tax allowances	Previous sales tax system[c]	Various sales tax rates
Israel	July 1976	Increase	17.9	(9.0)	—	—	No	Various sales taxes	0, 8
Italy	Jan. 1973	Equal yield	6.3	Nil	—	Increased wages	No	Central and local government sales tax	3, 12, 18
Ivory Coast	Jan. 1960	Equal yield	—	—	—	—	No	Manufacturers' VAT	8
Korea	July 1977	Equal yield	4.1	Minor	Changed excises	Proposed VAT rate of 13 percent reduced to 10 percent	Yes	Eight sales taxes representing 40 percent of revenue	0, 10
Luxembourg	Jan. 1970	Equal yield	3.5	Nil	—	—	No	Cascade wholesale tax	2, 4, 8
Madagascar	Jan. 1969	Increase	3.2	Nil	—	—	No	Cascade production tax	6, 12
Mexico	Jan. 1980	Equal yield or increase	—	—	Lower border VAT of 6 percent	—	No	Cascade production taxes	10
Morocco	Jan. 1962	Equal yield	2.4	Nil	Change in corporate and production taxes	—	No	Cascade production tax	5, 12
Netherlands	Jan. 1969	Equal yield	6.2	1.5	Lower income tax	Increased wages	Yes	Cascade wholesale tax	0, 4, 12
Nicaragua	Jan. 1975	Equal yield	[e]	Nil	Reduced customs	—	No	Multistage ring system	6
Norway	Jan. 1970	Loss	7.8	5.8	Reduced income and property taxes	Increased transfers and wages	Yes	Sales taxes on 65 percent of consumption	20
Panama	Mar. 1977	Increase	5.0	(3.1)	Stamp taxes reduced and increased excises	Increase in utility rates	No	Wholesale tax	5
Peru	July 1976	Increase	27.1	(13.5)	—	—	No	Cascade production tax	3, 20, 40
Senegal	Mar. 1961	Equal yield	—	—	1 percent payroll tax to offset lost revenue	—	No	Manufacturers' VAT	
Sweden	Jan. 1969	Equal yield	1.6	Nil	—	—	No	Retail sales tax	11, 1
United Kingdom	Apr. 1973	Loss	4.9	0.7	Selective employment tax removed	—	No	Multirate wholesale tax	0, 10
Uruguay	Jan. 1968	Equal yield	66.3	(53.0)	—	—	No	Manufacturers', wholesale, and retail taxes	5, 14

aThe Consumer Price Index (CPI) for the quarter before VAT is deducted from that for the quarter after VAT and the difference expressed as a percentage increase.

bFigures in parentheses represent broad estimates based on examination of the data. Other figures are based on external and contemporary commentaries.

cThis column is an accurate as a brief summary can be. "Cascade production tax" refers to a cascade tax on business turnover restricted to the production stage; "cascade wholesale tax" extends the turnover tax to include the wholesale stage; "cascade retail tax" extends the turnover tax to include the retail stage; "manufacturers'," "wholesale," or "retail" taxes are single-stage taxes—some operated on a ring system, others on a credit system.

dOn tax-exclusive prices.

eMonthly data unavailable for part of the period covered.

Source: Compiled by the author from International Monetary Fund data.

only five or so years ago. Today the cry is for stable revenues. This makes VAT, a stable revenue producer, a more desirable revenue source now than it was a few years ago. What was bad has become good (Hall and Rabushka 1983).

Neutrality

When applied to VAT, neutrality reflects the position that a substantial level of VAT collections can be made without changing the most efficient mix of resources and level of activity. The VAT is seen to place a proportionately equal burden on wages, profits, and interest, even when its rate is applied to the level of sales and not to these income aggregates.

The manner in which VAT causes a burden on aggregate income sources is one of its more difficult aspects to understand. The base available to VAT is the difference between VAT paid by providers of resources and the price at which the product is sold. The selling price is a base for taxation only to the extent the product includes costs that have not previously been subject to VAT rates equal to those applied to the sale being taxed. The VAT is a cost that must be paid as a constant portion of the selling price minus the amount of VAT paid throughout the entire production process (Kaldor 1955).

Consumption

The VAT is not a tax on consumption. Consumption enters directly into the base of VAT only to the extent that resources previously untaxed by VAT enter into the sales price paid by a final consumer. The VAT is a tax on production required to make a good or service a part of the economic process from man-made production to man-enjoyed consumption.

When VAT is called a tax on consumption, as is often done, a very undesirable simplification is being made. It communicates that VAT is only a national retail sales tax. In fact, when a journal refers to VAT, the editor frequently explains what VAT is by referring to it as a national sales tax. A tax on sales is, of course, also a tax on purchases. A tax that becomes due when a sale is made is also a tax paid when a purchase is made. The VAT becomes due for a business establishment qua purchaser when supplies, machines, and the like are purchased to permit the conduct of the enterprise's activities. The same establishment becomes liable for a VAT as a tax on sales when a customer makes a purchase. The VAT due as a result of the sale is the net VAT. The VAT due from the purchaser is the gross

VAT. Therefore, almost every economic transaction includes both a net and a gross VAT. It also includes, of course, both a sales and a purchase (Norr and Hornhammar 1970).

Calling VAT a national sales tax is a shorthand expression of the relationships briefly mentioned above. However, more than likely most nonexperts reading that "VAT is a national sales tax" would understand it to mean that "VAT is like the state and local government retail sales taxes except that it is on a national basis." In attempting to provide a shorthand description of VAT, journal editors are starting their readers down the wrong road (Schiff 1974).

International Treatment

The fact that VAT is something more than a retail sales tax on a national scale is demonstrated most clearly by discussions concerned with VAT and international sales and purchases. Obviously, most exports are not made at the retail level. Therefore, the refund of VAT on retail international sales would give little support to export sales. Here, because the characteristics of the VAT base are different from those of a retail sales tax, a refund of VAT provides a quite different impact. A substantial refund equal to all the VAT paid during production, transportation, and marketing processes provides a substantial stimulant (Studenski 1940).

The levy of a border tax equal to all of the VAT levied in the importing nation on the type of service or product being imported would total approximately the same reduction of imports as a retail sales tax of equal revenue productivity. This relationship demonstrates that VAT is less useful in restricting imports than in stimulating exports.

These relationships show VAT to be a tax that avoids many of the shortcomings of other transaction taxes. Deduction of previous VAT taxes paid through the production, transportation, and marketing processes removes the "piling on" or "cascade" weakness of the turnover tax. European countries that have found the use of VAT desirable have accompanied the move with an elimination of their general turnover tax. The United States, not having a turnover tax, cannot act in a similar way. The introduction of VAT with revenues being held constant would require reduction of some excise taxes, but mostly it would require reduction of profit, income, and estate taxes.

Concluding Remarks

The question of difference in type of tax to be reduced when VAT is introduced quickly leads to the question of whether prices are affected differently by transaction taxes as opposed to income taxes. The introduction of VAT in Europe had little observable effect on prices. One wonders if this would also be true if the taxes repealed had been income and estate taxes. This question is answered to a degree by the International Monetary Fund in its study of the price impact of introducing VAT. The tentative answer is that the introduction of VAT generally had little or no effect on prices. The data, however, are not sufficiently complete to say definitely that VAT introduction, whether as a replacement tax or as an additional revenue-raiser, increased or reduced price levels.

BRIEF COMPARISON OF A FLAT-RATE INCOME TAX WITH A VALUE-ADDED TAX

Both a flat-rate income tax (FRIT) and a value-added tax apply a fixed rate to the base being taxed. Neither of these taxes pretend to be personal taxes. Both aim at collecting a given percentage of the base identified for use by the government to pay for its services and products (Penner 1982).

In many cases government-provided goods and services possess the highest priority. Therefore, having adequate government revenues is of the highest importance. In carrying out this revenue provision function both the VAT base and the FRIT base possess the strength to provide stability as well as a substantial level of economic power.

Although both VAT and FRIT are not personal taxes, it is possible through use of broad exemptions and deductions to give these taxes a limited ability to adjust to the taxpayer's personal and economic situation. For example, FRIT may provide for the deduction of a given quantity of income for each dependent and VAT may provide for the exemption of a given value of food and shelter (O'Neill and Schwartz 1982).

When exemptions, deductions, or allowances are provided for in VAT and FRIT, the taxes become complex and costly to administer. In addition, both taxes soon suffer from collection inadequacies and attract all the weaknesses so apparent in the existing federal tax system. One basis of judging whether VAT or FRIT should be introduced in order to put in place a federal tax system that meets the required revenue and needed private enterprise supports is the built-in resistance of the tax base and rates to adjustment to meet special interest demands.

Here one can rely to a degree on the European experience. The VAT as it has developed in Western Europe during the past 25 years has demonstrated a strong resistance to special provisions. Its good record exists largely because the VAT collected by each business firm as it makes a sale is reduced by VAT paid on purchases the firm made from other businesses subject to VAT. As a result, each business subject to VAT is anxious to make its own purchases from other VAT-paying firms because this minimizes its VAT liability. Under the VAT a business firm wishes to be either fully covered by VAT or subject to zero rating.

Under zero rating VAT taxes paid on purchases are refunded. Under exemption taxes paid on purchases are not refunded, but the firm's sales are exempt from VAT. Under FRIT any exemption directly affects the income of the exempt taxpayer and does not cause a deterioration of the tax position of other income receivers, as does exemption under VAT (Wiedenbaum 1973).

The FRIT is levied directly on the income earned by wage earners, which is the same base on which the employee portion of the social security tax rests. This results in a heavier tax burden on wage earners than on those with income from dividends and rent (Hall and Rabushka 1983).

Under VAT the tax payment is made by all sellers of goods and the purchasers become liable to a price that includes this tax cost along with all other costs. The final user of the good or service does not have the potential of directly shifting the tax burden backward onto resource providers or forward on to resource users. The FRIT taxpayer can only reduce tax payments by earning less, thereby reducing productivity. The VAT taxpayer can reduce tax liabilities by purchasing less, thereby making more resources available for investment (U.S., Treasury Department 1977).

International Considerations

One final but very important advantage of a VAT over a FRIT is the different treatment they receive in the international community through the General Agreement on Tariffs and Trade. The VAT has been declared by GATT and by the worldwide economic community to be an indirect tax. The FRIT, on the other hand, is generally accepted and treated as a direct tax because its base is income that is judged to be affected by personal adjustments. Also, the VAT holds the indirect label because it is judged to be shifted forward in higher prices. The FRIT is considered to be a direct tax because its collections result in lower income, not in higher prices (Pohmer 1983).

These differences in direct and indirect tax burdens result in GATT allowing VAT nations to deduct VAT from exports and to add on the domestic VAT as a border tax on imports. A nation using FRIT cannot deduct its FRIT on exports without becoming guilty of export subsidies and cannot add on a border tax equal to FRIT on imports without violating general freedom of trade and tariff treaties.

The international trade advantage of VAT over FRIT and all types of income- and profit-based taxes is direct and understood by businesses engaged in international commerce. The export-stimulating and import-restricting impact of indirect taxes strengthens a nation's economy. The advantage of indirect taxes in the allocation of tax burdens is frequently denied by economists who emphasize a general macroeconomic approach. They see the commercial advantage of indirect taxes to be washed out in international exchange-rate adjustments (Wonnacott 1971).

Concluding Remarks

If the commercial advantage of indirect tax treatment of exports and imports does not exist (as macroeconomists argue), then nations using a substantial VAT should be willing to abandon the special export and import advantage enjoyed by users of VAT. This they have been unwilling to do. Instead, in doubtful areas such as social security financing they have successfully pushed for wider application of the indirect tax approach to the international allocation of taxes.

A tax refund's impact on prices of exported goods can be countered through interest-rate policy. Recent U.S. experience indicates this possibility quite clearly. The tight monetary policy of the Federal Reserve Board acted to attract funds from abroad and to increase the dollar's international price. The relative prices of U.S.-produced goods increased. Higher prices reduced the competitiveness of U.S. exports. The result was increased international trade deficits or reduced surpluses for the United States. Lower export prices owing to the refund of taxes on exports would be countered by the U.S. indirect tax policy.

TREATMENT OF CERTAIN INCOME SOURCES
UNDER THE VALUE-ADDED TAX

A logical way to commence a discussion of introducing a major VAT in the United States would be to reproduce all the regulations and court decisions required to carry out the federal individual and corporate income taxes. It would also be appropriate when discussing the individual hedonistic justice of VAT to explore the horizontal tax equality of average income receivers that is provided by the individual income tax through its special legal provisions that allow breathing holes for high income receivers. The point at issue does not require lengthy belaboring. It can be satisfactorily handled for our purpose by looking briefly at two very generally accepted premises: (1) that the federal government's ability to tax according to ability-to-pay and to distribute the tax burden to encourage economic growth is seriously handicapped by its nearly complete reliance on revenue sources using as a base a legal definition of personal income, wages, and corporate profits and (2) that there is no particular divine or economic principle requiring the federal tax system to use a tax on personal income and business profits to finance general government costs.

Depletion

One thorny aspect of eliminating the federal individual and corporate income tax is how depletion would be treated under VAT. If depletion is seen as a using up of capital similar to depreciation, the basic treatment is that expenditures made to acquire and develop resource properties are eligible to enter into a presale tax payment only if the bill of sale shows tax payment. The sale of oil or other resource products would be subject to the value-added tax rate. The seller of the oil could deduct the amount of tax paid on purchases during the tax period.

However, an adjustment period is appropriate. This is because firms that had purchased mineral properties in the past would not have any prepaid VAT to deduct from VAT liability arising from sales of minerals.

Capital Gains

Conceptually, VAT is only interested in value added to a product through application of production factors. The increase in sale price of assets that is not the result of additional productive activity is not a portion of GNP and therefore not a portion of VAT. It is the capital gains arising from inventory or basically short-term capital gains, as the concept is used in the United States and other Western industrial nations, that could become the base of VAT. This is true even though the gains are not completely included in the gross domestic product or the GNP. The GNP and national income include the gains from inflation as they become a portion of wages, profits, dividends, and rents and as the incomes are used to save and to directly purchase goods and services.

The economic problem in applying VAT is to separate trading gains from the exchange of assets with additional value owing to inventory service from monetary increases or decreases owing to interest rate and price shifts. Basically, the same kind of problems and shortcomings encountered under the income tax arise in the application of VAT. However, because of the much lower maximum tax rate under VAT, the degree of difficulty should be much less (Arthur Anderson and Company 1980).

Finance Industry

The VAT envisaged for the United States would be on the product base; that is, it would be applied through the subtractive method used in Europe. However, where administrative or political considerations make it appropriate, VAT administration could take advantage of the income (or additive) method. For example, application of VAT to the finance industry would be appropriately administered by the additive method. This is basically the type of VAT used by Michigan. It appears likely this approach would also be helpful in applying VAT to capital gains (see Chapter 1).

The exemption of the finance industry from VAT in France and Germany is not due to a theoretical or administrative weakness of VAT. Rather, it arose largely from traditional procedures of taxing finance that the respective legislative groups did not wish to dislodge. Because all federal income taxes, with the exception of the social security payroll tax, would be eliminated in this federal tax reform, the European "out" would not be available (Stein and Foss 1981).

Rental Income

Rent is charged and facilities are rented by large and small economic units. The rent required is a price charged for a service sale, and it is taxable under VAT. Also, owner-occupied facilities that do not produce rent would be a portion of a comprehensive base for VAT. These rents are excluded from the base of individual income tax in the United States. The compromise procedure used in France and Germany includes the costs of constructing as a portion of the VAT base and exempts owner-occupied "rents" (Sullivan 1963). This would be an appropriate approach for the United States to take (Sullivan 1967).

The European approach gives an economic advantage to structures constructed before VAT's introduction. This windfall could be picked up by levying a special tax equivalent to VAT on the undepreciated value of all physical capital and all durable consumer goods. However, the efficient functioning of VAT does not require such retroactive action because the renter not currently buying goods will not have tax prepayments to deduct from tax liability.

The renter will receive invoices from those VAT-paying firms from which he or she makes purchases. These will be deductible from VAT liability on rent charges. If no receipts are received, no deductions are made. This is the technical position of the owner renting property purchased before VAT was introduced, and it is the usual situation in France because of exemption.

The VAT in both Germany and France considers the home or industrial plant built for the owner as an end-use product. The VAT is paid by the contractor and is included in the invoice. Under one conception of VAT the owner treats this charge in the same manner as a VAT charge made when stocks or capital equipment are purchased (Lindholm 1975). Section 4, paragraph 12 of the German VAT lists limited exemptions of rents and property transfers. It ends with the following sentence: "Accommodation in apartments and bedrooms made available by an entrepreneur for the temporary accommodation of guests and the leasing of machinery and other equipment of any description which forms part of an industrial plant (even if they are essential elements of real estate) are not exempt."

Depreciation

The value added used as the base of VAT can consist of a firm's net sales. The base is calculated by deducting from current sales the intermediate purchases on current account and depreciation and depletion correctly allocated to current sales. The base is equal to payments to factors of production, assuming sales totals do not include indirect taxes and inventories remain constant. This is the income variety of VAT base, or income value added (IVA). The problem of trying to calculate depreciation has not been avoided. Also, because of the problems of treating indirect taxes, inventory changes, and depreciation and depletion, the IVA type of VAT base is best administered through withholding the tax from factor payments. However, the problem remains of treating depreciation to calculate profits that are not distributed as dividend payments. If the remaining income is a major federal revenue source, the problem of treating depreciation must be continued and whether depreciation is deducted in developing the VAT base (as it must if IVA is used) does not pose a new difficulty.

The consumption VAT, or consumption value added (CVA), levies the tax on net sales. No depreciation deduction is permitted. Purchases of capital goods are treated instead like purchases on current account. This means that capital purchases are treated like raw material purchases; all interfirm purchases are treated alike. We have instant depreciation (Oakland 1967).

Retail-Level Sales

The general procedure in Europe is to make VAT a portion of the quoted retail price. However, the procedure is not always followed in the case of restaurant meals and hotel bills.

When VAT is made a portion of the selling price, the cashier need not calculate the different VAT rates applying to basic foods and to luxury items.

Including VAT in the retail price is a justified practice not only because of added efficiency, but also because (1) other taxes—for example, social security and property taxes—are not separated out and listed on the sales slip or calculated by the cashier and (2) the amount of VAT paid is not needed for the vast majority of retail sales because the item or service is an end-use purchase. However, some sales are made for business purposes and they need receipts to be used as deductions from VAT liability.

The French have met this difficulty by requiring the retailer to keep a separate account for customers subject to VAT, that is, the non-end-use purchasers. It is generally agreed that this answer provides too much administration to meet a minor problem. In Sweden a business buying at retail keeps its cash slip or bill and the portion of price consisting of VAT is deductible when the business calculates its VAT liability.

There really is no good reason why VAT should be treated differently from other taxes paid by business. In the United States where retail sales taxes are well developed and the two taxes could possibly be confused, there is even stronger justification for the administrative procedure that includes VAT in price than exists in Europe.

Collection at Each Stage

The VAT is collected at each stage of production. This procedure appears to be complex. However, the collection approach has not caused difficulties. Real-world experience has not justified fears expressed before the adoption of VAT. France uses the most complicated of all VATs (although the new Italian VAT uses even more rates). But even under these conditions France has been able to administer the tax with personnel released when numerous small excises were repealed upon VAT's introduction. The changeover in Germany from the turnover tax to VAT was remarkably smooth (Mehus 1969).

When VAT is used as a major tax, complete and current sales data are provided for useful economic forecasting and planning. The multistage base of VAT and the Western European procedure using monthly tax payments based on invoices are credited with increasing the accuracy of economic forecasting and planning. Analysis of all VAT returns, which computer processing permits, would provide a virtually complete transactions matrix by region as well as by industry. These data could replace much of the statistical material now collected on a less comprehensive and less reliable base. The serious inventory recessions suffered by the United States in 1975 and 1982 might have been largely avoided if data VAT could provide had been available (NET 1969).

Service Businesses

Small service firms are perhaps best treated as small retailers. However, the Michigan Business Activity Tax (BAT) of the 1950s made special provision for service industries through special base allocation provisions. The law provided that if statutory deductions did not total at least 50 percent of taxable receipts, the taxpayer had the right to deduct a flat 50 percent. In addition, if payroll alone exceeded 50 percent of taxable receipts, an additional 10 percent or one-half of the excess, whichever is smaller, could be deducted.

As a result of these provisions any Michigan firm (including a service firm) with gross receipts of less than $25,000 was exempt from VAT. In the case of service firms the exemption was greater if payrolls made up more than 50 percent of taxable receipts (Lock 1955).

Because service firms have been widely exempt under state and local retail sales taxes, they are likely to protest being taxed under a federal VAT. However, the very exemption they enjoy under state retail sales taxes justifies their taxation under a federal VAT. In Europe certain service industries have been granted the option of being exempt or taxed. If the industry opts for exemption, it is unable to recover the VAT included in cost of supplies and capital goods purchased. This treatment is proper because the industry itself does not pay VAT on its value added. The disadvantage is considerable and has brought about an unheard-of situation in taxation. In Holland some service industries have actually requested they be included under VAT.

In Europe the liberal professions (that is, dentists, lawyers, accountants, and so forth) are exempt from VAT. The exemption, of course, really means that their liability is limited to the VAT included in their purchases from businesses paying VAT (Carlson 1980).

Although application of VAT to the liberal professions, financial institutions, and other service businesses causes problems, the difficulties are not insurmountable. The different environment in the United States would allow a U.S. VAT that breaks away from European tradition in this respect. A U.S. VAT would be applicable to value added by the liberal professions. This approach would make a considerable addition to the VAT retail base.

Concluding Remarks

Although difficulties will be encountered, the very broad, potential base of VAT is more likely to be realized than that of an income tax. This is because pressures internal to the tax continue to work toward expanding, not reducing, the base. Also, because VAT is broad based, additional revenues can be collected without raising rates so high that evasion becomes irresistible.

In Western Europe the VAT did not originally include retail markups in its base. Now it does. Before this was accomplished, it was believed great administrative difficulties would be encountered. This has not proved to be the case (see Table 8.2).

8

THE
VALUE-ADDED TAX
IN ACTION

DATA OF USE OF THE VALUE-ADDED TAX

The data found in Table 8.1 are not available for all countries using the value-added tax (VAT). However, the principal VAT-using nations are included. Brazil and France, the two nations relying most on VAT, are also nations that have a history of fiscal difficulties. Denmark makes the greatest use of VAT as a percentage of the gross domestic product (GDP), and it is also the nation that allows the fewest exemptions and makes use of very simple administrative procedures.

The data in Table 8.1 make clear that VAT has the capability of making a very substantial contribution to a nation's revenue total. The VAT is a proved efficient tax-revenue provider. It is also, because of the base used, a tax that does not fall heavily on savings and investment or the income of the middle classes.

Rates used during the life of the VAT in the states of the European Economic Community (EEC) are shown in Table 8.2. The rates and exemptions provide an idea of the portion of total VAT potential that is being utilized in each nation. The VAT collections could be increased substantially by increasing the breadth of VAT, bringing the standard rate in all member states up to around 20 percent, and having all users of VAT adopt a broad base. In addition, the finance industry, which is now entirely exempt, could be readily included in the VAT base (see Chapter 7).

Small Business Encouragement

The VAT can be made relatively simple to administer at both the taxpayer and tax collection levels. The $20,000 gross receipt exemption of House Resolution (HR) 7015 is an example of this type of provision.

TABLE 8.1

Value-Added Tax Collections in the European Economic Community,
1976 and 1977
(in percent)

Country	Value-Added Tax as a Percentage of All Tax Revenues	Value-Added Tax as a Percentage of Gross Domestic Product
Belgium	17.3	7.2
Brazil	32.8	3.3
Denmark	19.1[a]	8.1[a]
France	36.4	7.5
Ireland	15.2[b]	6.0[b]
Italy	15.5	5.2
Netherlands	15.9	7.4
United Kingdom	8.4	3.0
West Germany	13.0	5.2

[a]Estimate.
[b]Data given for 1976.

Source: Organization for Economic Cooperation and Development, National Accounts Statistics.

Exemption from VAT not only eliminates VAT-related book-keeping for a small business, but under the program examined in this book the federal individual and corporate income taxes are repealed. Therefore, small businesses will be left with only the required social security records at the federal level. The small business will be given real encouragement to experiment and grow.

International Trade Treatment

Both VAT drafts proposed by the Ways and Means Committee in the late 1970s included provision of zero rating on exports and the levy of border taxes on imports equal to the VAT rate existing on those goods and services in the United States. When the United States does not have a VAT and its trading partners do use a substantial one, U.S. exports must overcome a border tax equal to the VAT of the importing country but an equal border tax cannot be levied on imports.

TABLE 8.2

Rates since Introduction of the Value-Added Tax for
Domestically Distributed Goods and Services
(in percent)

Country	Effective Date	Rate*				
		Zero	Reduced	Standard	Inter-mediate	Increased
Belgium	1/01/71		6.00	18.00	14.00	25.00
	1/01/78		6.00	16.00		25.00
Denmark	7/03/67			10.00		
	4/01/68			12.50		
	6/29/70			15.00		
	9/29/75			9.25		
	3/01/76			15.00		
	10/03/77			18.00		
	10/01/78			20.25		
Ireland	11/01/72		5.26	16.37	11.11	30.26
	8/03/73		6.75	19.50	11.11	36.75
	3/01/76		10.00	20.00		35.00
						40.00
	3/01/79	0	10.00	20.00		
Italy	1/01/73		1.00	12.00		18.00
			3.00			
			6.00			
			9.00			
	1/01/75		1.00	12.00	18.00	30.00
			3.00			
			6.00			
			9.00			
	2/08/77		1.00	14.00	18.00	35.00
			3.00			
			6.00			
			9.00			
Netherlands	1/01/69		4.00	12.00		
	1/01/71		4.00	14.00		
	1/01/73		4.00	16.00		
	10/01/76		4.00	18.00		
United Kingdom	4/01/73			10.00		
	7/29/74			8.00		
	11/18/74			8.00		25.00
	4/12/75			8.00		12.50
	7/18/79	0		15.00		
West Germany	1/01/68		5.00	10.00		
	7/01/68		5.50	11.00		
	1/01/78		6.00	12.00		
	7/01/79		6.50	13.00		

*All national rate structures include a zero rate for exports.

Source: Compiled by the General Accounting Office, based on information provided by foreign officials.

When the exporting nation does not have a VAT, its exporters do not benefit from a tax refund that can be used later to pay the border tax levied by the importing nation. This is currently the situation for the United States (General Accounting Office 1981).

The European countries adopting VAT experienced a common trend of export growth after VAT was adopted compared with the three previous years (Hoeffs 1980). The United Kingdom in the single year 1975 was the only exception. One can hardly deny that the addition of VAT was an important stimulant to the exports of these major European industrial nations. Also, one can say with some confidence that a VAT would stimulate employment in major U.S. exporting industries and reduce the competitive position of many imports in the United States.

The Value-Added Tax and International Trade

Use of VAT as a revenue-raiser permits the levy of substantial revenues without changing the relative desirability of decisions to use more labor or more machines, and the like. The VAT is basically a neutral tax. However, it is also possible to use a variety of VAT rates and exemptions to reduce the burden on particular sectors of the population and to change the relative competitive position of selected products and services.

The VAT is now the major tax of the industrial nations of the free world. There are two exceptions, the United States and Japan. In the case of Japan social basics and low military needs reduce the push for revenues. In the United States great wealth, income, and a strong federation tax system have retarded the need for a tax based on total production.

Now, however, the time has come for the United States, and maybe Japan, to develop a national revenue source that is equal to the job of providing both huge and stable tax collections. Also, these taxes must be raised in such a way that investment and production efficiency are encouraged.

The different VAT rates used by EEC member states have tended to decline through the years, as have the special exemptions. This, of course, is the reverse of U.S. experience with income taxes that get ever more complicated as new pressure groups push through tax reducing, special-interest legislation (General Accounting Office 1981).

The data in Table 8.3 provide a useful summary of exemptions in effect in seven EEC member states. As mentioned above, the finance industry and professional services make up a major VAT-expansion potential, as do a number of others in the general-use services area such as hospitals and funeral services (Carlson 1980). One

TABLE 8.3

Exempt Goods and Services, as of November 1, 1979

	Belgium	Denmark	Ireland	Italy	Netherlands	United Kingdom	West Germany
Land and buildings	X	X	X		X	X	X
Rentals and leases	X	X	X		X	X	X
Medical care, doctors, and dentists	X	X	X	X	X	X	X
Hospitalization	X	X	X	X	X	X	X
Fuel, power, utilities, electricity				X			
Heating oil and gas		X					
Telephone services							
Water					X		
Credit/lending operations	X	X	X	X	X		
Insurance	X	X	X	X	X	X	X
Local public transportation		X	X	X		X	X
Accountants' services			X				
Lawyers' services	X		X				
Education/schools	X						X
Funeral services		X	X	X	X	X	
Lotteries, betting, and gaming	X	X	X	X	X	X	
Postal services	X	X	X	X	X	X	X
Art		X			X	X	X
Nonprofit organizations	X	X	X	X	X	X	X

Note: The table shows general application for goods and services. Since there are numerous exceptions to the basic rules, the individual countries' tax laws should be consulted for a complete application of rates and exemptions.

Source: Compiled by the General Accounting Office, based on information provided by foreign officials.

must conclude that VAT's potential, particularly in the breadth area, is underutilized in the EEC.

Definitions and Economic Considerations

Before leaving this discussion of some of the nuts and bolts of VAT, a few of the concepts utilized are worth a brief analysis. For example, an exempt product or service need not apply a VAT rate to its sales. However, the VAT included in purchases is not refunded. When a product or service is zero rated, the sales are not subject to VAT and the business firm receives a refund of the VAT paid on its purchase from other firms. Zero rating applies to all exports to non-EEC nations and to most exports to EEC member states. The concept has also been used on domestic transactions to some extent, particularly in the United Kingdom and Ireland. Generally speaking, producers or merchants are stimulated through zero rating to increase foreign sales. If they export, they enjoy a tax favor that acts as an export subsidy. On the other hand, imports into a VAT–using nation are liable to a border tax equal to the VAT rate applying to the product or service in the importing country. Of course, if it wishes, the importing nation may exempt imports from the border tax. This flexibility gives VAT a clear advantage over exchange-rate shifts that retard or stimulate imports or exports.

The adoption of VAT by Mexico in 1980 and the continued use of a major manufacturers' tax in Canada place the United States in an unfavorable trade position vis-à-vis its two closest neighbors. An exporter from both Mexico and Canada benefits from a tax refund or exemption. Also, any export from the United States to Mexico and Canada faces, respectively, a border tax equal to VAT or a border tax equal to the Canadian manufacturers' tax.

Relative to the rest of the world the United States is operating to a degree with an unharmonized tax system. The trading partners of the United States occupy a more favorable competitive position because of their use of indirect taxes (largely the VAT) and because of expansion of the portion of total cost consisting of costs of government services.

Basic Administrative Form

The VAT is collected and administered through use of an invoice like the British form reproduced here as Table 8.4. The invoice changes as office procedures become more sophisticated in individual countries. However, the basic data remain constant and are relatively simple.

TABLE 8.4

Illustration of a Value-Added Tax Invoice

SALES INVOICE No. 74   14 August 1979
To A Retailer Ltd.
48 North Road, London N12 5NA.

From: Foundation Trading (UK) Ltd.
Bowman Street, Chester.   VAT Regd. No. 987 6543 21
Sale

Quantity	Description and Price	Amount Exclusive of VAT	VAT Rate	VAT Net
		£	%	£
6	Radios, SW14 at £21.30	127.80		
12	Record Players P38 at £9.80	117.60		
6	Amplifiers J27 at £11.80	70.80		
		316.20	15	45.06*
	Delivery (strictly net)	6.00	15	0.90
Terms: Cash Discount of 5% if paid within 14 days		322.20		45.96
	VAT	£45.96		
Tax Point: 14/8/1979	TOTAL	£368.16		

*Calculated on the discounted price.

Source: Her Majesty's Customs and Excise, Value-Added Tax: General Guide, Notice no. 700 (London: Her Majesty's Customs and Excise, 1979), p. 76.

Government administrative costs of VAT in the United Kingdom are estimated at about 2 percent of gross VAT revenue. A Belgian study places administrative costs at 1.2 percent of VAT revenues.

Amendments through the years have móved toward greater VAT simplicity. With a pure VAT being more simple than a pure income tax, and with amendments and special provisions of the income tax moving toward greater complexity while VAT moves toward greater simplicity, adoption of VAT and elimination of the federal individual income tax will sharply cut tax administrative requirements. In addition, VAT will push toward better business decisions of all kinds. What more can one expect a tax shift or any economic reform to accomplish?

RELATIVE INDUSTRY TAX BURDEN UNDER VALUE–ADDED AND INCOME TAXES

The data used to arrive at the percentages shown in Tables 8.5 and 8.6 are to a degree affected by the type of tax—value-added or income—now in effect. For example, the portion of gross national product (GNP) produced by an industry is reduced when income taxes rather than value-added taxes are used. This is the case because production does not take place until the price received is high enough to increase profits that they provide a fair return after taxes, that is, a return that is over 46 percent—the corporate profit tax rate. The value-added tax, on the other hand, need not provide additional profits sufficient to cover the total tax increase. In the case of the value-added tax, the profit percentage increase need be no greater than that of the wage, net interest, or net rent figures.

Of course, these tax-incident differences are always subject to a variety of opinions. Therefore, a simplified assumption is used in this discussion; that is, prices are seen to be affected in the same way and to the same degree under a value-added tax as under business income taxes.

Tax Impacts

In the tax area the term income has served as a useful concept to those wishing to give the impression that taxes are levied on the basis of ability-to-pay. Also, the particular concept of income that should be used as a tax base (if an income tax is to be levied according to ability-to-pay) has remained uncertain. For example, does the taxation of corporate profits to both the corporation and the individual (on the portion of profits distributed as dividends) constitute an ability-to-pay income tax?

Does the taxation of profits at high rates while interest payments are deductible as an expense really constitute taxation according to ability-to-pay?

In terms of the personal income tax should a deduction be allowed for the costs of educating a child as a kind of personal deprecia-

TABLE 8.5

Income Tax versus Value-Added Tax

Industry	Income Tax of Specific Industry (billions of dollars)	Percentage of Total Income Tax	Gross National Product of Specific Industry (billions of dollars)	Value-Added Tax (15 percent rate) of Gross National Product of Specific Industry (billions of dollars)	Percentage of Total Value-Added Tax
Agriculture, forestry, fisheries	0.132	0.16	85.6	12.840	3.35
Mining	2.009	2.48	127.2	19.080	4.98
Construction	2.208	2.72	127.2	19.080	4.98
Manufacturing	38.246	47.12	644.0	96.000	25.22
Transportation and public utilities	3.574	4.40	261.9	39.285	10.26
Wholesale	6.747	8.31	212.2	31.830	8.31
Retail	5.942	7.32	260.5	39.075	10.20
Finance, insurance, and real estate	19.645	24.20	448.2	67.230	17.55
Services	2.672	3.29	386.9	58.035	15.15
Total	81.175	100.00	2,553.7	383.055	100.00

Source: U.S., Department of Commerce, Survey of Current Business (Washington, D.C.: Government Printing Office, July 1982).

TABLE 8.6

Comparison of Percentages, Income Tax versus Value-Added Tax

Industry	Percentage of Total Income Tax	Percentage of Total Value-Added Tax
Agriculture, forestry, fisheries	0.16	3.35
Mining	2.48	4.98
Construction	2.72	4.98
Manufacturing	47.12	25.22
Transportation and public utilities	4.40	10.26
Wholesale	8.31	8.31
Retail	7.32	10.20
Finance, insurance, and real estate	24.20	17.55
Services	3.29	15.15
Total	100.00	100.00

Source: U.S., Department of Commerce, Survey of Current Business (Washington, D.C.: Government Printing Office, July 1982).

tion charge? One cannot but become convinced (1) that the basic philosophy of sound economics and the justice of the income tax are largely destroyed in the tax's administration and (2) that this is necessarily the case. The concept of income does not provide a useful tax base.

Table 8.6 shows that agriculture, forestry, and fisheries are nearly entirely exempt from income taxes. A VAT would increase these industries' tax payments from 0.16 percent of total income taxes to 33.5 percent of total value-added taxes. On the other hand, manufacturing pays 47.12 percent of total income taxes and would contribute only 25.22 percent of a VAT. Finally, wholesaling would contribute as large a share of a VAT as it does of federal income taxes. Retailing would experience a modest increase of its portion of taxes under VAT.

Business Tax on Profits

Study of the taxation of business continues to be limited to profits that for some reason are labeled income. This was true of a recent study by the federal Joint Committee on Taxation. The Wall Street Journal reported that 20 large commercial banks paid taxes to the federal government equal to only 2.7 percent of U.S. income (Wall Street Journal 1983c). This statement means that of the profits earned domestically only 2.7 percent was paid as corporate income taxes. Taxes paid by employees on their earnings or on the properties owned domestically are not considered. The study does not differentiate between capital provided by borrowing and capital provided as equity, and it therefore fails to take into consideration that interest paid is a cost, while profits (that is, income) are not a deductible expense.

When one digs a little deeper, one sees that provisions of the domestic income tax law account for a large portion of the low tax paid on domestic earnings of large commercial banks. For example, interest on debts incurred to purchase tax-exempt municipals can be deducted. Domestically, banks can also deduct from their income tax base the funds set aside as reserves for bad debts. These tax breaks are not available on bank profits earned abroad.

The tax on profits kept abroad by large commercial banks is reported at 38 percent. This is comparable to foreign taxes paid by other industries. However, data indicate that the domestic income taxes of large banks are relatively low. The study reports the effective domestic income tax rate in the automobile-production industry to be 47.7 percent, the highest of any major industry. The aerospace industry and the chemical industry pay income taxes as a percentage of profits at the 6.8 percent and 5 percent level, respectively.

Data from the study summarized in Tables 8.5 and 8.6 demonstrate with a somewhat different industrial breakdown that manufacturing accounts for nearly one-half of income taxes paid by industry and for only about one-fourth of GNP allocated by industry. The data relating income taxes to GNP demonstrate a great variation in the relative tax burden as measured by percentage of GNP paid as income taxes and value-added taxes.

Value-Added Tax Introduction

One must be careful not to read too much into the relationships developed in two studies mentioned above. With this in mind it is appropriate to examine the relationships between use of the income tax and the value-added tax as highlighted by the studies.

Under a value-added tax system the percentage of total tax paid by each industrial grouping varies from 3.35 percent to 25.2 percent. The percentage of total income taxes paid by each industrial grouping varies from 0.16 percent to 47.12 percent. The portion of taxes paid by each industrial grouping varies much more under the income tax system than under the value-added tax system. The bottom line of this relationship is that the value-added tax treats industrial groupings more evenly than does the income tax. The tax system becomes less important in determining the industrial area that will prosper. This is just another aspect of the basic advantage of equality and stability possessed by the value-added tax.

In these days of high unemployment in the manufacturing sector its very high relative tax burden under the income tax is particularly undesirable. Introduction of a VAT would increase the relative tax burden of industries producing raw materials. This would encourage conservation, which is generally considered to be a desirable goal.

The industry currently enjoying considerable expansion—the services industry—would have its relative tax burden substantially expanded under the value-added tax. The increase would undoubtedly arise because a large portion of the value-added in this industry is represented by individual salaries, which are not included under the corporate income base but are taxed as personal income. These salaries are, however, a portion of the value-added tax base, as are all earnings and payments for the factors of production.

CHARACTERISTICS OF THE VALUE-ADDED TAX

In both the United States and the United Kingdom the VAT has suffered from the bias in favor of income taxes on the part of academic and government tax specialists. In April 1971 the United Kingdom finally broke through the prejudices of its tax specialists. The quicker the United States does the same, the sounder the world and U.S. economies will be.

Professor Nicholas Kaldor (1955), famed British economist and author of the best-selling tax book, An Expenditure Tax, is of the opinion that British economists have been completely mesmerized in their efforts to define income and that much too little has been done on the usefulness of income, however defined, to measure ability to pay taxes. Kaldor, a member of the Labour party's inner advisory group, is a long-time critic of the income tax's ability to reach the right individuals or the correct element of society if economic growth or tax justice are to be maximized.

Coverage and Rate

The European experience teaches that only one VAT rate should be used. If one product or service is to be subject to a heavier or lighter VAT burden, the goal is better accomplished by differences in percentage applied to the price in arriving at the base. The administrative characteristics of VAT are such that complete exemption is only possible through tax refund or zero rating.

In France the VAT spread from an original tax on manufacturing to a tax including a large portion of private sector GNP in its base. The built-in expansion characteristic of VAT is now recognized, and all VAT lesiglation (except in Italy) extends down through the retail level. Even Italy, however, has replaced local retail taxes with a national tax.

Although an excellent study sponsored by the American Retail Federation demonstrated that a VAT can be administered without difficulty alongside state and local retail sales taxes, the European practice of eliminating these local taxes must be the preferred route because it has proved in Europe to be the best. A national VAT of 20 percent with one-quarter of collections distributed to the states on the basis of population, as is done in Germany, would be a possibility. If this were done, the following consequences would obtain:

1. The U.S. VAT rate would become comparable to European rates, while avoiding most of the upward pressure on prices.

2. The growing and very serious inefficiencies and difficulties arising from the diverse and ever-expanding state and local sales taxes would be somewhat reduced.

3. Revenues would become available for state and local government, and therefore the financing of decentralization would be expanded.

The Hidden Tax Paradox

A double standard exists in taxation. The amount of corporate income tax and the amount of property tax and social security contributions included as part of the price paid for a pair of shoes are unknown. These taxes are all hidden in the price. In fact, they are so well hidden that a buyer is generally unaware the shoes cost more because these taxes have been paid. This type of hidden tax is accepted.

On the other hand, an excise tax or a sales tax must be an add-on. The product must be sold at a price plus tax. This difference in treatment is largely a U.S. paradox and does not exist in Western Europe or Australia. In the United States a transactions tax is unfair and underhanded when it is hidden in the price, while to hide other taxes is accepted as normal practice.

This situation is not easily changed, as demonstrated by the federal air ticket tax that was at first hidden completely and then was only partially hidden. This attitude has retarded development of transaction-based taxes in the United States. A VAT at the retail

TABLE 8.7

Danish Value-Added Tax Form

Value-Added Tax
TAX ACCOUNTING

Date	Purchases			Sales			Comments
	1 Purchase Price Including VAT	Tax Credit		4 Sales Price	5 Tax Payable	6 VAT Deductible on Exports	
		2 Domestic Purchases	3 On Own Imports				

Value-Added Tax
DECLARATION

Taxable Period

LETTER

Official
Paid

194

Kroner (rounded)	Specification
	Tax payable
	Tax deductible
	Tax liable

To
Tax Service
Postbox 297

Copenhagen V

. . . .
Signature

Space reserved

Source: Kingdom of Denmark, Revenue Department, 1980.

154

level in the United States should be included in price just as it is in Europe and just as other taxes are included in price in the United States.

The Value-Added Tax: A Simple Tax

The use of a VAT along the lines set down in the previous section does not require an elaborate administrative machinery. One of VAT's great advantages is the simplicity of the concept.

Table 8.7 shows the tax-due VAT report form used by the Danish government. A VAT for the United States that is carefully drafted can be as simple as the Danish tax.

USE OF NATIONAL INCOME ACCOUNTS TO DEMONSTRATE TAX BURDEN LOCATION

Introduction

It is generally agreed that the treatment of incomes, taxes, receipts, payments, investment, consumption, exports, and imports in determining the national income account (NIA) conceptual aggregates provides a fundamental insight into the functioning of the U.S. economy. Such agreement does not exist as to the contribution NIA makes in providing an understanding of the location of the burden of taxes and the impact of taxes levied on NIA components.

The VAT is often said—and assumed—to be a tax on the consumer. It is frequently concluded from this burden assumption that VAT is a retail sales tax that has been made unnecessarily complicated because of some European political requirements.

The VAT base is as limited or as broad as the money value of sales adjusted as the legislative bodies of the various countries using the tax have decreed. Inclusion of all sales in VAT's base means that a distinction is not made between the sale of goods and services conventionally identified as consumer or as investment transactions. However, as a firm makes its VAT payment it can deduct the VAT previously paid. This is demonstrated in the calculation of a subtractive VAT in Table 8.7.

The final user (usually a consumer) does not develop a VAT liability through a future sale, and therefore the VAT included as a portion of costs cannot be used later to reduce a VAT liability. The VAT liability becomes a portion of costs to be covered by future sales prices. This, like all other costs, becomes an element in wage and price settlements.

The relationship existing when a VAT liability is not developed from which VAT paid can be deducted also exists when the purchase price (excluding the VAT portion) cannot be used to decrease taxable income or be used as a tax credit. There is a reduction in degree under the second situation, but the concept of "the buck stops here" is the same; that is, taxes can be deducted from taxes due only when the law so provides or when a tax liability arises from a commercial transaction. The use of a tax paid to reduce a tax due ends with the sale of a product to someone not recognized as being engaged in a commercial transaction. This is true of a property tax, an income tax, and a transaction tax. Such similarity, which is so often denied, is accepted and demonstrated in the NIA.

With the introduction of NIA in 1934 and the availability of data back to 1929, a method evolved for measuring a defined concept of economic activity and, indirectly, economic well-being. Now and again the concept measured has been modified and refined, but basically the structure remains as developed just before and during the Great Depression. The data were widely utilized in the 1940s to demonstrate the Keynesian theoretical economic structure. Here the data are used to demonstrate the macrodistribution of taxes.

Public Sector Size and Revenue Balance

Some 50 years ago government activities, particularly federal government spending and tax collecting, were not considered to be an important element in providing goods and services to households and in employing production factors. The federal government's receipts from all sources were $3.9 billion in 1929, and total state and local government revenues were about $7.5 billion, thus making a total of $11.4 billion. The GNP for the same year is estimated to have been $103 billion. The federal government had a surplus of $734 million, and state and local governments enjoyed a surplus of about $100 million. Government tax collecting and spending were about 10 percent of GNP, and budget surpluses existed. Therefore, through its financing and spending government was making a contribution to funds available for investment and was not crowding out private borrowers from the money market in order to cover its own deficits, as tends to be true today with a federal debt of $1.36 trillion.

Under these public sector conditions the manner of treating taxes in national economic accounts was established. The impact of the selection that was made was not seen to be great. Nobody with power in the decision process apparently wished to tie government economic activities closely to private sector buying, selling, producing, investing, and trading abroad.

At hand for use as a working tool was the constitutional distinction between direct and indirect taxes. It had developed in nineteenth-century literature and had proved to be useful to the writers of the United States Constitution when they were looking for ways to restrict the taxation powers of the new national government. This direct and indirect tax concept became the dichotomy around which the NIA treatment of taxation was built. In addition, the textbook definition of incomes of the factors of production was used to establish a national income total that was distinct from gross national product.

A summary of the National Income and Product Accounts for the period 1980-82 is given in Table 8.8. It is in sufficient detail to demonstrate the direct and indirect tax dichotomy. It also shows the failure of the accounts to relate taxes to government purchases of goods and services and to generally integrate the public sector with the private sector.

One line includes indirect business taxes and another line includes profits tax liability. No mention is made of taxes paid out of wages or out of incomes from other sources. On the product side of the accounts one line shows government purchasing of $435.6 billion in goods and services. However, the total of the two tax lines on the income side is only $262.6 billion. Obviously, the NIA in such summary form does not provide a useful understanding of how taxes affect prices, incomes, and wealth, or for that matter, the relation between taxes and government income and spending. The source of public sector funds is not clear, nor is it clear how the public sector is integrated with the private sector. These relationships needed to measure tax collection impacts are not identified or analyzed.

Circular Flow of Taxes and Government Spending

The national accounts can be presented in another way: as a circular flow of income between households and the factors of production. Under this approach, in order to finance government activities, private control over resources takes the form of the gross product or income of the factors of production, land, labor, and capital. These are usually called business and income taxes.

Preservation of the Factor Income Concept

As noted, the separate accounts of the national income accounts are frequently shown as a circle of incomes and products with the beginning and ending point being gross national product/gross national income; that is, the value of all products sold is equal to the value of

TABLE 8.8

National Income by Type of Income, Seasonally Adjusted at Annual Rates
(in billions of dollars)

	1980	1981	1981				1982	
			I	II	III	IV	I	II
National income	2,117.1	2,352.5	2,293.7	2,324.4	2,387.3	2,404.5	2,396.9	2,425.1
Compensation of employees	1,598.6	1,767.6	1,718.0	1,750.0	1,789.1	1,813.4	1,830.8	1,850.6
Wages and salaries	1,356.1	1,494.0	1,452.8	1,479.4	1,512.6	1,531.1	1,541.5	1,556.5
Government and government enterprises	260.1	283.1	276.2	279.8	284.0	292.3	296.3	300.0
Other	1,095.9	1,210.9	1,176.5	1,199.6	1,228.6	1,238.8	1,245.2	1,256.5
Supplements to wages and salaries	242.5	273.6	265.2	270.6	276.5	282.3	289.3	294.1
Employer contributions for social insurance	115.3	133.2	129.9	132.1	134.3	136.5	140.2	141.6
Other labor income	127.2	140.4	135.3	138.4	142.2	145.8	149.1	152.5
Proprietors' income with IVA and CCAdj	116.3	124.7	123.4	123.8	127.5	124.1	116.4	118.1
Farm	19.4	24.0	21.6	22.5	27.1	24.6	17.8	18.0
Proprietors' income with IVA	26.4	31.8	29.1	30.3	35.1	32.8	26.0	26.2
CCAdj	-7.0	-7.9	-7.5	-7.8	-8.0	-8.2	-8.2	-8.2
Nonfarm	96.9	100.7	101.8	101.2	100.4	99.5	98.6	100.1
Proprietors' income	99.9	100.3	103.2	100.9	99.3	97.7	93.8	94.2
IVA	-3.1	-1.6	-2.5	-1.4	-1.2	-1.2	0.0	-0.5
CCAdj	0.1	2.1	1.2	1.8	2.3	3.0	4.7	6.5
Rental income of persons with CCAdj	32.9	33.9	34.4	34.0	33.6	33.6	33.9	34.2
Rental income of persons	65.3	69.4	68.7	68.9	69.5	70.5	71.0	70.6
CCAdj	-32.4	-35.5	-34.3	-34.9	-35.9	-36.9	-37.1	-36.4
Corporate profits with IVA and CCAdj	181.6	190.6	200.3	185.1	193.1	183.9	157.1	154.9
Corporate profits with IVA	199.4	207.5	217.6	202.6	210.3	199.4	167.2	160.8
Profits before tax	242.4	232.1	253.1	225.4	233.3	216.5	171.6	168.7
Profits tax liability	84.7	81.2	91.5	79.2	82.4	71.6	55.8	53.7
Profits after tax	157.8	150.9	161.6	146.2	150.8	144.9	115.9	115.0
Dividends	58.1	65.1	61.5	64.0	66.8	68.1	68.8	69.3
Undistributed profits	99.7	85.8	100.1	82.2	84.0	76.9	47.0	45.7
IVA	-43.0	-24.6	-35.5	-22.8	-23.0	-17.1	-4.4	-7.8
CCAdj	-17.8	-16.8	-17.3	-17.5	-17.1	-15.5	-10.1	-5.9
Net interest	187.7	235.7	217.6	231.6	244.0	249.5	258.7	267.4
Addenda:								
Corporate profits after tax with IVA and CCAdj	97.0	109.5	108.9	105.9	110.7	112.3	101.3	101.2
Dividends	58.1	65.1	61.5	64.0	66.8	68.1	68.8	69.3
Undistributed profits with IVA and CCAdj	38.9	44.4	47.3	42.0	43.9	44.3	32.5	31.9

IVA = inventory adjustment   CCAdj = consumer-cost adjustment

Note: Roman numerals indicate quarters of the year.

Source: U.S., Department of Commerce, Survey of Current Business (Washington, D. C.: Department of Commerce, August 1982).

all incomes received. The first step in breaking down the aggregates is the reduction of gross national income (GNI) to national income. This is done by subtracting indirect business taxes and depreciation from GNI.

The national economic accounts use the term indirect taxes partially in the way it was defined by nineteenth-century economists. The taxes included in this group are all sales, excises, gross receipts, customs duties, and property taxes paid by businesses. The group also corresponds to some extent to that of indirect taxes as provided in the United States Constitution.

The grouping together of taxes in the national economic accounts that are deducted before national income is calculated has helped to perpetuate the idea that some taxes increase prices and others do not. The group of taxes categorized as indirect business taxes is treated in the same way as depreciation is treated. The justification for doing this is apparently because they both bring about an increase in price prior to the price becoming an income of the factors of production. They are a cost but not an income of the factors of production and therefore not a part of national income.

Depreciation is not received first as dividends by the owners and later paid back to the firm to cover depreciation. Also, indirect taxes are not received first by wage earners and then paid back to the firm so that the business can cover its indirect tax liabilities. This relationship is obviously accurate. However, it is also true that both depreciation and indirect taxes are costs like wages and a normal return on equity. So why the special treatment? Apparently, it is because of (1) traditional separation between indirect and direct taxes, (2) some vague economic theories, and (3) the established way of defining national income, that is, to limit it to payments to the factors of production.

National income equals the income of the factors of production (profits, wages, interest, and so forth). All are treated in the NIA as though tax liabilities did not go along with payments of all types. Later adjustments are made to provide for various tax payment allocations.

The treatment of taxes seems to imply that real income is the income before taxes and real price is the price after indirect taxes. This unequal treatment of taxes must be kept in mind as the locations of tax burdens are considered. Profits are higher because corporate profits taxes must be paid, wages are higher because social security and income taxes must be paid, and prices are higher because these taxes and indirect business taxes must be covered by prices received. Taxes are included in all payment and receipt quantities.

The Income-Product Match-Up

The Summary of National Income and Product Accounts reports profits-tax liabilities (U. S. , Department of Commerce, various dates). The adjustment is made quickly and Profits before Tax is the title of the line. Therefore, confusion as to what the profits really are is avoided. The NIA clearly reports profits after taxes. The summary does not report a similar after-tax figure for wages, business and professional income, rent, interest, and so forth. However, there is a widely used national accounts concept called disposable income, which is the after-tax total of income available to individuals and unincorporated businesses. This adjusted total of income is available to pay for consumer goods and services that are placed on the market. Some of it is saved, also. The savings finance investments of unincorporated businesses and become deposits of savings institutions, payments on mortgages, and the like.

Disposable income in many respects is the bottom line of the NIA, but not quite. The real honest-to-goodness bottom line is personal consumption expenditures. This aggregate is reported in the NIA but it is incomplete because spending for financing housing is not reported.

At this point, the bottom of the income-product circle, the products that match the reported incomes appear. They are divided into four groups: (1) personal consumption expenditures (excluding residential structures), (2) gross private domestic investment (including residential structures), (3) net exports of goods and services, and (4) government purchase of goods and services.

End-Use and Intermediary Goods

The price paid for consumer goods is the payment for end-use. All investments in both the private and public sectors have been made to put these end-use goods on the market. Although gross private domestic investment is one of the four sectors of GNP, it is, of course, an intermediary good and not an end-use good. And government spending includes large investment, consumer goods, and service components that are not separately reported.

Investment, both private and public, only has value because it is useful in producing an end-use consumer good. The value of capital goods arises because the investment is required to produce the consumer good and service or because the consumer satisfaction can be produced more cheaply through use of machines. The accounts can make investment a separate sector because along the way they have subtracted depreciation and savings from gross incomes. These gross incomes arose from the sale of goods and services at prices high enough to cover the cost of capital as well as wages, energy, raw materials, and so forth. Also, these prices were high enough to permit payment of taxes by the sellers. The taxes were deducted along the way as the gross income from sales worked its way down to the bottom line. This is demonstrated with NIA data in Table 8.8.

Taxes as Prices

If taxes were increased to provide more free consumer goods (in other words, if taxes were used to pay the price for a larger portion of consumer goods such as medical services), the prices of market-provided goods and services would go up to permit this resource transfer. However, consumers would have more money to cover the higher prices because medical services would be free. Prices would be up but inflation would not have taken place. However, the higher prices would bring about a reallocation of consumer satisfaction. Those not using medical services would have a reduced scale of living. Large users of medical services would have their scale of living expanded.

Treatment of Taxes under National Income Accounts

The concepts of national income and taxation incidence as included in the NIA were satisfactory in 1929 but they no longer meet the test of helpfulness in the 1980s. Taxes at nearly one-third of incomes bring about too great an adjustment of factor incomes to allow continuation of reporting the before-tax income figure and the after-tax price figure. Wages, profits, and other factor incomes must be reported as the after-tax figure. Indirect business taxes and depreciation must be treated in the same way as other taxes and business-production costs. The NIA must be moved up to gross national income.

Taxes are prices. Every consumer purchase includes a tie-in purchase of government spending and a tie-in purchase of capital goods. The present special treatment of indirect business taxes and depreciation as deductions separated out of the regular adjustments of factor incomes is confusing. In addition, this treatment perpetuates the idea that depreciation costs and indirect business taxes affect prices more directly than other costs. The more appropriate stance at this point in our understanding of the economic process is one of neutrality. This means abandoning the national income total

TABLE 8.9

Gross Domestic Product of Corporate Business in Current Dollars, Seasonally Adjusted at Annual Rates
(in billions of dollars)

	1980	1981	1981 I	1981 II	1981 III	1981 IV	1982 I	1982 II
GDP of corporate business	1,635.5	1,837.1	1,788.9	1,818.6	1,867.8	1,873.1	1,863.1	1,883.8
Capital consumption allowances with CCAdj	181.2	206.2	196.2	202.9	209.7	216.0	218.9	223.3
Net domestic product	1,454.2	1,630.9	1,592.7	1,615.7	1,658.1	1,657.1	1,644.2	1,660.6
Indirect business tax and nontax liability plus business transfer payments less subsidies	155.8	186.1	180.8	186.9	187.8	189.1	184.0	189.3
Domestic income	1,298.5	1,444.8	1,411.9	1,428.8	1,470.3	1,468.0	1,460.2	1,471.3
Compensation of employees	1,107.3	1,224.5	1,190.4	1,213.5	1,242.5	1,251.5	1,259.5	1,270.6
Wages and salaries	929.2	1,024.8	996.2	1,015.7	1,040.5	1,046.6	1,049.7	1,057.7
Supplements to wages and salaries	178.0	199.7	194.2	197.8	202.1	204.9	209.8	212.9
Corporate profits with IVA and CCAdj	151.3	167.8	176.5	164.3	172.2	158.3	140.2	138.3
Profits before tax	212.1	209.3	229.3	204.6	212.3	190.9	154.7	152.1
Profits tax liability	84.7	81.2	91.5	79.2	82.4	71.6	55.8	53.7
Profits after tax	127.5	128.1	137.8	125.4	129.8	119.3	99.0	98.4
Dividends	39.7	50.8	46.8	48.9	52.7	54.6	56.0	59.6
Undistributed profits	87.8	77.3	91.0	76.4	77.1	64.7	42.9	38.9
IVA	-43.0	-24.6	-35.5	-22.8	-23.0	-17.1	-4.4	-7.8
CCAdj	-17.8	-16.8	-17.3	-17.5	-17.1	-15.5	-10.1	-5.9
Net interest	39.9	52.5	44.9	51.0	55.6	58.3	60.5	62.4
GDP of financial corporate business	97.8	104.8	105.6	103.6	104.2	106.0	106.6	112.7
GDP of nonfinancial corporate business	1,537.7	1,732.3	1,683.3	1,715.0	1,763.6	1,767.2	1,756.6	1,771.1
Capital consumption allowances with CCAdj	172.0	195.8	186.3	192.6	199.1	205.1	207.8	212.0

IVA = inventory adjustment   CCAdj = consumer–cost adjustment

Note: Roman numerals indicate quarters of the year.

Source: U.S., Department of Commerce, Survey of Current Business (Washington, D.C.: Department of Commerce, August 1982).

162

and working down from only a gross figure, as is done on the product side.

The national economic accounts illustrated in Table 8.9 demonstrate that national income includes employer social security taxes and corporate profits taxes within its total. Although the procedure deducts the indirect business tax before national income, these taxes have the same dollar-for-dollar impact on national income and prices.

Concluding Remarks

The proper treatment of taxes in the NIA has been the subject of considerable difference of opinion through the years. The problem that continued to bother the developers of the accounts was the following: the theory taught that indirect and direct taxes had quite different incidences, but the accounts system resulted in all taxes being in the same pot—prices. Also, the difference between business taxes and personal taxes (a difference that lay behind the concept that democracies possess only the ability-to-tax according to the ability-to-pay) disappeared when collections from both direct and indirect taxes had the same effect on disposable income as treated in the NIA. Both direct and indirect tax payments reduced disposable income and became basically the same kind of tax when considered in terms of aggregate spending power for end-use goods and services.

These tax effects on prices must be considered in assessing the international competitive position of U.S. products. Because all taxes are included in price (with the possible exception of natural resource taxes), countervailing U.S. duties are needed to harmonize the prices of U.S. goods with those of nations using the VAT. Adoption of a U.S. VAT would provide an alternative solution.

The gross national product and disposable income are the two major national income aggregates, one the gross base available to support economic activity and the other total end-use income, that is, personal saving and consumption. The size of each is not affected directly by the type of taxes used. Just as much tax is included in the GNP aggregate whether income or transaction taxes are used, and the same is true of deductions in calculating disposable income.

The concept of a stable public revenue source resting evenly on all of GNP and not related to income redistribution or monopoly returns is attractive. It is generally accepted that all economic activity benefits from public sector services that are best financed as an even portion of GNP rather than by collecting a price through attempts to reach surpluses of one type or another. The VAT functions in this general manner.

The Organization for Economic Cooperation and Development (OECD) makes studies to determine the tax benefit position of typical workers in its member nations (Western industrial nations and Japan). The most recent study is based on 1981 data (1982).

Tax data included in the study are limited to individual income taxes and employee-paid social security payroll taxes. The study treats the taxes as though the tax receipts reduced by an equal amount the ability of workers to purchase goods and services. By using this approach the study implied this was not true of other taxes. In this concept the dichotomy is continued of the direct tax being carried by the buyer while indirect taxes are shifted forward in price.

In the limitations section of the OECD report the researchers write, "Nothing is said about who finally bears the burden of these taxes as this depends upon how they are shifted and this is something upon which there is still no agreement amongst economists." The analyses made in this book and the evidence of relative prices in different nations lead to the conclusion that all taxes (direct or indirect) are reflected in prices.

APPLICATION OF THE DESTINATION PRINCIPLE

In the 1977-79 Tokyo Round held in Geneva under the General Agreement on Tariffs and Trade (GATT) the United States became a party to an international tax and trade negotiation somewhat along the lines of the Kennedy Round 15 years earlier. International economic changes have occurred unusually rapidly during the past 15 years. However, with the exception of developments related to the Organization of Petroleum Exporting Countries (OPEC), most of the pressures and changes—even devaluation of the dollar in August 1971—were foreseen in 1964.

On the other hand, the economics of border taxes, the value-added tax, the destination principle, and the relationship of each to the other were only dimly perceived in 1964. At that time U.S. negotiators failed to give high priority to the manner in which the relatively unimportant turnover and other indirect taxes were treated under GATT understandings. New studies of the incidence of the corporate income tax (CIT) and indirect business taxes such as VAT were not yet digested. In addition, little attention was given to the alternative of a declining exchange rate, which was provided by use of border taxes on imports and tax refunds to exporters.

Today the VAT is used by over 30 nations and by the state of Michigan. The rates are generally substantial. Also, CIT is now seen to be a basic cost of production (as is true of VAT), not a tax of a surplus. As a result of this new attitude, many industrial nations have reduced their CIT through integration with the personal income tax. In Germany, for example, the CIT is treated like a tax withheld on dividend payments.

Domestic Tax Policy

Neglect of the domestic tax aspects of international commercial operations in the Kennedy Round was harmful to U.S. interests. Just how harmful cannot be calculated. Amazingly, similar neglect existed in the Tokyo Round of trade negotiations. The neglect in 1964 spawned U.S. capital exports. Continuation of such an approach is destined to increase capital hemorrhaging.

Immense problems of international finance and continued uncertainty over energy prices cause a neglect of the daily impact of border taxes levied at national VAT rates on U.S. exports to Western European nations. The refund of VAT and production taxes on exports from Europe and Japan reduce the competitiveness of U.S. goods in all international markets. Exports from the United States have not benefited by a tax refund equal to 15 to 20 percent of the free-on-board price, while products exported from Europe and Japan have.

Tax Rules under the General Agreement on Tariffs and Trade

The tax-related rules under GATT are basically limited to (1) consideration of the direct effect of expenditure of taxes that cause prices of export products to be lower than domestic prices, (2) refund of taxes that are shifted forward, and (3) levy of border taxes with rates equal to domestic indirect tax rates.

It is possible to demonstrate that a tax-trade-price-impact policy based on this approach is much too limited. However, it is a concept that comes up with amounts that can be measured with reasonable accuracy and, therefore, can be monitored. In addition, it is an area of government fiscal actions where the acceptable approach is firmly fixed. It also constitutes international fiscal policy according to the destination principle. The approach's incidence assumption is that indirect taxes are shifted forward in higher prices and that direct taxes are shifted backward in lower returns to the factors of production. A destination principle aimed at treating all taxes alike would permit the refund of all taxes on exports and a border tax covering all taxes of the importing nation.

Fundamental Shortcomings

The limited destination principle now permitted under GATT owes a considerable portion of its acceptability to the theory that (1) government expenditure of funds cannot decrease costs of production, (2) tax incidence is constant and can be measured, and (3) taxes related to goods produced and marketed should be paid by consumers.

The limited destination principle combines these ideas of government expenditure and benefit with tax incidence and shifting concepts to justify the refund of only indirect taxes on exports and a border tax on imports equal only to the level of indirect taxes used by the importing nation. The destination principle concludes that collection of the same taxes on exported goods as on goods used domestically amounts to collection of higher taxes on exports than on goods consumed locally. This is true because taxes on exports are paid by citizens of a nation not benefiting through consumption of public goods that have been financed with taxes included in the price of goods and services they purchase at home. On the other hand, the levy of border taxes on imports ensures that those who enjoy the use of imported goods also bear the taxes needed to meet some public sector costs of the importing nation.

The conceptual framework of the destination principle is shaky. Rather horrendous assumptions are required.

Treatment of Nations with a Large Public Sector

Application of the destination principle by all nations on all taxes would avoid the problem of different incidence impacts. It would, on the other hand, favor a nation utilizing the least amount of private resources. A producer in a nation with a large public sector would benefit from large refunds on exports. In addition, in order to enter this market importers would have to pay very high border taxes. If resources are used equally efficiently in all nations producing the product, the producer in the nation with a large public sector would be favored. The effect of the border tax is to allocate to imports government costs within the importing nation, not government costs in the nation of export. At a maximum the nation of exports can only refund its government costs. The limited destination principle followed by GATT encourages expanded government expenditures and financing of them with indirect taxes.

The traditional and most effective producer may be located in a country that is a relatively large user of private resources. Under the broad destination principle the efficient producer becomes a smaller supplier. The relatively inefficient nation with a large public sector becomes a larger supplier. Efficiency of resource use is reduced.

Concluding Remarks

The destination principle is an unnecessary additional element restricting freedom of economic exchange. Elimination of the destination principle should have been a basic demand of the United States in the Tokyo Round of international trade negotiations.

The refund of any domestic tax on exported goods or services should become a trade subsidy prohibited by GATT. The levy of border taxes on imports should be treated as tariff duties limited under GATT through the Kennedy and Tokyo rounds. If this change is not acceptable, the United States should adopt a basic tax reform that would permit use of the destination principle in the treatment of taxes on its exports.

9

NET WEALTH
TAX BASICS

CHARACTERISTICS OF THE NET WEALTH TAX

Net physical wealth consists of two quite disparate parts: land (natural resources) and reproducible capital. These basic components of all wealth are represented in many cases by debt and equity rights such as bonds, mortgages, and common and preferred stock shares. The total value of physical wealth is often represented by financial assets and liabilities, which are called intangibles.

The concept of net wealth provides a much better base for equal treatment of people (that is, horizontal justice) who are in approximately similar economic circumstances than do the income, estate, and gift taxes. A person with a large taxable estate at death may be liable for large estate taxes, or a person may enjoy large incomes but may have a temporary taxable base and a very small estate at death. These situations do not arise under a net wealth tax because the base is taxed after the debt is deducted. The debt instruments themselves become net wealth to the holder of bonds, stocks, mortgages, and so forth.

The base of the net wealth tax (NWT) is broad and a low rate can provide substantial revenues. Net wealth is often the source of relatively stable income; therefore, NWT has income tax characteristics. In addition, appropriate portions of net wealth can be sold or used as borrowing security to finance investments (Andrews 1973).

An individual with a substantial net wealth base possesses economic security. Decisions of the holder can be of such a nature that the capital spinoff is maximized or minimized. These decisions often do not affect the immediate net wealth tax liability of the holder. In addition, net wealth can be the source of satisfactions that are not measured in the marketplace, thereby avoiding income and capital gain bases (Cutt 1969).

Net Wealth Tax Relationships

In recent years the net wealth tax has been used by 14 countries. The tax has experienced some recent growth, particularly in South America. The Indian net wealth tax provides about three times the revenues that are collected from death taxes (Eiger 1959).

There is no doubt but that administrative problems exist in the use of the net wealth tax. However, it is also true that where an honest effort is made at both the legislative and administrative levels, the net wealth tax can provide revenues in a manner that stimulates productive use of wealth. France realized this and adopted a net wealth tax in 1982 (Paglin 1975).

The Shoup mission to Japan just after World War II favored the use of a net wealth tax in its report. At that time the Japanese tax used rates from 0.5 to 3.0 percent, which are relatively high and progressive. The tax was repealed in 1954 as Japan moved back to greater reliance on graduated income taxes (Tanabe 1967).

Rates

Net wealth tax rates in effect are generally progressive. For example, in Western Europe the rates tend to go from around 0.5 to 1.8 percent. One basic advantage of the net wealth tax is that it can react actively on concentrations of economic power without using high tax rates. In fact, a proportional net wealth tax has the impact of a relatively high-rate graduated income tax. It works out this way because as the level of income increases, the portion of income arising from wealth holdings also increases (Bird 1972).

Administrative Procedures

The tax base can be developed with the active assistance of owners of capital through legislation providing that insurance companies in case of loss or destruction need pay only the amount declared as the value to administrators of the net wealth tax. Another useful method is to list in a public place all the values declared for possessions such as houses, automobiles, and furniture. An old approach is to provide for self-assessment with the government having the right to purchase the property at the value given—or other bona fide would-be purchasers could make offers (Flemming and Little 1974).

Although Switzerland has had a successful net wealth tax for many years, laws providing for secrecy of bank accounts should be lax and coupon bonds should be prohibited. Tight secrecy laws caused much of the difficulty that Japan encountered with its net wealth tax. This is an unnecessary barrier for a government to erect against itself in carrying out its fiscal responsibilities.

A net wealth tax that includes household possessions and houses in its base will have some impact on use of consumer purchasing power. The portion of consumer expenditures made for durable goods will tend to decrease.

Also, under NWT the mortgage on a house and the debt on consumer goods will be deductible from the tax base. This will encourage housing and general consumer indebtedness. The tendency toward expanded credit use at the household level will be countered somewhat by increased financial assets owing to increased credit purchases (Organization for Economic Cooperation and Development 1982).

Improved administration of local property taxes is another expected impact from a federal net wealth tax. Federal valuations would permit local governments to improve both the efficiency and the justice of their property taxes.

Comparison to Income and Profit Taxes

As we all know, true income (that is, consumption plus change in net wealth) cannot possibly constitute a tax base (Simons 1930). This fact of life has brought about creation of an artificial tax base for the income tax that more or less resembles true income or true profits. The created tax base is called taxable income and it varies substantially between tax jurisdictions (Tobin et al. 1967).

An anomaly has developed out of the use of the created tax base for the income tax: a very rich person may pay very little taxes, while a skilled employee or professional may be liable for payment of a very substantial tax assessment. If ability-to-pay is related more closely to how rich one is, why is a tax on wealth not used instead of a tax on income or profits? Is it because wealth is more difficult to locate and to calculate in terms of value? Or is it because the use of wealth as a tax base would really result in taxation according to ability-to-pay? We have not spent enough time in analyzing these questions. The data are very sparse. An effort has been made at this point to gather some helpful numbers and understandings.

Wealth Distribution

It is estimated that about 50 percent of the people above 25 years of age in a typical Western industrial nation are without wealth in the conventional sense (Atkinson and Harrison 1978). They possess some social security income rights, a small balance to meet emergency needs, and some equity in a home, automobile, and household appliances. That is about it (Ture 1972).

Introduction of a net wealth tax and repeal of corporate and individual income taxes and the estate and gift taxes would make it easier for an average income earner and corporation to accumulate some wealth. The existing tax obstacles to accumulation of a little nest egg and some equity capital are substantial (Tanzi and Iden 1969).

Point of Tax Assessment

The corporate income tax uses profits as its base. The profit base is a mangled version of the accountant's and the economist's concept of profits. Inflation becomes the source of much of the profit base. Increased inventory values push profits up and accelerated depreciation pushes them down. In addition, corporate income tax law is filled with special deals for investing or holding ownership in various ways.

What is really considered in our proposal for a substantial tax change is a removal of taxes on profits and estates at death. It is recommended that taxes be assessed instead on the holders of wealth. A tax liability under the recommended approach develops if nothing happens as well as if the property under the taxpayer's control is turned over many times. The amount of taxes due only changes if the market value of net assets on valuation day is less or more than the previously established level.

Market Value as Income

The market value of everything arises from the capitalization process in the broadest sense. Assets or capital have a value because of the expected income from use and holding. The production process and resulting income often occur without any particular guidance or owner determination. The owner and the market place a value on an object or a right because it will produce benefits, that is, income of four kinds.

First, the possibility exists of increasing value over time in real terms or only in money terms. Ownership is seen as an inflation hedge.

Second, the object will directly produce a flow of services (for example, a house or a horse).

Third, money income is received by the owner (for example, interest or dividends).

Fourth, possession of the wealth extends prestige and power to the possessor. These, in turn, increase the satisfaction enjoyed by the owner in a variety of ways.

Legislation is still influenced by the old idea that a tax not paid out of income or sales is bad because it acts to kill the goose (capital) that lays the golden egg (income). For example, several nations' net wealth taxes set a limit on tax payable as a proportion of realized cash income. When this is done, some inducement not to shift assets to most productive use has been stimulated (Pryor 1973a).

Calculation of Wealth

In April 1982 the Federal Reserve Board set the total value of wealth owned by households, personal trusts, and nonprofit organizations to be $10.7 trillion. The calculated net worth of U.S. households is set at $9.1 trillion. Some $2.7 trillion of this wealth consists of owner-occupied real estate. About 37 percent of the value of owner-occupied real estate is mortgage financed. On the basis of these data the net wealth base provided by homesteads if all owner-occupied homes were included in the taxable base would be about $2.0 trillion, and assuming one-half of these fall within the minimum exemption, the taxable homestead portion of the net wealth tax base would be around $1.0 trillion (Federal Reserve Board 1981).

TABLE 9.1

Net Wealth Tax Base and Revenues,
Fiscal Year 1981

	Billions of Dollars
Corporation income taxes	61[a]
Estate and gift taxes	7[a]
Total repealed taxes	68
2 percent net wealth tax	120[b]
Revenue increase	52[c]

[a]Repealed.
[b]New revenues.
[c]Net new revenues to be applied to deficit.

Source: Calculated by author from federal and state data.

The approximately $7 trillion of net wealth existing outside the base made up of homesteads will not be entirely free of net wealth exclusions. Exclusions would total around $1 trillion. This leaves a total net wealth tax base of about $6 trillion. A flat 2 percent federal net wealth tax would produce around $120 billion of revenues (see Table 9.1).

Tax Replacement

It is quite possible that removal of the retardant of the heavy tax on corporate profits and the one-time tax on estates and gifts would stimulate the economy. More efficient use of capital would increase the net wealth tax base. As a result it is quite possible the federal deficit would be reduced while both the corporate income tax and the estate and gift taxes were repealed.

Impact Comparison

What is the difference in impact on productivity and income and wealth distribution of two different tax policies, one consisting of a net wealth tax and the other of estate and corporate income taxes? In both cases the taxes are levied on a base consisting of wealth and income related to wealth. However, the timing of payment is very different. Annual payment of the net wealth tax causes it to become routinized. The once-in-a-lifetime payment of an estate tax makes the planning process very uncertain, as does the cyclical nature of profits (Covey 1973).

The annual net wealth tax provides constant pressure to increase the productivity of capital included in the tax base. The estate tax, on the other hand, is a distant sometime liability. Setting aside funds to make the estate tax payment does not increase the productivity of capital, but rather, it stimulates the holding of liquid assets in excess of normal needs. Highly liquid assets are generally thought of as uncommitted and therefore are dedicated to performing the rather low-level goal of meeting emergency requirements.

The small group with substantial wealth would also be induced to be more productive. The cash outflow required to pay the net wealth tax on an expensive vase that is increasing in value at a compound 10 percent rate must come from somewhere or the vase must be sold (Balough 1969).

The need for a cash flow to pay the tax on the valuable vase induces the wealthy person to press for more productive use of his or her other accumulations of purchasing power. He may sell his Trea-

TABLE 9.2

Comparison of Corporate Income Tax and Net Wealth Tax

Characteristics	Corporate Income Tax	Net Wealth Tax
Ability-to-pay	Location of burden divided between consumers, owners, and labor at uncertain proportions	Exemptions can be large and payment limited to owners of wealth
Resource allocation	Levies a heavy tax on profits out of which equity and loan capital must come	Encourages full use of capital and increases private enterprise
Foreign activities	Discourages return of foreign earnings to the United States and encourages foreign investment of U.S. capital	Provides some inducement to foreign use of U.S. capital
Foreign trade	Discourages exports and encourages imports, thus reducing employment and economic growth in the United States	Because of low rate and broad base, impact is of little importance
Revenue potential	Decreasing collections now approximate $45 billion	A 2 percent rate with large exemptions would provide $120 billion of revenues
Administrative costs	Substantial as tax expenditures increase	Because of the low rate and a large base that is largely a matter of record, costs are low
Inflation effect	Through increase in cost of capital supply is reduced, thereby raising prices	Tends to push for lower prices through supply expansion
Level of government spending	Presses for government subsidies and stabilization spending because of instability of receipts	Spending is stabilized because of tax revenue stability

Source: Compiled by the author.

174

TABLE 9.3

Comparison of Estate Tax and Net Wealth Tax

Characteristics	Estate Tax	Net Wealth Tax
Ability-to-pay	Carrier of burden, uncertain, avoidance pressures very strong as due only at death	Paid annually and in regular amounts, making avoidance and evasion rather difficult
Resource allocation	Liquidity large to hold estate together after death; gifts to nonprofit groups encouraged	Tends to stimulate productive use of capital to meet annual tax liability; somewhat encourages labor use
Foreign activities	Encourages export of capital to low-tax countries and discourages foreign investment in the United States	Low annual rate causes tax to be capitalized in lower price; therefore, effect on foreign-use decisions is very small
Foreign trade	None direct	Only very indirectly
Revenue potential	Raises around 1 percent to 2 percent of revenues	Could be very large if considered as a substitute for both estate taxes and wealth-concentration-reduction aspect of the income taxes
Administrative costs	Government light but private very substantial	Because base changes are a matter of record, costs are not substantial at either private or government level
Inflation effect	Through less productive use of capital it tends to increase costs and prices	The pressure will be toward lower prices and increased efficiency
Level of government spending	Perhaps encourages when tax on large estate is collected	People with substantial wealth are made more interested in economy in government; this should push a bit more toward less spending by government

Source: Compiled by the author.

175

sury bills and replace them with newly issued stock of a firm within a developing industry. Or he may decide to sell a painting to meet the tax liability. After all, a vase is not very productive in the sense of providing the basics of the economy—jobs, goods, and services.

Detailed analyses do not exist of (1) NWT-generated pressure to use capital more efficiently and (2) whether this outweighs the tax's tendency to encourage present consumption. It can be said, however, that the NWT impact on increased productivity is much more direct than its impact on level of consumption. Also, under inflationary tendencies such as those experienced since 1974 the annual NWT encourages the shift from cash and low-realized-return investments to ownership of operational capital earning an annual income.

Table 9.2 summarizes and compares the characteristics of a net wealth tax and a corporate income tax. Table 9.3 compares the net wealth tax with the estate tax. This analysis of the desirability of the net wealth tax permits a brief but comprehensive look at the basic relationships.

Concluding Remarks

The net wealth tax is being used in countries with economies that differ widely. The tax has proved to be adaptable. When the large revenue needs are compared with the tax bases in use, tax policy makers must become open to suggestions to bring the net wealth of a nation under the tax base umbrella.

The idea that current income and consumption make up the total usable tax base cannot be accepted. Tax needs are much too great to exclude the $10 trillion or so of U.S. net wealth. Net wealth is a legitimate tax base. Its current neglect in the United States is not justified.

ESTABLISHING THE NET WEALTH TAX BASE

The theoretical support for a net wealth tax is impressive indeed. This is particularly true when one considers the tax in terms of the income effect and the substitution effect arising from demand for leisure. The NWT reduces income as much when the wealth is used intensively as when it is idle. Therefore, the desire to earn additional income is stimulated when the tax is introduced. Use of the tax stimulates more productive activities. The substitution effect works in the same direction as the income effect. Removal of the income tax means that a higher portion of income is no longer required to meet tax payments as more is earned. Therefore, effort aimed at a higher level of production will certainly be stimulated. Under a wealth tax the tax liability does not increase as the income level goes up.

The net wealth tax, like all general taxes, is subject to exemption and reduced rate pressures. These have been handled in different ways by the nations now using the tax. With the exception of Uruguay these nations have continued their income and death taxes. Revenues from the income and death taxes reduce the need for a truly general net wealth tax that completely exploits its potential.

There is much to be said for use of a general, flat-rate tax when the base is broad and the basic justification of the tax is not ability-to-pay. For example, in the case of NWT the aim of the tax is to somewhat reduce the holdings of wealth while encouraging more productive use of wealth. At the same time NWT has an initial impact that would generally correspond with ability-to-pay goals.

A convenient way to administer the portion of a net wealth resting on furniture, jewelry, paintings, and other personal property is to make use of insurance information and insurance liability in case of destruction or theft. For example, the NWT used in 14 Swiss cantons has as its base a percentage of insured value. In Norway insured values less a deduction are used.

Automobiles and boats in excess of small mass-produced vehicles are included in the net wealth tax base, as are more valuable pieces of art and furniture. Insured values are again used. However, apparently none of the NWT users have found it necessary to take the final insurance-based step, that is, restricting the insurance payment in case of destruction or theft to the amount declared as the NWT base.

Character of Wealth

The deposit of funds or rare goods in safety deposit boxes effectively eliminates enjoyment beyond that provided by a knowledge of the power of wealth. If coupon bonds are eliminated in one way or another, then the portion of net wealth consisting of securities can be readily included in the NWT base. All European users of NWT have excluded pension rights from the tax base. This exemption follows from social policy and not from administrative difficulties. It may also be argued that the purpose of NWT is not being served when pensions are included in the base. The tax is levied to capture some of the additional taxable capacity provided by wealth ownership. Obviously, pension rights are a portion of the compensation for services performed. On the other hand, it is also true that possession of pension rights by one of two with equal incomes imparts a superior financial position to the possessor of pension rights. Therefore, strict horizontal equity requires the inclusion of pension rights in a NWT base.

Annuities are usually included in the NWT base. Again, exemption sometimes exists when the annuity cannot be sold and is not yet providing income. When income is arising from possession of the annuity, then it is often included in the NWT base.

Life insurance lies between a pension right and regular savings. It can be the security for low-interest-rate loans. The compromise is to exempt from the NWT base a given, relatively small capital value of insurance policies. When acting like an annuity, insurance can be the source of funds for payment of a pension. When this stage is reached, the entire capital value of the insurance is included in the net wealth base.

The general approach to taxing monetary savings is to provide exemption while not abandoning the purpose of the net wealth tax. Savings in the form of art objects are intrinsically different from most monetary savings because they are not the source of interest or other investment income, as are monetary savings. Therefore, the NWT must be paid either out of earnings sourced at some other location or from receipts received from the sale of some of the objects. Nevertheless, the exemption of art objects is not a workable procedure, as this would offer a means of minimizing the tax. As a result, a compromise is generally provided, both in type of art objects and in value of holdings.

If a very valuable art object is declared to be part of the national heritage, then it must be open to the public for observation and enjoyment. This requirement socializes the gratification the art or historical object provides. Normal furniture and objects important for education frequently enjoy special treatment. For example, only a portion of their value may be included in the NWT base (Usher 1976).

There is undoubtedly some undervaluation in establishing the value of items of wealth not sold frequently in the market. These examples can be reduced. In the case of jewelry, for example, exempting the insurance company from any payment in excess of declared value and making the declared value available to NWT administrators can help to raise the NWT base consisting of valuable personal property.

The value of structures and land need not be established each year. Valuation adjustments can be made annually through application of the inflation or deflation rate. Then every three or five years a careful evaluation of the property can be made on the basis of sales of similar properties and special features affecting the value of the property under consideration. Valuation work would most likely be done cooperatively with the local and state government tax officials being responsible for establishing their property tax base.

In terms of treatment of homes some NWT laws favor owner-occupied homes over homes occupied by renters. Under other NWT laws the minimum taxable net wealth is set high enough to largely, if not entirely, exempt owners of one-family homes who do not have other substantial wealth holdings (Ernst and Whinney various dates).

Justification of favorable treatment of owner-occupied residences rests on two principal legs. One is the social-political justification. Homeownership should be encouraged, as it often promotes a more stable environment for raising children and a less mobile citizenry, which in turn promote social stability. The second point is that an owner-occupied home does not directly earn money income for use to pay the NWT. Also, because some nations levy the income tax on a base including imputed income of owner-occupied homes, the levy of a full net wealth tax on this base appears to overtax people in this position.

It is also true, of course, that giving a tax break to net wealth consisting of homeownership detracts from horizontal equity between the house renter and the occupant of an owned home. Another expected impact is that more capital will go into owner-occupied homes than would exist under a neutral tax system. This acts to somewhat reduce the productivity of capital.

The value of goodwill, patents, and copyrights is generally included in the NWT base. This is accomplished without separate treatment when the rights are owned by a public corporation with outstanding stock. Ownership of legal rights by individuals or a family corporation requires rather complex valuation procedures in order for them to be accurately included in the NWT base. This valuation problem has prompted some countries to exempt the legal rights. However, because they are generally realizable, they should be included in the NWT (Cartter 1953).

The final portion of a NWT base is the capitalized value of the future earning power of taxpayers. Earning power was one result of additional investment in formal education and on-the-job training. Personal capital is a source of money income and other satisfactions, but it is not net wealth (Harberger 1962).

Many characteristics of earning-power capital distinguish it from personal capital. In the first place, the ability to earn is not property. More important, it cannot be sold nor is it transferable. Also, earning power is very uncertain and often temporary.

No user of the NWT includes capitalized personal income in the base. The concept has been raised, however, as a smokescreen by opponents of net wealth taxation. This occurred, for example, when the tax was under consideration in Canada, Australia, and the United Kingdom (Field 1979).

More Detail on Assessment Practices
of the Net Wealth Tax

In 1979 the Organization for Economic Cooperation and Development (OECD) prepared a summary of assessment and valuation procedures used by its member nations in the administration of NWT. The OECD member nations are all European. Therefore, of course, procedures used outside of Europe are not included.

In 1979 there were ten European nations using a NWT. Today there are still ten, but Ireland has repealed its NWT and France has introduced one.

The OECD breaks down the base into 11 parts. These 11 types of wealth are supplemented by a general category called special concessions. Six of the eleven nations annually establish new valuations; three complete valuations every three years and one, every two years.

In varying from one to three years in setting values, the European users of NWT are making a larger investment in administration than is typical of property tax administration in the United States. Even if the assessments are less thorough than those made in the United States, it remains true that the much broader range of assets covered by NWT requires a more careful examination of valuation than in the United States, where the property tax is largely limited to real estate and uses gross value as its base.

Open market value (OM) is the principal element in establishing the NWT base. For example, in the first category of wealth—personal chattels—eight European nations using NWT rely on OM. The OM and stock exchange valuations continue to dominate establishment of the NWT base. Only Norway and Switzerland make use of insurance value of the personal chattels in setting the base.

Switzerland generally excludes personal chattels from its canton-level NWT. However, those cantons using personal chattels as a portion of the NWT base use a percentage of insurance value.

The next category, immovable property, is used as a portion of NWT base in all the European users. The procedure widely used in the United States in administering the property tax is generally utilized by European nations to set values on this second and very important portion of the NWT base.

The law in this area, however, varies substantially between countries in terms of the frequency with which values are set and the difference in treatment of business and nonbusiness property. A building's portion of immovable nonbusiness property is revalued from once every nine years to once every four years.

Most European nations using NWT value the land separately. Taxpayers having agricultural land are treated as owners of business assets. Most nations value this land on the basis of full-use yield.

Basically, the procedure amounts to a capitalization of expected net revenue (Gaffney 1969).

Sweden sets the value of land in the same way as that of immovable property in general. The procedure sets land at 75 percent of market value. Market value is established every five years.

Forests or woodlands are also treated as business assets. A number of nations treat this land in the same way as agricultural land. There are some variations, however. For example, Finland multiplies by ten a three-year moving average of net yield.

In setting the value of businesses that do not have their stock listed on one or more exchanges, the going-concern valuation procedures are used. This works out to be a capitalization of profits. Of course, businesses with marketable shares and bonds are readily valued by using the values set in stock and bond markets.

Values set by bid and ask prices of the exchanges take into consideration the NWT liability faced by all security holders. When this is done, the value of securities held by nonbusiness investors decreases. If NWT is a flat-rate tax, this has the effect of a capitalized cost.

Tax Goals

The economic result of raising taxes in the fashion described above has some similarity to corporate and individual income taxes. However, one major difference is that both profitable and nonprofitable operations would be included in the tax base. This, of course, is a just approach. The costs of government services do not end at the water's edge of profitability.

Valuation of life insurance, pensions, and annuities has become an area of considerable concern to NWT administrators. The problem arises from governments' failure to operate actuarially sound death, medical, and income assistance programs. As a result of these valuation difficulties, capitalization of payments made has proved to be a generally adequate procedure. This approach can be used to set a market value for all pension and insurance programs. The weakness of the approach arises from the lack of a general market in which pension and annuity rights can be traded. Only about 50 percent of the European nations with a NWT attempt to place a value on these rights and balances and to subject the amount to NWT.

The OECD reports that NWT in Europe does not generally exempt owner-occupied dwellings. However, a special concession to this category of immovable property is rather common.

Concluding Remarks

Establishment of the NWT base is made easier by exemption of wealth holdings up to a rather substantial level. The fact that valuation tools vary considerably demonstrates the seriousness with which NWT is utilized. Political pressures the wealthy can exert on NWT administration are evident. However, considerably greater administrative strength is exhibited by some nations than by others. This demonstrates the potential for developing a sound and fair NWT.

With its highly developed state and local property tax based largely on real estate, the United States provides an opportunity for a cooperative administrative setup. Existing fiscal development in the United States can be helpful in developing a national NWT.

NET WEALTH TAX POSSIBILITIES

As the discussions of European administrative procedures have shown, the net wealth tax encounters many of the same administrative hurdles as the U.S. property tax. Assessments must be made in such a fashion that valuations are both current and sound. These difficulties are minor when stacked up against those faced by tax administrators trying to locate income and its owner and controller in order to apply a progressive tax rate that can go as high as 50 percent.

By being a flat-rate tax at a low rate, the NWT avoids many difficulties that overwhelm the federal income tax enforcers. To save a dollar of NWT taxes, property underassessment must be $50 dollars. To save a dollar of income taxes at the 50 percent rate, only two dollars of income need to be hidden from the eyes of the tax collector.

Some rather good things can be expected to happen if NWT is introduced along with a substantial federal value-added tax and if the federal income tax is eliminated. First, the market value of going business enterprises will increase substantially. The ability to retain each dollar earned will be increased by between 30 and 50 percent. There will be an expansion in the ability of going firms to cut prices and to modernize plant and equipment. New investment funds will become available, thereby raising the level of net wealth and the ability of U.S. businesses to meet foreign competition. One can also expect reduced unemployment and an increased ability of U.S. firms to raise wages. There are many other likely desirable results. At this time we will consider only one more expectation: the general feeling of optimism that will be generated as profits are retained by business firms. The optimism is likely to promote expanded willingness to take risks and strengthened capitalistic spirit.

A second group of impacts is related to the effect of NWT on use of wealth. One possibility would be to establish a general, stan-

dard percentage yield of capital. If the capital is used in such a way
that the return is above this general yield, the NWT tax rate as a percentage of income would be reduced. On the other hand, if earnings
are below this standard rate, the NWT as a percentage of income
would be increased. Such investment-stimulating impact would promote
efficient use of capital above that naturally attached to NWT.

Before leaving this point, one must note that NWT has been
criticized for discouraging savings and capital accumulation, whereas
it is said, the income tax cannot be avoided by spending and not saving.
This is not entirely true of the income tax, where wasteful business
spending can reduce the tax due (for example, holding conventions in
expensive resort locations). Nevertheless, the point that NWT reduces savings (and does so more directly than income or transaction
taxes) requires examination.

Impact on Use of Savings

Why do people save and when is it possible for them to fulfill
this desire?

Personal and business savings are made so that resources will
be available for further expansion or for meeting emergencies. The
ability to carry out this desirable and productive action is dependent
on continuing possession of earnings above the current needs. Even
under the best conditions, high income taxes decrease the ability to
save and, therefore, to meet the savings goal. The NWT avoids the
savings reduction associated with the income tax because under NWT
(1) the tax due does not increase along with earnings and (2) the very
broad base permits large collections with a low rate.

Another characteristic of NWT is that the increased demand for
savings owing to economic growth does not decrease the availability
of funds, as happens under the income tax. The NWT base remains
approximately the same in good and bad times. The income tax as a
cost varies widely during the economic cycle and therefore its impact
on the availability of savings fluctuates widely.

Another aspect of NWT is its great potential for expanding tax
expenditures in a much more expeditious manner than taxes based on
income. For example, the NWT rate on the value of jewelry might be
much higher than the rate on new power production facilities. The
same pressures would be developed if the exempt level on power production is greater. The result, of course, is to reduce the funds invested in jewelry while stimulating people with funds to invest in power
production facilities.

The NWT used in Europe includes personal property while excluding household furniture from its base. Only in Switzerland does

household furniture come under the NWT, and even there some nine cantons exempt it. One approach uses the insurance valuation of household effects and deducts from this value the amount it would cost to purchase furniture to perform the basic function, that is, utilization value.

In this instance the NWT is being used to discourage luxurious household rugs, furniture, and so forth. This tax expenditure reallocates in a very precise manner the use of economic resources. It does so in a much more precise way than income taxes could (Organization for Economic Cooperation and Development 1979).

Obviously, one could argue that a tax affecting resource use in such detail is undesirable. In reply one can point out that the free market system is too valuable to be weakened. But at the same time if the shortage of capital assigned to productive use is in short supply, what better way to correct the balance than to encourage decisions through relatively minor tax actions that shift the balance of capital use toward productive uses.

All nations using NWT, with the exception of Uruguay, continue to use income and death taxes. This approach weakens the tax impacts that can be gained through NWT legislation. The income tax raises the earnings level required to justify an investment, while NWT causes holders of capital to put into effect actions that increase the efficiency of capital use. The approach developed in this book avoids such a contradictory relationship; the income, profit, and death taxes are repealed and are replaced with a net wealth tax and a value-added tax.

Concluding Remarks

The continuation of a democratic, capitalistic economic system requires encouragement of investment and low-cost productive effort. At the same time, however, capital and purchasing power cannot become concentrated in only a few hands. Wealth must be stimulated while being broadly held and efficiently used. The NWT works to bring about this condition.

DIFFERENCE BETWEEN WEALTH
AND INCOME AS A TAX BASE

Wealth is of two major types. One type possesses the ability to assist in the production of salable goods and services. Wealth coming within this category includes land, structures, natural resources, machines, inventories, and the like.

The other type of wealth has value because of certain desirable features and relative scarcity. Wealth of this type includes precious metals, works of art, pleasure-giving objects, and the like.

The two types of wealth blend into each other at the margin. This is particularly true of wealth providing satisfactions only to the owner because it is one or a limited number of a kind and more cannot be easily produced. Wealth consisting of bank deposits and other defined monetary or near monetary assets constitutes largely representative assets supported by the existing legal structure and having value because they can legally demand wealth of the two basic types. If the market value of these representative assets is included in the amounts added up to determine society's total wealth, double counting of wealth is being practiced.

Income is received by persons because they possess all types of wealth including representative assets. Typically, an increase or decrease in the value placed on wealth does not affect income as defined for tax purposes or as a statistical quantity. In a broad sense the relationship of wealth to income is one of substitution except when human activity is included. Human productivity does not have a market value because it is not traded or valued in the market. Slavery has been abolished.

Productivity

Increased productivity of capital reduces the need for capital (that is, wealth) to reach a certain level of productivity. Under these conditions real income has increased per hour required to produce the wealth needed to maintain a given level of real income. The increase in productivity of capital reduces wealth while increasing income. The market can keep wealth in its former relationship to income only if supply of the new, more productive capital can be limited. Therefore, wealth, even when primarily possessing value because of productivity, enjoys a varying portion of its value through limitation of supply. Wealth and income measured through enjoyment or productivity are less closely related than is often assumed. Nevertheless, wealth can be generally taken as a measure of income and income, in turn, as a measure of wealth. A person is wealthy because his or her income, realized and unrealized, is large. A person with substantial income and, consequently, a high ability to pay taxes may not be wealthy.

Administration

Use of either wealth or income as a tax base requires that the base be located (that is, that its ownership or control be identified) and that the tax assessed be collected. In neither case is this process carried out without difficulties. The large owners of wealth and large earners of income are also generally the possessors of political and social power.

Wealth and Income

Wealth as a tax base is favored over income because its value once established requires only minor adjustments for a period of years. Taxable income, on the other hand, can move from a substantial sum to zero or a loss within a single year. As a measure of an individual's taxpaying ability either as controller of physical property or as owner of indebtedness certificates, wealth is relatively stable. The income receiver enjoys stability to the degree that income is sourced in wealth. The earnings of the typical professional person or worker provide as stable a tax base as does wealth. Such economic stability, however, is best tapped by a transaction tax rather than by an income tax. This is the situation because (1) personal income is already used as a base for a heavy social security tax and (2) the General Agreement on Tariffs and Trade permits a tax refund on exports and permits the levy of a border tax on imports equal to domestic taxes based on transactions.

CONSTITUTIONALITY OF A NET WEALTH TAX

The Supreme Court has used three measures in evaluating the constitutionality of a tax under the Constitution's direct-tax limitation. They are in brief (1) the legislative intent, (2) the apportionability of the tax, and (3) the true nature of the tax. The last has been used most often and most thoroughly. The first two measures seem to have been used only as occasional side arguments have required, and then only in such a way as to be consistent with results from evaluating the true nature of the tax in question.

Basic Decisions

This approach was demonstrated when the Pollock Court stressed that the legislative intent of the Constitutional Convention far outweighed any intent of Congress. This was determined, however, after the Court had found the true nature of the tax in question to be direct and unapportioned and, therefore, unconstitutional (Pollock 1895).

In the Speckels Sugar case, 1904, the Court seemed to reverse itself, saying that since Congress had defined the tax in question an excise, "it must be assumed, for what it is worth, that Congress had no purpose to exceed its power under the Constitution." But the Court had already found that the tax in Speckels was an excise in nature. The Court made clear which sort of intent held the most weight in Flint v. Stone, 1911, saying that although Congress could not change the real nature of a tax by mere declaration, such a declaration was entitled to weight in evaluating the nature of the tax. Again the Court found the tax was not direct in nature and thus constitutional. However, taking the same stance while weighing Eisner v. Macomber, 1920, the Court found that in "truth and substance" the tax in question was direct and that this outweighed the congressional intent. Clearly, the "true nature" of a tax outweighs the intent or interpretation of Congress when constitutional limitations on legislative acts are considered.

Similarly, the Court has always evaluated a tax's apportionability consistently with its true nature. In Hylton v. United States, 1796, the Court found a tax on the use of carriages neither direct nor apportionable. In the Pollock case the Court found a tax on income from invested property both direct and apportionable.

Evaluation of a tax's true nature, then, seems to be the primary method by which the Supreme Court determines its directness and constitutionality. In evaluating the nature of a tax, the Court discerns if it is significantly the same or sufficiently different from a tax upon property merely because of ownership. If the tax is found significantly the same as a tax based upon ownership, it will be declared direct and unconstitutional unless it comes under the Sixteenth Amendment.

True Nature

Two factors that the Court will take into consideration in evaluating the true nature of a tax are its range and the conditions under which it is effective. If the subject of taxation reaches property over too broad a range, the tax may be declared direct. For example, a tax upon the sale of property "made in any place" has been declared a tax really and practically upon property. Similarly, prior to the enactment of the Sixteenth Amendment the Court found that a tax on gross receipts "from every source whatever" was a direct tax. To avoid the apportionment restriction, a tax that reaches property must be in some substantial way limited in scope.

Range or Scope

The range or scope of a tax is also limited by the limitations or conditions under which it may be levied. A direct tax makes little or no reference to the origin or use of the property reached, while a tax that does refer to such conditions is a specific excise rather than a general direct tax. If the conditions of a tax are not met, no tax is payable. Given specific enough conditions, even a tax levied on the subject of holding business assets and measured by the value of those assets has been classified an excise (Flint v. Stone Tracy Company 1911).

In another example a tax limited to the income of corporations was classified an excise prior to the Sixteenth Amendment, even though a general income tax had been held to be direct because it reached income from invested property. The Court has also found that the conditions of an option to receive a stock dividend are sufficiently restrictive to be taxed without apportionment, even though the receipt of a stock dividend without an option may only be taxed through an apportioned tax. It is important to note, however, that in all cases thus far the conditions limiting unapportioned taxes have been inclusive rather than exclusive. That is, to avoid being direct, the taxes included rather than excluded a specific type of property. It is possible that the Supreme Court would view a tax that merely excluded specific types of property as an effort to avoid the constitutional limitation of apportionment by an arbitrary exclusion, and thus the Court would void the tax. This position could not be taken when the exclusion was all land from a wealth tax base.

Use of Measure

In Eisner v. Macomber, 1920, the Court commented that market values could not be used as a measure of income because an unrealized market value was no more than the stockholder's property interest in the corporation. This principle, that the measure of a tax may have as much bearing on the constitutionality of a tax as the tax's subject, can be derived from the famous case of Brown v. Maryland, 1827. In that case Justice Marshall gave an example of improper use of federal taxing power by outlining an excise tax based on the occupation of exporter but measured by the value of the exports. Congress has power to tax occupations through an excise but is barred from taxing exports. Could Congress overcome the restriction on taxing exports by using its power to tax occupations? Justice Marshall thought not (Eisner v. Macomber 1920).

Constitutionality under Direct Tax Clause

As interpreted by the Supreme Court, the Constitution's direct tax clause requires that a general tax upon property must be apportioned on the basis of population. However, a tax upon some other subject need not be apportioned if both the subject and the measure of the tax are sufficiently restrictive to not produce the results of a general tax upon property. The Supreme Court has listed some subjects acceptable for nonapportioned taxes: manufacturing of goods, consumption of goods or services, occupations, privileges, business activities, employments, vocations, specific types of property in reference to origin and use, and bank notes and other documents.

The Court has also stated that business activities alone embrace everything at which a person can be employed. Thus, a tax on the subject of business activities measured on the value of assets used in business would touch all invested real and personal property. In such a case, however, the Supreme Court could rule much as it did in the Pollock case and declare that a tax upon all business activities so measured is not sufficiently restrictive to be different from a tax directly upon all invested property merely because of ownership. A similar argument could be made against the other acceptable subjects in the list unless additional circumstances of taxation were given to limit the scope of the tax. Therefore, uncertainty is lessened when the NWT base is substantially less than all property. Also, property may be owned without becoming subject to NWT.

Given a reasonable set of conditions, the Court would prefer not to limit congressional power to tax incomes. Second, an income tax measured by the value of assets used in producing revenues would be limited; it would not touch all invested property. Property held and not invested, property invested but not producing revenues, and property of an individual or firm not producing income could not be measured for taxation. There is also a third economic advantage to this form of tax. An income tax would touch a broader range of property than a tax on business activities.

The Supreme Court could affect such a tax in two ways. First, the Court could use the principle outlined by Justice Marshall in Brown v. Maryland, 1827, wherein a constitutional limitation on taxing power was judged sufficient to cancel a constitutionally granted power to tax. Second, the Court could alter or restrict its judicial definition of income, most likely using reasoning similar to that used in the Eisner v. Macomber case of 1920. By this reasoning the Court might construe the meaning of income such that only property actually producing a net profit could be taxed. If some assets could be shown not to produce profits, although they contribute to gross revenues, then those assets would not be measurable for taxation.

Constitutionality Requirements

Accurately predicting the Supreme Court's reaction to any given subject or measure of a net wealth tax cannot be done without doubt.

Suffice it to say that an acceptable subject or measure could not touch a body of property so broad as to include all or nearly all property, no matter how it may be utilized. The tax must be sufficiently restrictive to avoid producing a tax equivalent to a property tax merely because of ownership, and this requirement is easily met by the NWT considered in this book. Under a net wealth tax the base is restricted in three ways: (1) a minimum level is set on taxable wealth, (2) debt is deductible from the base in calculating taxable net wealth, and (3) land can be excluded from the base.

An unapportioned net wealth tax affirmed by the Supreme Court would have the same properties that are open to excises. The tax could repeatedly measure the same property. Furthermore, the amount of tax could be increased and the difference could be levied within the same tax period. Thus, annual taxes could be levied. The reasonableness of the tax level would not be open for judicial review. Like an excise, the tax would not be invalidated if part of its measure reached nontaxable property such as state and municipal bonds (Flint v. Stone Tracy Company 1911). However, if the tax could be shown to reach all state and municipal bonds, it would be invalidated. There is no doubt but that the potential constitutional difficulty of NWT is lessened when the tax exempts a substantial amount of wealth owned by people not controlling enough wealth to reach the minimum taxable level.

Concluding Remarks

The framers of the United States Constitution, realizing they had established a legally strong central government, wanted to exclude from its power the right to tax land. They were in most cases wealthy landowners and had no desire to make such wealth subject to taxation.

Times have changed and the states have not become large users of land taxes. Therefore, the limitation of federal government's power to tax land as a capital asset does not serve a useful purpose. Realization of this by the Supreme Court has led to a gradual erosion of the special protection given to land.

CONCLUSION

This is the end of the tale.

The U.S. economy produces and sells a prodigious quantity of goods and services. The problem to be solved is how to balance a federal budget at approximately the current level without destroying much of the efficiency and new product and service developments required to support an economic system based on the concept of free and private enterprise.

The solution offered in this book brings together revenue sources that have a proved track record when combined with income and estate taxes, but not when these taxes have been eliminated. Nowhere does there exist a private sector as productive as the one in the United States.

It is possible to develop a national tax system that can abandon taxes on income, profits, gifts, and estates. In doing this the system can rid itself of harmful impacts on savings, investment, and economic growth. The two taxes proposed as revenue replacements for the United States are the value-added tax and the net wealth tax. Use of these new taxes (new for the United States but widely used in other nations) would free wage income from all national taxes except the social security (payroll) tax.

A new approach to fiscal policy is needed to modernize the federal tax system and to meet expenditure requirements without reducing efficiency.

The heritage of the new tax system will be a much less complex administrative environment. Taxes paid under the value-added tax will be calculated and paid like all other prices charged for goods and services. The net wealth tax will be paid only by those possessing substantial wealth. This will provide a more economically desirable way to reduce the unequal distribution of economic power than death or income taxes. A wealth tax chips away year after year at concentrations of economic power. Repeal of the income, estate, and gift taxes will make the U.S. net wealth tax much stronger than those used in Europe, India, and other nations.

Anyone who considers the background material presented in this book must agree with the conclusion that it offers a new tax system capable of raising revenues of around one-fourth to one-third of gross national product without destroying work and investment incentives, while preserving a domestic market economy that is internationally competitive.

BIBLIOGRAPHY

Aaron, Henry, ed. 1981. The Value Added Tax: Lessons from Europe. Washington, D. C.: Brookings Institution.

Adams, T. S. 1921. "Fundamental Problems of Federal Income Taxation." Quarterly Journal of Economics 35: 527.

Advisory Commission on Intergovernmental Relations. 1983. Changing Public Attitudes on Government and Taxes (S-12).

_____. 1981. "Federal Preeminence in the Income Tax." In The Dynamics of Growth, pp. 143-51. Washington, D. C.: ACIR.

_____. 1980. Flows of Federal Funds, 1952-76 (A-75). Washington, D. C.: ACIR.

_____. 1973. The Value-Added Tax and Alternative Sources of Federal Revenue (A-78). Washington, D. C.: U. S. Government Printing Office.

_____. 1961. Coordination of State and Federal Inheritance Estate and Gift Taxes. Washington, D. C.: U. S. Government Printing Office.

Ainsworth, Kenneth G. 1980. "State Taxation of Multinational Firms: The Federal Role." Seventy-third National Tax Association-Tax Institute of America Conference. Columbus, Ohio: NTA-ITA.

Akhton, M. A. 1980. "Income and Price Elasticities of Imports in Industrial Countries." Business Economics 15: 69-75.

Akin, John. 1973. "Fiscal Capacity and the Estimation Method of the Advisory Commission on Intergovernmental Relations." National Tax Journal, vol. 26.

American Bar Association. 1977. Tax Lawyer 30: 565-85.

American Economics Association. 1950. "The Problem of Economic Instability." American Economic Review 40: 521.

Andrews, W. O. 1973. "What's Fair about Death Taxes?" National Tax Journal 26: 465-69.

Arthur Anderson and Company. 1980. VAT in Other Countries. New York: Arthur Anderson and Company.

Atkinson, A. B., and A. J. Harrison. 1978. The Distribution of Personal Wealth in Britain. New York: Cambridge University Press.

Bachrach, Peter. 1967. The Theory of Democratic Elitism. Boston: Little, Brown.

Baird, Charles W. 1981. "Proportionality, Justice and the Value Added Tax." Cato Journal, Fall, pp. 405-19.

Balough, T. 1969. "A Note on the Wealth Tax." Economic Journal, March, pp. 222-23.

Barlow, Robin, Harvey E. Brazer, and James N. Morgan. 1966. Economic Behavior of the Affluent. Washington, D.C.: Brookings Institution.

Bartlett, Bruce, and Timothy P. Roth. 1983. The Supply Side Situation. Chatham, N.J.: Chatham House.

Bastable, C. F. 1903. Public Finance. 3d ed. London: Macmillan.

Bell, Rauiel. 1976. The Coming of Post-Industrial Society. New York: Basic Books.

Bernard, Michael M. 1979. Constitutions, Taxation, and Land Policy. Lexington, Mass.: Lexington Books.

Bhatia, K. B. 1982. "Value-Added Tax and the Theory of Tax Incidence." Journal of Public Economics 19: 203-23.

Bird, R. M. 1980. "Taxing Personal Wealth." Canadian Taxation, vol. 2, no. 1.

_____. 1974. Taxing Agricultural Land in Developing Countries. Cambridge, Mass.: Harvard University Press.

_____. 1972. "The Case for Taxing Personal Wealth." Proceedings of the Twenty-third Annual Tax Conference. Toronto: Canadian Tax Foundation.

Blakey, Roy G., and Gladys C. Blakey. 1941. The Federal Income Tax. New York: Longmans.

Blinder, Alan S. 1976. "International Transfers and Life Cycle Consumption." American Economic Review 66: 87-101.

Blum, J. 1948. Noble Landowners and Agriculture in Austria (1815-48. Baltimore: Johns Hopkins University Press.

Boskin, Michael J. 1982. "Reaganomics and Income Distribution." Journal of Contemporary Studies 5: 31-44.

Boskin, Michael J., ed. 1978. Federal Tax Reform. San Francisco: Institute for Contemporary Studies.

Boskin, Michael J., and E. Sheshinski. 1978. "Optional Redistribution Taxation when Individual Welfare Depends on Relative Income." Quarterly Journal of Economics.

Bradford, David F. 1981. "The Incidence and Allocation Effects of a Tax on Corporate Distributions." Journal of Public Economics 15: 1-22.

Bradley, J. F. 1975. "Economic Aspects of a Net Wealth Tax for the Republic of Ireland." British Tax Review, no. 3, pp. 142-51.

Brannon, Gerard M. 1973. "Death Taxes in a Structure of Progressive Taxes." National Tax Journal 26: 451-57.

Break, G. F. 1977. "Social Security as a Tax." In The Crisis in Social Security, edited by M. J. Boskin, pp. 107-23. San Francisco: Institute for Contemporary Studies.

Break, George F. 1978. "Corporation Tax Integration." In Federal Tax Reform, edited by M. J. Boskin, pp. 55-73. San Francisco: Institute for Contemporary Studies.

_____. 1957. "Income Taxes and Incentives to Work." American Economic Review 47: 539-41.

Brennan, G., and D. Nellor. 1982. "Wealth Consumption and Tax Neutrality." National Tax Journal 35: 427–36.

Brennan, Michael J. 1965. Theory of Economic Statics. Englewood Cliffs, N.J.: Prentice-Hall.

Brinner, Roger E. 1981. "The Proper Medicine for Stagflation." Technology in Society 3: 45–62.

Brittan, S. 1980. "HAYEK, the New Right and the Crisis of Social Democracy." Encounter, January.

Brookings Institution. 1964. The Role of Direct and Indirect Taxes in the Federal Revenue System. Princeton, N.J.: Princeton University Press.

Browning, Edgar K. 1975. "Why the Social Insurance Budget Is Too Large in a Democracy." Economic Inquiry 13: 373–88.

Bullock, C. J. 1900. "The Origin, Purpose and Effect of the Direct Tax Clause in the Federal Constitution." Political Science Quarterly 15: 217–39, 452–81.

Bundesministerium. 1981. Verteilung der Unstatzsteuer. Art. 106, Abs. 3 and 4, Satz IGG, May 9.

Burnett, Edmund C. 1963. Letters of Members of the Continental Congress. Reprint. Pittsburgh: Carnegie Institution.

Burns, Arthur F. 1967. "The New Stagnation Theory." In American Fiscal Policy, edited by Lester C. Thurow, pp. 51–61. Englewood Cliffs, N.J.: Prentice-Hall.

_____. 1946. "Economic Research and the Keynesian Thinking of Our Times." Twenty-sixth Annual Report of the NBER. New York: NBER.

Business Taxation Presidential Task Force. 1970. Business Taxation. Washington, D.C.: U.S. Government Printing Office.

Carlson, George N. 1980. Value-Added Tax: European Experience and Lessons for the United States. Washington, D.C.: U.S. Government Printing Office.

Carlson, Keith M. 1981. "Trends in Federal Revenues: 1955–86." St. Louis: Federal Reserve Bank of St. Louis.

Carson, G. 1977. "The Golden Egg": The Personal Income Tax, Where It Came from, and How It Grew. Boston: Houghton Mifflin.

Cartter, A. M. 1953. "A New Method of Relating British Capital Ownership and Estate Duty Liability to Income Groups." Economica, August.

Carver, T. N. 1904. "The Minimum Sacrifice Theory of Taxation." Political Science Quarterly 19: 66–79.

Chambers, Charles L. 1976. "The Steel Products Decision: An Inquiry into the Treatment of the Value–Added Tax under the Countervailing Duty Law." Vanderbilt Journal of Transactional Law 9: 819–83.

Chickering and Rosa. 1982. "The Social Security Problem." Wall Street Journal, May 30, p. 30.

Chow, Gregory C. 1981. "Estimation and Control of Rational Expectation Models." American Economic Review 71: 211–16.

Clark, Peter B. 1974. The Effects of Exchange Rate Adjustments. Washington, D.C.: U.S. Department of the Treasury.

Clotfelter, Charles T. 1983. "Tax Evasion and Tax Rates." Review of Economics and Statistics.

Cnossen, S. 1982. "What Rate Structure for a Value Added Tax." National Tax Journal, vol. 35.

Cohen, Edwin S. 1982. "A Decade of DISC: Genesis and Analysis." Virginia Tax Review 2: 7–58.

Cohn, Gustaf. 1895. The Science of Finance. Translated by T. B. Veblen.

Collie, Marvin K. 1973. "Estate and Gift Tax Revision." National Tax Journal 26: 441–49.

Colm, Gerhard. 1934. "The Ideal Tax System." Social Research, August 1934, pp. 319-42.

Commerce Clearing House. Various issues. State Tax Reporter.

Covey, Richard B. 1973. "Estate and Gift Taxation." National Tax Journal 26: 459-63.

Cutt, James. 1969. "A Net Wealth Tax for Canada." Canadian Tax Journal 17: 298-308.

Dam, Kenneth W. 1970. The GATT Law and International Economic Organization. Washington, D. C.: U. S. State Department.

Davie, Bruce. 1981. The Congressional Budget Process after Five Years. Washington, D. C.: American Institute for Public Policy Research.

Davies, David G. 1963. "A Further Reappraisal of Sales Taxation." National Tax Journal, December, pp. 410-15.

_____. 1960. "Progressiveness of Sales Tax in Relation to Various Income Bases." American Economic Review 50: 987-95.

Deaton, A. 1977. "Involuntary Saving through Unanticipated Inflation." American Economic Review 67: 899-910.

Denison, Edward F. 1962. The Sources of Economic Growth in the United States and the Alternatives before Us. Committee for Economic Development, Paper no. 13.

Dernberg, Thomas F. 1974. "The Macroeconomic Implications of Wage Retaliation against Higher Taxation." International Monetary Fund, Staff Paper 21, no. 2.

de Wind, Adrian W. 1950. "The Approaching Crisis in Federal Estate and Gift Taxation." California Law Review, March.

Dickerson, W. E., and Leo D. Stone. 1966. Federal Income Tax Fundamentals. 2d ed. Belmont, Calif.: Wadsworth.

Diebold, William. 1983. "The United States in the World Economy." Foreign Affairs, Fall, pp. 81-104.

Dosser, D. 1963. "Towards a Theory of International Public Finance." Kyklos 16: 74-79.

Downing, R. I., et al. 1964. Taxation in Australia. Melbourne: Melbourne University Press.

Due, John F. 1960. "Net Worth Taxation." Public Finance 15: 310–21.

Dunlop, John Thomas, ed. 1980. Business and Public Policy. Cambridge, Mass.: Harvard University Press, Division of Research.

Eiger, Richard M. 1959. "Indian Wealth and Expenditure Taxes." National Tax Journal 12: 153.

Eilbott, Peter. 1969. "The Revenue Gain from Taxation of Descendants' Unrealized Capital Gains." National Tax Journal 22: 506–15.

Eisenstein, Louis. 1955. "The Rise and Decline of the Estate Tax." In Federal Tax Policy for Economic Growth and Stability, U. S., Congress, Joint Committee on Economics, November 9, pp. 820–31.

Eismemeier, T. J. 1982. "The Japanese Miracle." Journal of Contemporary Studies 5: 33–44.

Eisner v. Macomber. 1920. 252 U.S. 217.

Ernst and Whinney. Various dates. International Series, USA-Periodic revision. New York: Ernst and Whinney.

European Taxation. 1976. 16: 42–47.

Fabozzi, Frank J., and Robert Fonpueder. 1981. "Corporate Tax Rates in an Inflationary Environment: 1976 and 77." Business Economics 16: 55–58.

Fand, David I. 1970. "Monetarism and Fiscalism." Banca Nazinale del Lavaro Quarterly Review, September, pp. 274–307.

Faxen, Karl-Olof. 1964. "A Programme for Tax Policy." Skandinaviska Banken Quarterly Review, p. 77.

Federal Reserve Board. 1982. "Households." In Sector Balance Sheets. Washington, D. C.: Federal Reserve Board.

Feld, Alan L. 1981. "The Case for an Increase in the Personal Exemption." Taxation with Representation Newsletter 10: 2–3.

Feldstein, Martin. 1976. Charitable Bequests, etc. Prepared for Committee on Ways and Means. Washington, D. C.: U. S. Government Printing Office, pp. 1034-44.

_____. 1975. "The Income Tax and Charitable Contributions." In Conference on Tax Research, pp. 21-68. Washington, D. C.: U. S. Treasury.

Fellner, William. 1975. "Revisiting the 'Austrian' Time Periods with Current Tax Policy in Mind." In Conference on Tax Research, pp. 3-17. Washington, D. C.: Department of the Treasury, Office of Tax Analysis.

Fiedler, Lawrence E. 1965. "United States Income Tax Considerations with Respect to the Worldwide Marketing of American Products." Taxes, August, pp. 526-39.

Field, Frank, ed. 1979. The Wealth Report. London: Routledge & Kegan Paul.

Field, Tom. 1981. "Reagan Fails to Propose Cuts in Tax Expenditures." Taxation with Representation Newsletter 10: 1-4.

Financial Executive Resource Foundation. 1982. Economic Impact of International VAT. Morrison, N. J.: Financial Executive Resource Foundation.

Fischer, Stanley, ed. 1980. Rational Expectations and Economic Policy. Chicago: University of Chicago Press.

Fisher, Irving. 1942. Constructive Income Taxation: A Proposal for Reform. New York: Harper.

Fisher, Janet A. 1958. "Taxation of Personal Incomes and Net Worth in Norway." National Tax Journal 11: 84-93.

Flemming, J. S., and M. D. Little. 1974. Why We Need a Wealth Tax. London: Methuen.

Flint v. Stone Tracy Company. 1911. 220 U. S. 108.

Formby, John P., and Terry G. Seaks. 1980. "Paglin's Gini Measure of Inequality: A Modification." American Economic Review, June, pp. 479-82.

Frankel, H. 1970. Capitalist Society and Modern Sociology. London: Laurence and Wishart.

Freeman, Roger A. 1973. "Tax Relief for the Homeowner?" National Tax Journal 26: 485-90.

Friedlaender, Ann F. "Incidence and Price Effects of Value-Added Taxes." In Proceedings of National Tax Association, p. 278.

Fullerton, Don, et al. 1981. "Corporate Tax Integration in the United States: A General Equilibrium Approach." American Economic Review 71: 677-91.

Gaffney, Mason. N.d. "Land Rent, Taxation, and Public Policy." In Paper of the Regional Science Association 23: 141-53.

Galbraith, John Kenneth. 1971. The New Industrial State. 2d ed. Boston: Houghton Mifflin.

General Accounting Office. 1981. The Value-Added Tax: What Else Should We Know about It? Washington, D.C.: Comptroller General of the United States.

_____. 1980. The Value-Added Tax in the European Economic Community. Washington, D.C.: Comptroller General of the United States.

General Agreement on Tariffs and Trade. 1961. Basic Instruments and Related Documents. 9th supplement. Geneva: GATT.

Ghazanfar, S. M. 1982. "Retail Sales Tax Regressivity over Time." Western Tax Review 3: 80-94.

Gilbert, Milton. 1948. "Comments on Simon Kuznet's National Income and Capital Formation." Review of Economics and Statistics 30: 151-95.

Gillespie, W. Irwin. 1965. "Effect of Public Expenditures on the Distribution of Income." In Essays on Fiscal Federalism, edited by Richard Musgrave, pp. 164-65. Washington, D.C.: Brookings Institution.

Goldsmith, R. W. 1951. A Perpetual Inventory of National Wealth. Studies in Income and Wealth, vol. 14. New York: National Bureau of Economic Research.

Goode, Richard. 1976. The Individual Income Tax. Rev. ed. Washington, D. C.: Brookings Institution.

Greenwood, Daphne. 1983. "An Estimate of U. S. Family Wealth and Its Distribution from Microdata, 1973." Review of Income and Wealth, March, pp. 23-44.

Grossman, Gene M. 1978. "Alternative Border Tax Policies." Journal of World Trade Law 12: 452-60.

Grove, David L. 1971. Survey of Current Business, no. 7, pt. 2, pp. 91-92.

Gutman, Harry L. N.d. "Federal Wealth Transfer Taxes." National Tax Journal 35: 253-68.

Gutman, Peter. 1977. "The Subterranean Economy." Financial Analysis Journal, pp. 26-27.

Hale, David. N.d. "Rescuing Reaganomics." Policy Review, pp. 57-69.

Hall, J. K. 1940. "Incidence of Death Duties." American Economic Review, March.

Hall, R. E. 1982. A Simple Income with Low Marginal Rates. Stanford, Calif.: Hoover Institution.

Hall, R. E., and Alvin Rabushka. 1983. Low Tax, Simple Tax, Flat Tax. New York: McGraw-Hill.

Hamilton, ed. 1851. The Works of Alexander Hamilton. New York.

Hansen, Bert. 1960. "Aspects of Property Taxation: A General Report." Public Finance 15: 199-219.

Harberger, A. C. 1964. "Taxation Resource Allocation and Welfare." In The Role of Direct and Indirect Taxes in the Federal Revenue System. Princeton, N. J.: Princeton University Press.

_____. 1962. "The Incidence of the Corporate Income Tax." Journal of Political Economy, June, pp. 215-40.

Harvard Law School. 1964. World Tax Series on Colombia. Chicago: Commerce Clearing House, pp. 436-60.

_____. 1963. World Tax Series Taxation in the Federal Republic of Germany. Chicago: Commerce Clearing House, pp. 152-66, 699-742.

Hausman, Jerry A. N.d. Income and Payroll Policy and Labor Supply. National Bureau of Economic Research, Working Paper no. 610. Washington, D.C.: NBER.

Hazenberg, Werner. 1980. The Impact of Changes in the U.S. Federal Tax Structure on Its International Trade. Washington, D.C.: Department of Commerce.

Heclo, High. 1974. Modern Social Politics in Britain and Sweden. New Haven, Conn.: Yale University Press.

Hellawell, Robert. 1980. United States Taxation and Developing Countries. New York: Columbia University Press.

Hellerstein, Jerome R. 1963. Taxes, Loopholes and Morals. New York: McGraw-Hill.

Hinds, Dudley S., Neal G. Carn, and Nicholas Ordway. 1979. Winning at Zoning. New York: McGraw-Hill.

Hoeffs, Richard A. 1980. "HR.5665 Hearings Statement." In Tax Restructuring Act of 1979—Hearings, pp. 140-45. Washington, D.C.: U.S. Government Printing Office.

Holzman, R. S. 1969. Federal Taxation of Capital Assets. Lynbrook, N.Y.: Farnsworth.

Horsman, E. G. 1972. "Britain and Value-Added Taxation." Lloyds Bank Review, January, pp. 25-36.

Houthakker, Henrick S. 1969. "Income and Price Elasticities in World Trade." Review of Economics and Statistics 51: 111-25.

Hulton, Charles R. 1981. Depreciation, Inflation, and Taxation of Income from Capital. Washington, D.C.: Urban Institute Press.

Hunt and Scott, ed. 1850. The Debates in the Federal Convention of 1787 (James Madison). N.p.: Greenwood Press.

Institute for Fiscal Studies. 1978. The Structure and Reform of Direct Taxation. London: George Allen & Unwin.

Internal Revenue Service. 1976. Statistics of Income 1972, Personal Wealth. Washington, D. C.: U. S. Government Printing Office.

International Monetary Fund. 1982. Government Finance Statistics Year Book. Washington, D. C.: IMF.

Jantscher, G. 1969. "Death and Gift Taxation in the U. S. after the Royal Commission." National Tax Journal, vol. 22.

Johnson, Harry L., ed. 1969. State and Local Tax Problems. Knoxville: University of Tennessee Press.

Joint Committee on Taxation. 1983. Taxation of Banks and Thrift Institutions. Washington, D. C.: U. S. Government Printing Office.

Journal of Commerce. 1965. March 11, p. 23.

Jump, Gregory V. 1980. "Interest Rates, Inflation Expectations, and Spurious Elements in Measured Real Income and Saving." American Economic Review 70: 990-1004.

Kaldor, Nicholas. 1955. An Expenditure Tax. London: Unwin.

_____. 1942. "The Income Burden of Capital Taxes." Review of Economic Studies, vol. 9, Summer.

Kalita, Arthur. 1982. "Will Municipal Bonds Survive the Flat-Rate Tax Movement?" Weekly Bond Buyer: PSA Conference Supplement, October 10, p. 1.

Kat, John A., and M. A. King. 1978. The British Tax System. Oxford: Oxford University Press.

Katzman, Robert A. 1980. Regulatory Bureaucracy. Cambridge, Mass.: MIT Press.

Keith, Lord. 1983. Enforcement Powers over VAT. London: Her Majesty's Stationery Office.

Kenen, Peter, ed. 1975. Internation Trade and Finance: Frontiers for Research. Cambridge: At the University Press.

Kidron, Michael. 1970. Western Capitalism since the War. Rev. ed. Harmondsworth, Middlesex: Penguin, p. 20.

Knight, Frank. 1933. Uncertainty and Profit. Series of Reprints of Scarce Tracts, no. 16. London: London School of Economics and Political Science.

_____. 1923. "Some Fallacies in the Interpretation of Social Cost." Quarterly Journal of Economics 38: 582–606.

Kolm, S. 1973. "A Note on Optimum Tax Evasion." Journal of Public Economics 2: 265–70.

Krueger, Ann O. 1983. Exchange Rate Determination. New York: Cambridge University Press.

Kurz, Mordecai. 1978. "Negative Income Taxation." In Federal Tax Reform, edited by M. J. Boskin, pp. 145–69. San Francisco: Institute for Contemporary Studies.

Laffer, Arthur B. 1982. Foundations of Supply Side Economics. New York: Academic Press.

Lampman, R. J. 1962. "The Share of Top Wealth Holders in National Wealth." Princeton, N.J.: Princeton University Press.

Lane, Robert E. 1959. "The Fear of Equality." American Political Science Review, vol. 53, March.

"Legitimate Foreign Income Tax." 1980. Business Week, January 28, pp. 120–22.

Lent, George. 1982. "Property Taxes in the Caribbean Community." Bulletin for International Fiscal Documentation, October.

Lerner, Abba P. 1967. "Employment Theory and Employment Policy." American Economic Review 57: 1–18.

Lewis, Wilfred. 1962. Federal Fiscal Policy in Postwar Recessions. Washington, D.C.: Brookings Institution.

Lightman, Stuart. 1982. "Hotels and VAT." British Tax Review, no. 4, pp. 233–40.

Lindblom, Charles E. 1977. Politics and Markets. New York: Basic Books.

Lindholm, Richard W. 1980. The Economics of VAT. Lexington, Mass.: D. C. Heath, Lexington Books.

_____. 1976. Value Added Tax and Other Tax Reforms. Chicago: Nelson, Hall.

_____. 1975. New Tax Directions for the United States. Prepared for 94th Cong., 1st sess., Ways and Means Committee. Washington, D.C.: Government Printing Office.

_____. 1972. "Toward a New Philosophy of Taxation." Morgan Guarantee Survey, January, pp. 3-8.

_____. 1971. "Death and Gift Taxes." In A Description and Analysis of Oregon's Fiscal System. Eugene.

_____. 1970. "VAT: A Short Review of the Literature." Journal of Economic Literature 8: 1178-89.

_____. 1948. "General Appraisal of State Income Tax Administrative Problems." In Income Tax Administration, pp. 263-72. New York: Tax Institute.

_____. 1944. The Corporate Franchise as a Basis for Taxation. Austin: University of Texas Press.

Lock, Clarence W. 1955. "The Michigan Value-Added Tax." National Tax Journal 8: 360.

Luger, Michael I. 1982. "Tax Incentives and Tax Inequalities." Journal of Contemporary Studies 5: 33-47.

Lunberg, Ferdinand. 1968. The Rich and the Super Rich. New York: Bantam Books.

Lundberg, Erik. 1968. Instability and Economic Growth. Studies in Comparative Economics, no. 8. New Haven, Conn.: Yale University Press.

Lutz, Mark A., and Kenneth Lux. 1979. The Challenge of Humanistic Economics. Menlo Park, Calif.: Addison-Wesley, Benjamin-Cummings.

Lydell, Harold. 1968. The Structure of Earnings. London: Oxford University Press, p. 153.

Lynn, Arthur D. 1967. "Property Tax Development." In Property Taxation USA, edited by R. W. Lindholm, pp. 7-20. Madison: University of Wisconsin Press.

Macdonald, Graeme. 1975. "The Wealth Tax—The Wrong Tool for the Job." British Tax Review, no. 5, pp. 283-88.

McIntyre, and Dean C. Tipps. 1983. Inequity and Decline. Washington, D.C.: Center on Budget and Policy Priorities, pp. 69-83.

McKie, J. 1970. "Regulation and the Free Market: The Problem of Boundaries." Bell Journal 1: 6-26.

McLure, C. E. 1979. Must Corporate Income Be Taxed Twice? Washington, D.C.: Brookings Institution.

McNeill, William H. 1963. The Rise of the West. Chicago: University of Chicago Press, pp. 661-64.

Madison, James. 1927. Formation of the Union of the United States. Washington, D.C.: Government Printing Office.

Maxwell, James. 1973. "Income Tax Discrimination against the Renter." National Tax Journal 26: 491-97.

Meade, James E. 1965. Efficiency, Equality and Ownership of Property. Cambridge, Mass.: Harvard University Press, pp. 38-39.

Mehus, Rudolph J. 1969. "The German VAT—Two Years After." Taxes 47: 554-56.

Melvin, J. R. 1979. "Short Run Price Effects of Corporate Income Tax and Implications for International Trade." American Economic Review 69: 765-74.

Messers, Ken. 1979. "A Defense of Present Border Tax Adjustments." National Tax Journal 32: 481-92.

Minarik, Joe. 1982a. Income Tax Policy Options. Washington, D.C.: Congressional Budget Office.

_____. 1982b. "The Future of the Individual Income Tax." National Tax Journal 35: 231-41.

Mitchell, William C. 1971. Public Choice in America. Chicago: Markham, chap. 4.

Morgan, D. C., Jr. 1964. Retail Sales Tax: An Appraisal of New Issues. Madison: University of Wisconsin Press.

Morgan, J. N. 1962. "The Anatomy of Income Distribution." Review of Economic Statistics 44: 270-83.

Morganstern, Oskar. 1979. National Income Statistics: A Critique of Macroeconomic Aggregation. Washington, D. C.: Cato Institute.

Mork, K. A. 1975. "Income Tax Evasion: Some Empirical Evidence." Public Finance 30: 70-76.

Multi-State Tax Commission. 1968-. Annual Reports. The Multi-State Compact.

Munnell, Alicia Haydock. 1977. The Future of Social Security. Washington, D. C.: Brookings Institution.

_____. 1974. The Effect of Social Security on Personal Saving. Cambridge, Mass.: Ballinger.

Mussa, Michael L., and R. Komendi. 1979. The Taxation of Municipal Bonds. Washington, D. C.: American Enterprise Institute.

Muth, J. F. 1961. "Rational Expectations and the Theory of Price Movements." Econometrica 29: 315-35.

Mutti, John. 1981. "Tax Incentives and the Repatriation Decisions of U. S. Multinational Corporations." National Tax Journal 34: 241-48.

Myrdal, Gunnar. 1953. Political Elements in the Development of Economic Theory. London: Routledge & Kegan Paul.

National Bureau of Economic Research. 1958. The National Economic Accounts of the United States. General Series 64. N. p.

National Institute of Education. N. d. Tax Wealth in Fifty States. Washington, D. C.: National Institute of Education.

NET. 1969. VAT. London: Her Majesty's Stationery Office.

"New Company Taxes for Old." 1981. Economist, November 14, p. 100.

Nichols, D. A. 1970. "Land and Economic Growth." American Economic Review 60: 332–40.

Norr, Martin, and Hornhammar. 1970. "The Value Added Tax in Sweden." Columbia Law Review 70: 392–93.

Oakland, William. 1967. "The Theory of the Value-Added Tax: A Comparison of Tax Bases." National Tax Journal 20: 119–36.

Oates, Wallace E. 1972. Fiscal Federalism. New York: Harcourt Brace.

Office of Management and Budget. 1982. Special Analyses, Fiscal Year 1982. N. p.

Okner, Benjamin A. 1975. "A Microeconomic Analysis." Review of Income and Wealth 21: 285–86.

Olson, Mancut. 1982. The Rise and Decline of Nations. New Haven, Conn.: Yale University Press.

O'Neill, and Schwartz. 1982. "Flat Tax Facts." Public Opinion, November, pp. 44–46.

Organization for Economic Cooperation and Development. 1982. The 1981 Tax/Benefit Position of a Typical Worker. Paris: OECD.

_____. 1979. The Taxation of Net Wealth, Capital Transfers and Capital Gains of Individuals. Paris: OECD, pp. 25–57.

Osterwei, Eric. 1980. "The Application of Belgian VAT to Foreign Suppliers of Services." Tax Management International Journal, March, pp. 3–6.

Ott, Attiat, and Ludwig O. Oittrick. 1981. The Federal Income Tax Burden on Households. Washington, D. C.: American Enterprise Institute.

Paglin, Morton. 1975. "The Measurement and Trend of Inequality: A Basic Revision." American Economic Review, September, pp. 598–609.

Parekh, C. V. 1958. The Law and Practice of Wealth in India. Bombay: Parekh.

Peckman, Joseph A. 1974. Who Bears the Tax Burden? Washington, D. C.: Brookings Institution.

_____. 1971. Federal Tax Policy. Rev. ed. New York: W. W. Norton.

Peek, Joe. 1982. "Interest Rates, Income Taxes, and Anticipated Inflation." American Economic Review 72: 980-81.

Penner, R. G. 1982. "More or Less Flat Tax." AEI Economist, August.

Penniman, Clara I. 1980. State Income Taxation. Baltimore: Johns Hopkins University Press.

_____. 1979. "In Defense of Tax Administrators." Western Tax Review, vol. 1 (June).

Phares, Donald. 1980. Who Pays State Taxes? Cambridge, Mass.: OG&H, pp. 29-58.

Phillips, A. W. 1958. "The Relation between the Level of Unemployment and the Role of Change of Money Wage Rates." Economica, November, pp. 283-99.

Pickerill, R. J. 1978. "European Attempts to Achieve Equity in Corporate Taxes." Tax Executive 30: 211-25.

Pohmer, Dieter. 1983. "Value-Added Tax after Ten Years: The European Experience." In Comparative Tax Studies, edited by Sijbren Cnossen, pp. 243-55. Amsterdam: North Holland.

Pollock v. Farmers' Loan and Trust Company. 1895. 158 U.S. 601.

Prest, A. R. 1980. Value Added Taxation: The Experience of the United Kingdom. Washington, D.C.: American Enterprise Institute.

_____. 1976. "The Select Committee on a Wealth Tax." British Tax Review, no. 1, pp. 7-15.

Projector, Dorothy, and Gertrude S. Wiess. 1966. Survey of Financial Characteristics of Consumers. Federal Reserve Technical Papers. N.p.

Pryor, Frederic L. 1973a. Property and Industrial Organization in Communist and Capitalistic Nations. Bloomington: Indiana University Press.

———. 1973b. "Simulation of the Impact of Social and Economic Institutions on the Size Distribution of Income and Wealth." American Economic Review 63: 50-72.

Ratner, Sidney. 1942. Federal Taxation 1789-1913. New York: Norton, p. 239.

Reese, Craig E., et al. 1980. "The Impact of a Federal Value-Added Tax on State Sales and Use Taxation." In Proceedings of the Seventy-third National Tax Association-Tax Institute of America Conference, pp. 198-203.

"Refund and Deferred VAT." 1982. European Taxation, September 22, pp. 291-92.

Reuss, Frederick G. 1963. Fiscal Policy for Growth without Inflation. Baltimore: Johns Hopkins University Press.

Rody, M. J., and H. H. Smith. 1960. Zoning Primer. West Trenton, N.J.: Chandler-Davis.

Roley, V. Vance. 1981. "The Financing of Federal Deficits: An Analysis of Crowding Out." Economic Review (Federal Reserve Bank of Kansas City), July-August, pp. 16-29.

Rolph, Earl R. 1948. "The Concept of Transfers in National Income Estimates." Quarterly Journal of Economics, May, pp. 327-61.

Rosen, Harvey S. 1982. "Taxes, Labor Supply and Human Capital." NBER Reporter, Spring, pp. 5-7.

Rothenberg, Jerome. 1967. Economic Evaluation of Urban Renewal. Washington, D.C.: Brookings Institution.

Royal Commission on the Distribution of Income and Wealth. 1975. Initial Report on the Distribution of Income and Wealth. London: Her Majesty's Stationery Office.

Rusett, Bruce M., et al. 1964. World Handbook of Political and Social Indicators. New Haven, Conn.: Yale University Press, p. 243.

Sacks, Jeffrey D. 1979. Wages, Profits, and Macroeconomics Adjustment: A Comparative Study. Brookings Papers on Economic Activity, no. 2, app. B, pp. 316-19.

Samuelson, Paul A. 1958. Economics. New York: McGraw-Hill, pp. 501-43, 598-613.

Sandford, C. T. 1981. Costs and Benefits of VAT. London: HEB.

_____. 1974. "The Relationship of Wealth Tax to Other Taxes." British Tax Review, no. 6.

_____. 1973. Hidden Costs of Taxation. London: Institute of Fiscal Studies.

_____. 1971. Taxing Personal Wealth. London: George Allen & Unwin.

Schiff, Michael. 1974. Value Added Taxation (Business Experience). New York: FEI.

Schultze, Charles L. 1971. The Distribution of Farm Subsidies: Who Gets the Benefits? Washington, D. C.: Brookings Institution.

Semple, Robert B. 1975. "Income Inequality in Britain Found to Change Little in Decade." New York Times, August 2.

Shapiro, Harvey, and David Klock. 1974. "Some Aspects of U. S. Treatment of Foreign Service Income." Journal of Economics and Business 26: 134-39.

Shoup, C. 1966. Estate and Gift Taxes. Washington, D. C.: Brookings Institution.

Shultz, William J. 1927. The Taxation of Inheritance. New York: Houghton-Mifflin.

Siemens, Wilhelm Von. 1921. Verdelte Umstatstener. 2d ed. Siemenstadt, Germany.

Simon, Carl, and Witte. 1980. The Underground Economy. Washington, D. C.: U. S. Government Printing Office.

Simon, Wayne M. 1975. Foreign Trade Elasticities for Twenty Industries. Washington, D. C.: International Trade Commission.

Simons, Henry. 1938. Personal Income Tax. Chicago: University of Chicago Press.

Sinai, Allen. 1972. "The Value-Added Tax and the U. S. Economy." Joint Economic Committee Hearings VAT, 92d Cong., 2d sess., March 21-24, pp. 132-48.

Sisson, Charles A. 1981. Tax Evasion. Washington, D. C.: International Monetary Fund.

Smith, Dan Throop. 1981. An Analysis of Value-Added Taxation in the Context of the Tax Restructuring Act of 1980. Morristown, N. J.: Financial Executive Research Foundation.

Smith, Dan Throop, et al. 1973. What You Should Know about the Value-Added Tax. Illinois: Dow Jones Service.

Smith, James D. 1975. "The Intergeneration Transmission of Wealth and Terminal Capital Gains Taxation." In Conference on Tax Research, pp. 199-287. Washington, D. C.: Department of the Treasury, Office of Tax Analysis.

_____, and Stephen D. Franklin. 1974. "The Concentration of Personal Wealth, 1922-69." American Economic Review 64: 162-67.

_____, and K. D. Stauntan. 1965. "Estimating of Top Wealth Holders from Estate Tax Returns." Annual Proceedings of American Statistical Association.

Soltow, Lee. 1965. Toward Income Equality in Norway. Madison: University of Wisconsin Press.

Somers, Harold. 1958. "Estate Taxes and Business Mergers." Journal of Finance, May.

Soule, Don M. 1959. "Shifting of the Corporate Income Tax: A Dynamic Analysis." Journal of Finance, no. 3, pp. 390-402.

"Sources and Methods, National Income Estimation." 1954. National Income, pp. 61-152.

South Carolina Tax Study Commission. 1961.

Special Analysis 'G.' 1982. Budget of the United States, Fiscal Year 1982, pp. 203-25.

Stein, Herbert, and Murray F. Foss. 1981. "Taxes and Savings." AEI Economist, July 1981.

Steuerle, Eugene, and Michael Hartzmark. 1981. "Individual Income Taxation 1947-79." National Tax Journal 34: 145-59.

Stockfish, J. A. 1956. "Capitalization, Allocation and Investment Effects of Asset Taxation." Southern Economic Journal 24: 28-40.

Stone, Joe A. 1979. "Price Elasticities of Demand for Imports and Exports." Review of Economics and Statistics 61: 306-12.

Stubblebine, Craig. 1983. Reaganomics: Midterm Report. San Francisco: ICS Press.

Studenski, Paul. 1940. "Toward a Theory of Business Taxation." Journal of Political Economy 48: 621-54.

Sullivan, Clara K. 1967. "Indirect Tax Systems in the European Economic Community." In Fiscal Harmonization in Common Markets, edited by Carl S. Shoup. New York: Columbia University Press.

_____. 1965. The Tax on Value-Added. New York: Columbia University Press, pp. 3-37.

_____. 1963. The Search for Tax Principles in the European Economic Community. Cambridge, Mass.: Harvard University Law School.

Summers, Lawrence H. 1981. Tax Policy and Corporate Investment. Working paper no. 605. Cambridge, Mass.: National Bureau of Economic Research.

Sunler, Emil. 1973. "Toward a More Neutral Investment Tax Credit." National Tax Journal 26: 209-20.

Swedish Institute. 1975. The Swedish System of Investment Funds. Stockholm: Swedish Information Services.

Tait, Alan A. 1981. "Is the Introduction of a Value-Added Tax Inflationary?" Finance and Development, June.

_____. 1972. The Value-Added Tax. New York: McGraw-Hill.

_____. 1967. The Taxation of Personal Wealth. Urbana: University of Illinois Press.

Tanabe, Noboru. 1967. "The Taxation of Net Wealth." IMF Staff Papers 14: 124-66.

Tanzi, Vito, and George Iden. 1981. The Impact of Taxes on Wages in the United States: An Example of Supply-Side Economics. DM Series. Washington, D.C.: International Monetary Fund.

_____. 1980. "Underground Economy Built on Illicit Pursuits." IMF Survey 9: 34-37.

_____. 1969. The Individual Income Tax and Economic Growth. Baltimore: Johns Hopkins University Press.

Taxation with Representation Newsletter. 1976. Vol. 5, no. 14 (June).

Taylor, Lester G., et al. 1977. The Effect of Direct Taxes and Other Changes on Money Wage Changes in U.S. Manufacturing. Technical Analysis Paper no. 50. Washington, D.C.: U.S. Department of Labor.

Teeters, Nancy. 1963. Federal Tax on Corporate Profits. Washington, D.C.: Federal Reserve Board.

Thompson, F., and L. Jones. 1982. Regulator and Policy and Practices. New York: Praeger.

Thurow, Lester C. 1982. "The Failure of Education as an Economic Strategy." American Economic Review 72: 72-80.

Titmucs, Richard. 1962. Income Distribution and Social Change. London: George Allen & Unwin, p. 198.

Tobin, J., et al. 1967. "Is a Negative Income Tax Practical?" Yale Law Journal 77: 198.

Toye, J. F. J., ed. 1978. Taxation and Economic Development. London.

Trimby, L. 1980. "Small Business versus Value Added Tax." Accountancy, January, pp. 52–54.

Ture, Norman B. 1978. "Taxation and the Distribution of Income." In Wealth Redistribution and the Income Tax, edited by Arleen A. Leibowitz. Lexington, Mass.: D. C. Heath.

_____. 1973. "Economics of the Value Added Tax." In Value Added Tax: Two Views, edited by Charles E. McClure and Norman B. Ture, p. 8–6. Washington, D. C.: American Enterprise Institute.

_____. 1972. White Paper on Long Range Tax Policy and Balanced Growth. Washington, D. C.: U. S. Chamber of Commerce.

United Kingdom. 1974. Wealth Tax Free Paper. Cmnd. 5704. Her Majesty's Stationery Office.

United States v. Butler. 1935. 297 U. S. 1.

Urban Land Institute. 1977. Large–Scale Development. Washington, D. C.: Urban Land Institute.

U. S., Congress, Committee on Finance. 1982. Flat Rate Tax Hearings, September 28–30.

U. S., Department of Agriculture, Bureau of Agricultural Economics. 1937. An Analysis of the Effects of the Processing Taxes Levied under the Agricultural Adjustment Act. Washington, D. C.: Department of Agriculture.

U. S., Department of Commerce. Various dates. National Income Report. Washington, D. C.: Department of Commerce.

U. S., Department of Labor, Bureau of Labor Statistics. 1980. National Survey of Professional, Administrative, Technical, and Clerical Pay, Bulletin 2081. Washington, D. C.: Government Printing Office.

U. S., Department of State. 1961. The General Agreement on Tariffs and Trade. Washington, D. C.: Government Printing Office.

U.S., Department of the Treasury. 1977. Blueprints for Basic Tax Reform. Washington, D.C.: Government Printing Office.

_____. 1968. Maintaining the Strength of the United States Dollar in a Strong Free World Economy. Washington, D.C.: Government Printing Office.

U.S., Department of the Treasury, Internal Revenue Service. Various dates. Estimates of Income Unreported on Individual Tax Returns. Washington, D.C.: IRS.

U.S., Securities and Exchange Commission. N.d. Volume and Composition of Individuals' Savings. Washington, D.C.: Government Printing Office.

U.S., Senate. N.d. Hearings, Revenue Act of 1963. Washington, D.C.: Government Printing Office.

U.S. Government Regulations. 1981. Washington, D.C.: Government Printing Office.

Usher, Dan. 1976. The Measurement of Capital. Chicago: University of Chicago Press.

Vedder, Richard K. 1982. "Rich States, Poor States (How High Taxes Inhibit Growth)." Journal of Contemporary Studies 5: 19-32.

Walker, Charles, and Mark A. Bloomfield. 1943. New Directions in Federal Tax Policy for the 1980s. Cambridge, Mass.: Ballinger.

Wall Street Journal. 1983a. August 30, p. 8.

_____. 1983b. May 13.

_____. 1983c. March 11, p. 28.

_____. 1979. September 27, p. 5.

Walter, Ingo. 1967. The European Common Market. New York: Praeger.

Wansermann, Ernst. 1973. The Austrian Achievement 1700-1800. London: Harcourt.

Ward, Benjamin. 1982. "Taxes and the Size of Government." American Economic Review 72: 345-50.

Weinrobe, Maurice D. 1971. "Corporate Taxes and the United States Balance of Trade." National Tax Journal 24: 79-86.

Weintraub, Sidney. 1981. Our Stagflation Malaise. Westport, Conn.: Quorum.

Weiss, Yoram. 1971. "Investment in Graduate Education." American Economic Review 61: 833-52.

White, Roger. 1982. "The Green Paper on Corporation Tax." British Tax Review, no. 2, pp. 79-86.

Wiedenbaum, Murray L. 1973. Matching Needs and Resources. Washington, D.C.: American Enterprise Institute, p. 47.

Wiles, Peter. 1974. Distribution of Income East and West. Amsterdam: North Holland, pp. 25, 48.

Winer, Stanley L. 1983. "Some Evidence on the Effect of the Separation of Spending and Tax Decisions." Journal of Political Economy 91: 126-40.

Wonnacott, Paul. 1971. "Tax Adjustments on Internationally Traded Goods." In United States International Economic Policy in an Interdependent World. N.p.

World Bank. 1982. Economic Memorandum on Uruguay, 3652-UR. Washington, D.C.: World Bank.

INDEX

ABOUT THE AUTHOR

RICHARD W. LINDHOLM was Dean of the College of Business Administration of the University of Oregon during the period of great turmoil on college campuses, 1959-72. At that time he introduced and developed the university's graduate school of management.

As early as 1951 Dr. Lindholm became involved in the economic development of Third World countries. Through the years he has acted as tax consultant to Turkey, Pakistan, Vietnam, Taiwan, and Papua New Guinea. Here and in his work with the U.S. Commerce Department, State Department, the Federal Reserve Board, and the revenue departments of Texas, Ohio, Michigan, and Oregon, Lindholm developed an interest in the broader effects of taxes beyond provision of a certain quantity of funds.

This broader interest led to publications such as The Corporate Franchise and Taxation, Introduction to Fiscal Policy, Taxation of the Trucking Industry, Land Value Taxation, Value-Added Tax and Other Tax Reforms, and The Economics of VAT. On December 15, 1975, the Committee on Ways and Means of the U.S. House of Representatives published Lindholm's New Tax Directions for the United States.

A New Federal Tax System incorporates the wisdom gained from Lindholm's lifetime of analysis and observation of tax systems in action and tax programs and concepts developed by economists, accountants, and lawyers. The time for taxation change has arrived and Lindholm, the analyst and observer, picks up the challenge.